# AFRICAN AMERICANS AT THE CROSSROADS

The Restructuring of

Black Leadership

and the 1992 Elections

**Clarence Lusane**

South End Press, Boston, MA

Copyright © 1994 by Clarence Lusane

Cover design by Cheryl Hanna
Text design and production by South End Press collective
Printed in the U.S.A.


Any properly footnoted quotation of up to 500 sequential words may be
used without permission, as long as the total number of words quoted does
not exceed 2,000. For longer quotations or for a greater number of total
words, please write for permission to South End Press

**Library of Congress Cataloging-in-Publication Data**

Lusane, Clarence, 1953-
African Americans at the Crossroads: the restructuring of Black leadership
and the 1992 elections/by Clarence Lusane
p. cm.
Includes bibliographic references and index
1. Afro-Americans—Politics and government. 2. Afro-American leadership. 3. Presidents—United States—Election—1992
E185.615.L9 1993 93-14034
323.1 196073—dc20 CIP
ISBN 0-89608-468-x:$16.00 paper
ISBN 0-89608-469-8:$40.00 cloth

**South End Press, 116 Saint Botolph Street, Boston, MA 02115**

99 98 97 96 95 94                    1 2 3 4 5 6 7 8 9

# Additional Praise for
## *African Americans at the Crossroads*

*This book represents a new genre of writings on Black politics, and is necessary reading for those interested in an analysis of Black political activism in the United States.*

Dr. James Jennings, William Monroe Trotter Institute

*A timely and important book that should put to rest theories that try to convince us of the declining significance of race and class.*

Cecilia Green, *Against the Current*

*Clarence Lusane offers a much needed analysis of the crisis of Black political leadership.*

Ron Daniels, Campaign for a New Tomorrow

*Everyone who wants to provide leadership in and for the African American community should read this book.*

Mel King, M.I.T.

*To Karen (of course);*

*To Mary, my mother, and Loretta and Lynn, my sisters, for their lifelong support and constant reaffirmation of my belief in the power of loving Black families;*

*To Eloise Greenfield, a brilliant, committed writer who has positively molded and inspired countless young minds, including this one long ago, and to whom I promised myself I would someday dedicate a book;*

*To James Boggs (1919-1993), writer, thinker, organizer, autoworker, political leader, my first political mentor, who more than anyone taught me to think philosophically and whose wisdom and teachings remain an inescapable part of my identity;*

*To Zoe E. Page (1937-1993), a dear friend, skilled sign language interpreter, and deeply dedicated humanist whose love for Africa and all Africans took her home where as an elder of the village of Brenu Akyinim in Ghana, she was released from this life.*

# Table of Contents

# List of Tables

# Acknowledgements

There are lots of folks to give shouts out to who assisted in the preparation of this book and in my reflections, projections, and corrections on my immature ideas and underdeveloped notions. More than I can convey, this book embodies countless discussions, arguments, debates, sharings, musings, intellectualizing, and kicking it with many friends, cohorts, homies, and comrades.

First, I need to thank the collective of folks who worked to research, write, produce, and distribute the newsletter *Black Political Agenda '92*—my posse, which includes: Keith Jennings, a good friend and confidant who served as managing editor and whose national and international travels always expanded our political family; Valerie Mims, whose editorial assistance and views were always valuable; Greg Moore, a multi-talented compadre whose analytical passions and humorous observations blended seamlessly; James Steele, whose political talents have been and continue to be invaluable to a growing number of movements and people, not the least of whom is me; and Carleen Windall, a highly skillful and professional editor. These were the folks who month after month toiled in the fields with me to produce what we believe was a quality and needed publication. We would like to believe that our modest effort to provide necessary commentary on the 1992 contest by some of the best Black political analysts in the nation, from the perspective of race and class concerns, was mostly successful.

I must also give deep thanks to James Jennings, Muriel Ridley, and the staff of the William Monroe Trotter Institute at the University of Massachusetts-Boston. Their critical, indeed, decisive support in our efforts to put out *Black Political Agenda '92* and their equally helpful and insightful comments on many of the ideas expressed in this book have earned my eternal gratitude. Much of Jennings' work on Black-Latino empowerment issues has influenced my own thinking over the last couple of years.

I also feel compelled to single out for appreciation a number of the professors in the Political Science Department at Howard University. As a graduate student in the Political Science Department, I found their critiques, insights, and analyses of the 1992 election and Black politics, in general, instructive and influential on my own perspectives. As engaged scholars, they approached the elections not only with razor-sharp analysis, but also with commitment and zeal. In particular, I want to thank Dr. John Cotman, whose radical worldview and critical mind I've come to enjoy immensely; Dr.

Joseph McCormick, whose research on the nature of Black politics promises important and timely contributions; Dr. Lorenzo Morris, one of the best political thinkers I've ever been exposed to, and a relentless mentor as well; Dr. Richard Seltzer, who is heroically (and hopefully, successfully) attempting to teach me everything I will ever need to know about quantitative research; and Dr. Ronald Walters, chairperson of the Political Science Department and a sage educator and friend of many years. All of these professors provided me with time, discussion, and critical documents.

There were countless individuals who provided me with data, materials, and often just an ear to hear my views and ideas about the 1992 election and what it meant to African Americans and the state of Black leadership. Some whose feedback permeates these pages, this includes: Michael Albert, co-editor of *Z Magazine*; Karen Bass, executive director of Community Coalition for Substance Abuse Prevention and Treatment; and one of my closest friends and political confidants; Cecelie Blakely, NAACP Washington Office; Christopher Booker, researcher and writer; Thomas D. Boston, economist; Maurice Carney, Joint Center for Political and Economic Studies and fellow graduate student; Sylvia Castillo, another close friend and sounding board and also a member of the Community Coalition for Substance Abuse Prevention and Treatment; Derrick Cogburn, fellow graduate student; Ron Daniels, former candidate for president in 1992 and president of Campaign for a New Tomorrow; Julius Davis, formerly of the Children's Defense Fund; Dennis Desmond, labor lawyer in Washington, D.C.; Eric Easter, editor of *One*; the staff of the Eisenhower Foundation; Guy Earl Wendell Deweever, graduate student, University of Maryland; Carla Feldpausch, editor of *Z Papers* ; April Green, fellow graduate student, Howard University; Daryl Harris, professor of political science at University of Connecticut; Mark Harrison, the Board of Church and Society of the United Methodist Church; Wade Henderson, executive director of NAACP Washington Office; Cedric Hendricks of U.S. House of Representatives; Joseph Hicks, executive director of SCLC-Los Angeles; Sylvia Hill, professor of criminal justice; Phil Hutchings of San Francisco; Geoffrey Jacques of Local 1199; Robin D.G. Kelley, professor at University of Michigan; Niani Kilkenney of Smithsonian Institute; Frankie King, staff of the Joint Economic Committee at U.S. House of Representatives; Acklyn Lynch, professor, University of Maryland; Cecil McDonald, Democratic National Committee; Gwen McKinney, co-director of McKinney and McDowell public relations firm; Julianne Malveaux, economist and writer; Manning Marable, professor at Columbia University; Charlene Mitchell of Committees of Correspondence; Askia Muhammad of WPFW-FM; Roger Newell, Jobs with Peace; Jack O'Dell, former director of international affairs for National Rainbow Coalition; Gwen Patton, former candidate for the U.S.

Senate in Alabama; Tom Porter, WPFW-FM; the staff of *Race and Class;* Carliotta Scott, staff of Rep. Ronald Dellums; Jerome Scott, southern and labor organizer; Karin Stanford, professor of political science at University of North Carolina; James Daniel Steele, professor at North Carolina A&T; Charles Stephenson, staff of Rep. Ron Dellums; Curtis Stokes, professor at University of Michigan; Bill Strickland, professor at University of Massachusetts-Amherst; Makani Themba, Marin Institute; Linda Williams, professor of political science at University of Maryland; and Michael Wynn, a brother always with his ear to the ground.

I am never short of admiration and appreciation for artists and the sacrifices they make for us all. My deep thanks, once again, to Cheryl Hanna for her powerful cover art and design, and for her friendship. Another great job! Also, my thanks to photographer Percy Davis.

The South End Press and I are both lucky to have an editor like Dionne Brooks. In the end, Dionne more than anyone has made this book a reality. She prodded, struggled, and made important suggestions that always made sense. With the most gentle of hand, she made me almost completely rewrite the first draft and produce what we both agree is a much cleaner and tighter manuscript. I feel thankful that I can count her as not only my editor, but also my friend.

Last and most special, I must thank my better half (more like two-thirds), who had to endure another season of my book writing isolation. Karen Jefferson remains the center of my personal universe, and her support and advice, wisdom and counsel, encouragement and needed criticisms, and overall strength guide me continually; for all of that, I am better. Her commitment to the advancement of African Americans is professional as well as personal. She is the manuscript curator for the Moreland-Spingarn Research Center at Howard University. She and the Center—which has contributed to countless projects including the widely heralded "Eyes on the Prize" and the Pulitzer-winning *Bearing the Cross,* to name only two—are invaluable resources to the Black community and the nation. It is this commitment that she brings to our family and to our life together. No one is as fortunate as I.

Of course, I claim all responsibility for the conclusions and viewpoints advanced in this book.

# by Lorenzo Morris

The problem with most conventional analyses and scholarly critiques of political change is that analysis and criticism always begin with old scenarios, well-worn frames of reference and second-hand guidelines for problem solving. Analysts begin by reviewing the "record"; the records of leaders, their stance on the current issues and their political backgrounds. Readers are told who counts now and who is likely to count in the near future based on who has counted in the past as a "key player." Criticism of the issues focuses on their clarity in relationship to recognized expectations and the conformity of current alternatives to established sides and lines of division. As a consequence, every new insight, every new assessment is constrained by an umbilical cord tied to a political heritage that may or may not be legitimate. To expand on a cliche, few things in the political world may be really new but nothing is born old.

The linkage of current politics to the past, however congenital, will only be clear once the "current" is consigned to the past. The task for issue-oriented analysis, therefore, is to assess the issues in the immediate context before consigning them to claims of political paternity. We need to know who is involved and what they are doing, not what happened to leaders who were involved and what is being done by leaders usually at center stage. If good political analysis sometimes requires a bit of name dropping, it should not require that we carry those names any further than necessary to clarify the issue.

Clarence Lusane is exceptional because he does not do that; he does not submerge his analysis in political background before he has committed himself and his readers to the issues at hand. He looks at an issue from all sides but he does not look first at the established black leaders to determine what the extent of the political problems before us is and what the significance of the issue is. He looks for what is in the background of an issue and where its roots are embedded, but only as the findings and needs of the present may dictate. In this study one finds, for example, analyses of the backgrounds of presidential candidates in 1992 who were virtually unknown to the electorate at large while the current difference between them and the major candidates is given extensive attention.

Only a tiny minority of voters know anything about the black presidential candidates of third parties such as Ron Daniels or Lenora Fulani. More likely, only a tiny minority know who they are. In all probability, only a minority can recall that Governor Douglas Wilder also ran. Yet, Lusane exposes a weak side of the central 1992 campaign figures which these candidates, like air to vacuum, rushed to fill. Who would have thought that offending Jesse Jackson at his own coalition meeting would give Clinton a significant electoral boost in spite of negative repercussions in the black community. Lusane not only shows that it is likely, he also describes the offense, castigating rap music performer, Sister Souljah, as a dreamed-of ingredient in the Clinton campaign strategy. The strategists in their logical concern for predictable voter turnout may have underestimated the unpredictable minority voters as well as Clinton's long term need for their support. Understandably, therefore, Lusane decides to look for predictive election factors outside the normal parameters of campaign strategy.

Why is it so important to reach around the established media centers and stars of national politics to determine where black politics is heading? For at least one reason that Lusane effectively argues, there has been no Black agenda, no national black issue consensus since 1992. However dispersed and disorganized national black politics may have been before, at least the civil rights and public elected officials could come together around central themes and promote a broad legislative agenda. In the last two presidential elections Jesse Jackson provided an organizing focal point for black politics by articulating consensual issues even where there was no uniformity among the positions taken by African American leaders. With the emergence of Clinton and his allies in the Democratic Leadership Council, progressive African American critics found themselves uncertain of the positions of Congress members like Mike Espy and John Lewis, who were visibly committed to the Democratic Party's standards and standard bearer.

To explain this loss of direction in the African American community, Lusane pays due deference to the historical perspective. He traces the search for a national political consensus among African Americans to the pre-Civil War struggles leading to the National Negro Conventions of the 1830s. Yet, rather than dwell on the historically incidental, a linkage is drawn through intervening conventions and organizations, including the 1972 Gary Convention in which nationalist sentiments and ambiguities mingled with integrationist electoral politics, to define the black agenda. The Gary Convention with its agenda brought briefly to the surface of national consciousness the uncertainties of nearly all African American leaders with the prospects and desirability of absorption into the major political parties. Here is an exceptional contribution to the study of black politics, the recognition that the nationalist influences have always been felt in the integrationist camp of electoral politics. It is a recognition that without diverse paths for political mobilization the African American presence in major party leadership circles would be greatly weakened.

A similarly exceptional insight into general American political behavior can be drawn from this study. Lusane suggests that some of the ambiguity and absence of consensus in the African American community may result from the failure to address social class divisions and issues that, along with urban disruption and decay, become ever more compelling. What happens in the ghetto of South Central L.A. affecting African and Hispanic Americans, he suggests, will ultimately require black leaders to take the initiative in tailoring race conscious concerns to meet the interracial cries for help emerging from the nation's more pluralist ghettoes.

On what basis does Lusane draw these conclusions? He draws from the usual data sources as well as from the extraordinary ones. For one, he studies rap music for its political content. To many of us that would require a greater commitment to scholarship and personal endurance than the future of American politics would seem to demand. Still, having published ground breaking work on rap, as popular culture, and politics, he knows it well. Few of us in American professorate would have discovered, as Lusane seems to have done, that rappers like "Public Enemy" would predict the uprisings in our urban malaise. The passage cited in the examination of the Rodney King disturbances is "Armageddon has been in effect. Go get a late pass." Particularly suggestive in the quote is the idea that in the midst of social disarray the "institutionalized," meaning public school, youth must bend the rules (get a late pass) in order to come to terms with the disarray. Of course, political perceptiveness among creative writers is hardly new, as James Baldwin's apt prediction of the late 1960s violent upheavals in *The Fire Next Time* shows.

What is new, however, is the search for non-institutional solutions to urban crises among the young victims and subjects of urban disorganization. Lusane attributes the chance for urban peace, in part, to the making of gang truces as happened in South Central L.A. He suggests that these kinds of resolutions will help to "rescue a generation of black males that society is ready to write off, incarcerate and marginalize." More than an ephemeral end to street confrontations, he projects the possibility for a sustained "politics of resistance" in the African American community that will confront a corresponding "politics of accommodation."

If accommodationists are most common among the black elected officials, these leaders are not necessarily submissive. There has been a gradual transformation in the composition of black political leadership from the domination of civil rights organizations to the ascendance of mayoral, congressional and related elected leadership. It is a complex evolution which Lusane puts in simple relief by comparing changes in *Ebony's* "100 most influential blacks" list since 1963.

That the evolution of leadership in the African American community is still going at full throttle is made clear. The leadership still seeks to justify itself on the basis of civil rights goals while confronting unrelenting economic and social pressures. "What does it mean for black leadership," Lusane asks, "that repressive authority is now in the hands of black city mayors and managers?" Among other things, it means that even the most race-conscious politics must use economic and social criteria for problem solving. It means that as long as the leadership relies on civil rights demands for guidance, however justified, there will be, as Lusane calls it, "a crisis of legitimacy."

This does not mean that civil rights is now on the backside of political evolution. On the contrary, President Clinton, by his inability to deal with more progressive black elected officials and interest group leaders, must focus on the old leadership. In so doing, he may well face a legitimation crisis of his own. Since his dispute with the "rainbow" coalition he has sought the support of the suburban white electorate according to Lusane. Yet, the white electorate clearly voted as a majority for George Bush in 1992. African American voters, however impassionately, rallied to Clinton's side. Faced with an active, reinforced and demanding Congressional Black Caucus, Clinton will regularly encounter pressure to redirect his attention.

Ironically, he will hardly be able to appease the black electorate or its leadership, as he once might have done, by symbolic gestures and token concessions because there is no clear black agenda to manipulate. With its size, diversity and some seniority the new Black Caucus can keep legislative pressure on the administration even without a consensual focus. Still, leaders on all side have come to a crossroads in black politics, as Lusane argues, and at this crossroads one does not have the choice of simply being better than the civil rights oppositions or of simply pursuing increased black representation in office if decisions are to be made. In order to venture the next step on the road, the mode of political leadership transportation will need to be altered.

Fortunately, this creative and reflective study sheds a light on the choices of leadership available and the steps to be taken.

# Preface

As a young man of fourteen growing up in Detroit in the summer of 1967, I was jolted into the brutal and punishing reality of race relations in the United States. The Detroit rebellion, sparked by the Black community's anger with racist police brutality and harassment, ignited only a few blocks from my home. On the second night of that traumatic interlude, my mother, sister, and about twenty of my neighbors were shot down in front of me. Miraculously and inexplicably, as the bullets flew by, I was the only one standing in the crowd that was not hit. Though they all survived—some with permanent injuries—my naïveté did not.

The sounds and images of that evening are indelible. I can still hear the shotgun blasts, the blaring sirens of fire trucks, police cars, ambulances, and the frightful screams of people as they fell to the ground on top of each other. I can still smell the sweat pouring from me and others on that hot, sweltering evening, as well as the putrid gun powder that blew through the air. I can still see the wildly dancing flames that seemed to come from every building, and, more disturbing, I can still visualize the bleeding from faces, chests, legs, and arms of people that I had known all my life. There was terror in the eyes of my mother and sister as a slow-motion panic gripped us all.

It was a pivotal and catalytic moment in my life. Without knowing it, I had reached my first crossroads. In the community movement that followed the rebellion, I and a whole generation of young African Americans in Detroit were rescued from the statistical destiny that had befallen poor, inner-city Black youth for decades. Community, city, and national leaders inspired, mobilized, and organized us away from self-destructive and society-imposed annihilation into socially responsible activities and a critical political consciousness. I made the decision to go down the path of social agency and seek answers and perhaps a resolution to the crisis of race. I have spent the rest of my life pondering questions and seeking solutions to the problem of race, class, and gender, inequality in the United States and throughout the world. In particular, from the vantage point of a fluid and reevaluated leftist ideological bent, I have sought to understand the relationship between leadership and social change. It's interesting to note that Geoffrey Jacques and Michael Dyson, two Black writers of my generation who grew up in Detroit during the same period, have written of the rebellion having had a similar impact on their lives.

I would like to say that my commitment to social change, equal rights, and human development started when I read Malcolm X's autobiography, or that my mother's admiration and love for Martin Luther King, Jr. transformed my way of thinking about the struggle the way it transformed her and countless other displaced Black southerners in the North. However, while I read Malcolm and reflected upon King, my commitment to fighting for progressive social change and eliminating racism was born in the fires of 1967.

Given my experience, I can't help but wonder how the Los Angeles rebellion of 1992, over the next ten to fifteen years, will impact the children and youth who participated in or were directly impacted by it. Will they become motivated by the experience to become the next generation of community and political leaders dedicated to bringing about progressive social reform? Or will they become cynical, bitter, and further alienated from society as a whole? Even before the smoke had all blown away, it was clear that even the limited interventions that came about in the wake of the 1960s riots on the part of the federal government, the private sector, the community, and national leaders would not be forthcoming in 1992.

It has been my fate to work within the prevailing institutions of power and outside mainstream U.S. politics—a political duality that I hope has been more complimentary than contradictory. I've studied politics at universities and on dirt roads in the Mississippi delta. I've walked the pavements of southeast Washington, D.C., organizing tenant associations, and I've been involved in organizing national peace demonstrations. I've worked on campaigns to get people elected at the neighborhood level and I've spent time in Port-au-Prince, Haiti reporting on that nation's turbulent and deadly election process. I hope that I've learned something about myself and human relations from all of these experiences, but ultimately history will be that judge.

For the last ten years, I've spent a considerable amount of time following and trying to understand the phenomenon of Jesse Jackson and the crucible of Black politics that he represents. I've been to virtually all of the National Rainbow Coalition's conferences and some semi-private meetings, attended many of its rallies and marches, participated in and helped organize some of its activities at the 1984 and 1988 Democratic National Conventions, and had ongoing discussions and relations with staffers, board members, Jackson admirers and dissenters, journalists who cover the NRC, and others who advise Jackson. Despite this familiarity with Jackson's style and ways, I must confess to always being marveled and impressed by Jackson's ability to grasp the political moment and re-articulate it in an accessible manner that conveys both a basic wisdom and a call to service. He paradoxically embodies the political soul of the Black freedom struggle and, at the same time, a Rainbow's arc of humanity's spirit. He remains the most fascinating political figure that I think I will see in my lifetime. In spite of the millions of words that have been written on Jackson and the Rainbow movement, the definitive study has yet to appear, unfortunately.

This book is in many ways an exorcism of the ideas and views that I have developed over the years. It seeks to be activist and advocates scholarship. There are issues around questions of race and class that avoid, deny, suppress, and ignore; which contribute to a social crisis that is needlessly wasting countless lives and will continue to do so unless fundamental reforms are implemented. My analysis, though left-of-center, assumes no leftist superiority. It only seeks to probe, confront, and challenge radical perspectives and assumptions that I and others have held for a long time, while at the same time critically engaging some of the central concerns of our time.

# Part I

# The Struggle for Black Leadership

# Chapter 1

# At the Crossroads

> The line of progress is never straight. For a period a movement
> may follow a straight line and then it encounters obstacles and
> the path bends...The inevitable counterrevolution that succeeds
> every period of progress is taking place.
>
> Martin Luther King, Jr.[1]

More than twenty-five years ago, Rev. Martin Luther King, Jr. posed the question, "Where do we go from here?" In his mind, Black Americans, indeed every American, had reached a crossroads. For African Americans in particular, many of the demands of the Civil Rights movement had been obtained and yet suffering, impoverishment, and a spiritual emptiness appeared not only to exist, but to be growing. On August 6, 1965, the historic 1965 Voting Rights Act was signed in an elaborate White House ceremony. Five days later, 3,000 miles and a world away, Watts erupted—to be joined within the next few years by hundreds of urban rebellions around the nation. These events and others fed King's frustration about a system that yielded little even when pushed to the maximum, and about a movement that appeared to have lost its way.

For African Americans now, a number of forces continue to drive the movement toward counterrevolution: the demise of the Cold War, the transformations in U.S. capitalism, the growth of Reagan-era racism, the rising influence and political hegemony of conservative ideology, and the social and economic deterioration of large sectors of the Black community.

Here in the last decade of the 20th century, African Americans have come upon new crossroads. To the surprise of few in the Black community, racism continues to play a decisive role in the destiny and life chances of people of color in the United States. As conditions worsen for the bulk of African Americans, Black leadership increasingly becomes the focus of criticism and disappointment. Many have come to believe that the current leadership is ineffective and incapable of leading the Black community into the next century. Black

3

leaders have responded that most of the factors of change are not in their control, that the Black community is under attack from within and without, or that the community must do more to uplift itself.

The issue of leadership is at the core of Black politics today. To advance the struggle against the persistent "American dilemma" of racism, the Black community and its leadership must make some critical political and strategic decisions about which direction to go in. Among the questions that must be tackled are: How can new leadership be developed? What is the current role of Black leadership? Has the Black community reached the limits of the benefits that can be obtained from electoral strategies? What is the relationship between electoral and non-electoral strategies? What should be the character of the Black community's relationship with the Democratic and Republican parties? Is a third party a viable option for African Americans? What role and impact will growing class differences within the Black community have in the future? And what role does gender politics play among African Americans? The responses to these questions and others will shape the practice of Black leadership over the next period.

Any analysis of the political behavior of Black leaders must be framed by the larger political, economic, and social contexts in which they function. For the most part, Black leadership confronts a deleterious social situation in the United States under which it has virtually no control. The economic and social salvos by the Reagan and Bush administrations and changes in the political economy of U.S. capitalism have profoundly impacted and limited the options available to Black leaders and activists in their efforts to address the conditions of the Black community. The economic collapse has been accompanied by a related social and cultural breakdown. These inter-related crises have crushed hope and eroded faith not only in Black leadership, but in the very system itself. Much of this book concerns the response of Black leadership to these changes.

First, it is necessary to discuss what has shaped the politics of the Black community and the context in which Black leadership has functioned. I will review in some detail the crossroads facing large sectors of Black America— one a rocky road of increasing desperation with side paths of anger, and bitterness, leading to a valley of barbarism, and the other a rough but passable road to hope and possibilities.

# Black Politics and the Demise of the Cold War

The end of the Cold War was highly significant for the African American community. Politically, ideologically, and economically, the Cold War shaped much of what Black leaders did and did not do for more than forty years. The U.S. war against communism sought to discredit leftist politics of any kind, Soviet-inspired or domestically grown. During the Civil Rights era, in particular, the charge of communist infiltration or communist influence was often used to attack the movement and its leaders, including Martin Luther King, Jr. and the youthful leaders of the Student Non-Violent Coordinating Committee. Even as late as the 1980s, presidential aspirant Jesse Jackson would be accused by right-wing forces of having too close an association with the Left.

The most important economic impact of the forty-year battle against communism was the diversion of billions of dollars over the years to build military and intelligence resources to fight genocidal wars in the name of anti-communism while badly needed social programs were underfunded, defunded, or never funded at all. During the Reagan era, military spending increased by 46 percent while housing was slashed by 77 percent and education by 70 percent.[2] In 1991 alone, while the United States was spending $295 billion on the military, its chief economic competitors, Germany and Japan, were spending only $34 billion and $32 billion respectively.[3] Despite the fact that there was never one act of aggression against the United States, the economy was militarized at the sacrifice of the future of the American people. Few Black leaders emerged as advocates of the Cold War, and more than a few were harmed by it, such as Paul Robeson and W.E.B. DuBois, but most accommodated themselves to it.

It was hoped that the end of the wasteful years of the Cold War would lead to a "peace dividend" of funding for social programs. While some political leaders began to recognize the destructiveness of a bloated military economy, to the point where virtually all major and minor party candidates and Independents in the 1992 elections called for some kind of cut in the military budget, those savings were quickly consumed by the debt left by the Republicans. The legacy of Reaganism is an economic crisis more critical and more permanent than any since World War II.

One benefit of the end of the Cold War is that it undermines the ability of conservatives to use anti-communism against the Black freedom movement. This kind of red-baiting has little support in the present era. The resistance to Black advancement is now being built around arguments that the system no longer has the ability to expand and that the crisis of capital means less for all.

# Race, Class, and the Crisis of Capital

When Reagan came into power, the United States was the globe's largest creditor nation. In 1992, by the time the Republicans left the White House, this country was the world's largest debtor and had a growing budget deficit in the trillions of dollars. Beyond the natural irrationality of a profit-driven political economy, key decisions by Reagan and Congress in the early 1980s laid the foundation for the current predicament. Most notably, feed-the-rich tax reform killed virtually any possibility of a fair, beneficial, and deficit-resolving tax system. The Tax Reform Act of 1986 was supposed to guarantee that no one in the country escaped paying at least some tax. Instead, the number of people paying taxes who made over $1 million fell by 85 percent.[4] Likewise, the outrageous funding given to Reagan's military buildup guaranteed more or less that the evils of Reaganism would live for several generations.

The nation's class divisions expanded widely during the 1980s. While the rich were getting richer, the poor and the middle class were getting poorer. In the 1980s, those with income under $20,000, saw their income increase by only 1.4 percent. Those whose income ranged from $20,000 to 50,000 saw an increase of 44 percent. In stark contrast, those whose income was over $1 million saw an increase of 2,184 percent![5] One of the tragedies of the 1980s, according to journalists Donald L. Barlett and James B. Steele, is that "the total wages of all people who earned less than $50,000 a year—85 percent of all Americans—increased an average of just 2 percent a year over those ten years. At the same time, the total wages of all millionaires shot up 243 percent a year."[6]

Central to the shrinking of the middle class was the loss of millions of manufacturing jobs. Japan and Western Europe, technologically ahead of the curve, grew economically as they decreased military spending and focused their attention on the acquisition of new technologies, and increased invest-ment in their workforce, and aggressive competition. Raising the overall standard of living and producing quality goods became the top priorities in these nations. U.S. manufacturers either failed to keep up or fled to nations where labor was cheaper, unorganized, and more exploitable. In 1981, 20.2 million people worked in manufacturing in the United States. A decade later, that number had shrunk to 18.4 million—a decline of 1.8 million workers. At the same time, the number of people who became sixteen years of age or older and would be entering the shriveling labor market grew by 19.4 million individuals.[7]

Reagan claims to have added millions of jobs to the economy during his presidency. But, those jobs were overwhelmingly in service and retail and offered less than half the salary of the manufacturing jobs that had disappeared. In 1992, the average weekly salary of retail workers was $204 compared to the average manufacturing workers' salary of $458. During the first three years of the Bush presidency, 300,000 jobs were lost in the United States according to a report by the Democratic Study Group. The country purged jobs, at an average of 9,419 per month from January 1989 through August 1991.[8]

The Reagan-born and Bush-matured economic recession had both class and racial consequences. One consequence was increased poverty among Whites—America's hidden secret. While political leaders and the mass media generally have come to expect high concentrations of poverty among inner-city or rural Blacks, there has been virtually no serious coverage of White poverty. The class questions raised by a growing poor White population and the potential for a cross-racial class struggle have been shuttled to the horizons of political discourse.

In 1991, half of America's poor, 49.7 percent, were non-Latino Whites which translated into 17.7 million Whites below the poverty line. This represented a 14 percent increase from 1989 to 1991. Although poverty among Black children is three times that of Whites, it should not obscure the fact that the trend in White child poverty rates has been increasing. In 1989, it was 11.5 percent. Two years later, it had grown to 13 percent. In thirty-three states, Whites constitute the numerical majority of the poor, while Blacks are the largest in six states, Latinos in three states, and people of Asian or Pacific Island descent the largest in Hawaii.[9] According to one well-respected study that compared poverty rates in a number of Western countries, including Australia, Canada, France, Germany, the Netherlands, Sweden, the United Kingdom, and the United States, the White poverty rate alone "*in the United States is higher than the poverty rate for the entire population of every one of the other nations*" (emphasis in original).[10]

White poverty has been driven by factors similar to those that have perpetuated Black poverty: wage shrinkage, and cutbacks in government programs that would assist those in poverty to get out. Politically, there clearly exists a common bond for building cross-racial unity. However, many Whites who were fed racist stereotypes by Reagan, Bush, congressional conservatives, and the media, still view themselves as different and better than those non-Whites who caught the brunt of Reaganism. In particular, too many Whites have blinded themselves to the state of emergency that defines much of Black life.

The deterioration of conditions in the Black community flowed from and through the political and economic transformations of the last two decades. As writer Manning Marable notes, "The acceleration of Black unemployment and underemployment, the capitulation of many civil rights and Black power leaders to the right, the demise of militant Black working-class institutions and caucuses, and the growing dependency of broad segments of the Black community upon public assistance programs and transfer payments of various kinds; these interdependent realities within the contemporary Black political economy are the beginning of a new and profound crisis for Black labor in America."[11]

Even so, under Reaganism there were some impressive economic and political gains by a few African Americans. Economically, the Black middle class expanded. In 1967, 6 percent of Black families were in the middle class. By 1990, that figure had risen to 14 percent.[12] More African Americans are attending college than ever before while the numbers of Black professionals and elected officials are the highest in history.

Black athletes and entertainers garner riches and fame that few activists and leaders during the civil rights days could have even imagined Whites having. Bill Cosby became perhaps the wealthiest entertainer, Black or non-Black, in the world. Other entertainers and athletes, such as Michael Jackson, Michael Jordan, Eddie Murphy, Mike Tyson, and Oprah Winfrey, are worth hundreds of millions. These images of Black abundance have fostered the myth of the American Dream and its ideology of individual achievement and bootstrap capitalism.

Yet, these advances are negligible when compared to the growing misery of millions of poor and working-class African Americans. The National Research Council details the growing class cleavage in Black America. Its 1989 report notes that "In 1970, 15.7 percent of Black families had incomes over $35,000; by 1986, this proportion had grown to 21.1 percent." The report goes on to say, however, that "During the same years, the proportion of Black families with incomes of less than $10,000 also grew, from 26.8 percent to 30.2 percent."[13] Since 1969, median Black family income has stagnated at about 60 percent of Whites.[14] In 1987, African Americans owned only 3 percent of all businesses in the United States, according to the Census Bureau.[15]

Under Reagan and Bush, from 1981 to 1991, more than 1.6 million additional African Americans fell below the poverty line, with the period 1989 to 1991 accounting for 940,000 of that number.[16] The Bush era contributed significantly to the ongoing economic devastation in the Black community. According to the Children's Defense Fund, 841,000 young people, a disproportionate number of whom were African American, fell under the poverty line in the first two years of the Bush administration.[17] In the 1990s, more than 60 percent of poor Blacks live in center cities.[18] These drops in income explain why the official Black poverty rate for Blacks is 32.7 percent, 10.2 million people—one-third of Black America—which is higher than for Hispanics (28.7 percent), Asians (13.8 percent), or Whites (11.3 percent).[19]

For many observers, it is the persistence and seeming permanence of poverty and its associated ailments that is most worrisome. Community and labor activists William Fletcher and Eugene "Gus" Newport state: "The crisis threatening Afro-America is not simply that there is Black poverty. Rather it centers around the chronic nature of that poverty."[20]

Growing poverty among inner-city Blacks has led to many debates over the term "underclass." Conservatives tend to view it as a behavioral category, i.e., the problems of the hardcore poor are a result of cultural or social practices that perpetuate their own poverty. Progressives have criticized that view and argue that the underclass is a consequence of an economic and political system prepared to write off large sectors of the population who are no longer needed in a post-industrial world. While many have decried the expansion of the so-called Black underclass, some have seen that growth as a natural manifestation of an inequitable society. Political scientist Mack Jones states that "the presence of the Black underclass is not a result of either malfunctioning of the American economic process or of the pathology of the members of the underclass. The underclass results from the sum of the routine systematically prescribed actions of the constituent elements or institutions of the political economy."[21]

Middle-class as well as working-class African Americans are trailing Whites when it comes to economic cushions. According to the Urban League, Blacks have fewer savings accounts than Whites (44.5 percent vs. 76.6 percent), fewer checking accounts (30.1 percent vs. 50.9 percent), fewer stocks (7 percent vs. 23.9 percent), less equity in their homes (43.5 percent vs. 66.7 percent), and fewer IRAs (6.9 percent vs. 26.4 percent).[22] Black family income is about 54 percent of Whites—the same as it was thirty years ago—but the net worth of Black households is even less than that. Black household net worth is $26,130, compared to $111,950 for Whites.

Three decades ago, Black Americans fought and died to end segregation in U.S. society. As the nation heads into the next century, segregation, with a strong class bias, has returned and contributes to the perpetuation of negative social trends. About 30 percent of all Blacks still live in virtually totally segregation, i.e., about nine million Blacks live in high-segregation neighborhoods that are at least 90 percent Black. In many major cities, large stretches of the landscape are in stark Black and White colors. In Chicago, 71 percent of the Black population lives in high-segregation neighborhoods. In metropolitan Detroit, the figure is 61 percent. On the other side of the tracks, 68 percent of Whites nationally live in virtually all-White areas.[23] Poor communities feed upon themselves in a state of perpetual dire straits.

# Black America's Health Care Crisis

The result of this economic burnout and freefall was the nearly complete social breakdown in the Black community. A health care situation incapable of meeting the health needs of most African Americans and the ongoing criminalization of Black youth are only two areas that highlight the devastation raging in the Black community. Overall, about 33 million Americans, a significant proportion African American, have no health care insurance.[24] As one writer noted, major health issues confront African Americans who "die an average five years earlier than Whites, are twice as likely to die before their first birthday, [and] have the highest cancer rate of any U.S. group."[25]

In the late 1980s, the Black infant mortality rate of 18 per 1,000 births was nearly twice the national rate of 10.4 per 1,000 births. The infant mortality rate for African American children is higher than for children in thirty-one nations, including Cuba and Kuwait.[26] As researcher Chris Booker wrote, "For Black males, the disadvantaged health status is a cradle-to-grave experience."[27] At almost every age, Black men die at a substantially higher rate than White men. For those aged 5 to 14, Black males die at a rate of 195 per 100,000, while for White males it's 145 per 100,000. Between the ages 45 and 54, Black male mortality is 1,244 per 100,000, and White male mortality is 578 per 100,000.[28] Overall, Black male life expectancy (65.4), which fell during the Reagan years, is lower than it is for White men, White women, and Black women.[29]

African Americans as a whole die at extraordinarily higher rates of the eight major causes of death than Whites. For example, Blacks die of heart disease at a rate 39 percent greater than Whites. The numbers are equally alarming for other causes, including cirrhosis and liver disease (7 percent higher), strokes (82 percent), diabetes (132 percent), cancer (32 percent), accidents (24 percent), kidney failure (176 percent), and homicides and killings by police (500 percent).[30] AIDS and HIV-related deaths are increasing, as death rates for Black men have grown to three times that of White men and nine times greater for Black women than for White women.[31]

These untimely deaths and other health problems affect Blacks of all social classes and have led a number of leading Black medical professionals to believe that in addition to economic issues, racism plays a key role in the quality and deliverance of heath care. A study in the *American Journal of*

*Public Health*, echoing other reports, found that race was a significant factor in the medical health and health care received by people of color.[32]

# Criminalization of the Black Community

The Black community's health is also threatened by the persistent criminalizing of large sectors of Black youth. In 1990, there were 609,690 young Black males between the ages twenty to twenty-nine in prison or jail, on probation, or on parole, while only 436,000 were in college. For White males of the same age, 4,600,000 were in college while 1,054,508 were in the criminal justice system.[33]

The criminalization and incarceration of young Blacks, particularly males, is depopulating many communities. Young Black men aged 15-24, who constitute only 6 percent of population, make up 47 percent of the prison population.[34] According to a report by the Sentencing Project, 23 percent of all young Black males nationally between 20 and 29 are incarcerated, on parole, or on probation.[35] Broken down by cities, these figures are even more stunning. In Washington, D.C., the figure is 42 percent. In Baltimore, it's 56 percent.

The consequences are not just socially destructive to the community, but also economically costly. More and more jurisdictions are spending more in their budgets on criminal justice than on needed social programs or education. In Washington, D.C., for example, the city spends more on criminal justice than on education. In 1992, the city allocated $518 million for education while the criminal justice area was budgeted for $629 million.[36] It costs $6,500 annually to educate a seventeen-year-old; to jail that same teenager for a year costs $21,000.

Partially due to the homicides and incarceration rates, the Black male-female ratio outside of prison dropped to a low 89.6 in 1980 and has been virtually unchanged since that time. This disparity has created a "mating crisis" for marriage-age Black women. According to the Census, "In 1960, 60 percent of Black women 15 years and over were married; by 1991, that proportion had declined to 38 percent.[37]

These conditions present a daunting challenge to Black leaders. Legislative victories and increased political clout for Black elected officials have failed to stop the tidal wave of decline that marks many Black communities. African Americans are demanding more of their leadership than in the past, since available resources are rapidly disappearing.

# Black Leadership Under Attack

Over the years, Black leaders have been diverted from the struggle for equality by relentless harassment, from federal, state, and local authorities. While some Black leaders have attempted to shift the blame for their own weaknesses on outside forces, it is nevertheless true, and well-documented, that Black elected officials have been disproportionately targeted for investigation by law enforcement agencies. The media has also played a critical role in that harassment either through discriminatory coverage or lack of coverage of the activities of Black leaders.

In one study on the subject, it was concluded that "harassment was in fact occurring; that Black elected officials were prevented in a variety of ways from effectively and efficiently carrying out the duties they were elected to perform."[38] Among the tactics used against Black leaders were smear campaigns, IRS audits and investigations, surveillance, phone taps, burglaries, grand jury investigations and indictments, intimidation of voters, recall movements, personal threats, and bombings. Numerous Black elected officials have had to fight these tactics, including Birmingham Mayor Richard Arrington, former D.C. Mayor Marion Barry, former Georgia State Senator Julian Bond, former Mayor Eddie Carthan, former Rep. Shirley Chisholm, Rep. Ron Dellums, and Rep. Harold Ford, among others.

As a defensive measure, a prominent group of African Americans formed the Center for the Study of Harassment of African Americans. The Center was established to investigate and monitor the disproportionate indictments and investigations of Black leaders and activists.[39]

Black grassroots and civil right leaders have also faced these same assaults. In 1993, offices of the NAACP in Tacoma, Washington on July 20 and in Sacramento on July 27 were firebombed by what was believed to be a network of skinheads and White supremacists. The bombings sent 2,000 NAACP offices on national alert. Racial tensions in the Black and civil rights communities were already high because only a few weeks earlier it was discovered that a group of White supremacists had planned to assassinate a number of well-known Blacks in the Los Angeles area, including Rodney King, the victim of a police beating, and to launch a gun attack against a prominent Black Los Angeles church, the First African Methodist Episcopal Church, during Sunday service. The purpose of those planned killings was to begin a race war.[40]

These attacks occur at a time when hate crimes are on the rise in the United States. In 1992, of the 4,755 hate crimes noted by the FBI, 2,963, or about 62 percent, were racial. Blacks accounted for 1,689 (57 percent) of the victims of those crimes.[41] There was a 49 percent increase in hate-related vandalism since 1991.

## Black Politics in the 1990s

As this book goes to press, only months into the Clinton administration, the hope of racial progress through traditional politics seems distant. Conservative pressures to maintain status quo limits on opportunities, the appointment of moderate Blacks to the administration, the withdrawal of the nomination of Lani Guinier as Assistant Attorney General for Civil Rights, continuing and well-documented discrimination in employment and mortgage lending, the selection of Republican David Gergen as a key White House adviser, the Supreme Court rejection of majority-Black voting districts, and the avoidance of confronting head-on the racial problems of the nation bode unfavorably for African Americans. While some Black leaders, such as Johnnetta Cole, Jesse Jackson, Maxine Waters, Ben Chavis, Kweisi Mfume, and Mary Frances Berry, have spoken out on these issues, many others, including some in the Congressional Black Caucus and the Clinton administration, have been loudly silent.

There are some hopeful signs. Even at this early stage, the 1990s have begun to generate a renewed political energy in the Black community from sectors other than the traditional leadership. From the Clarence Thomas nomination and the 1992 presidential campaign to debates about rap music, the Malcolm X phenomenon, the Los Angeles rebellion, and more, battles are once again being fought over what strategies can best deliver the Black community politically. Emerging out of these activities are new strains of radical leadership that are challenging the hegemony of the traditional liberal Black leadership and the growing influence of the new moderates.

## Non-Electoral Struggles

While much of the focus of Black politics in the recent period has been on the election of Blacks and the issues that accompany those efforts, such as voting registration and turnout, a wide range of non-electoral campaigns have been waged that also constitute arenas in which Black leadership develops. In 1992, though most of the Black leadership was keyed in on the presidential election, other important campaigns involving Black activists and leaders also occurred. Among these campaigns were the battles against environmental racism, the struggle for D.C. statehood, efforts around multicultural and Afrocentric education, campus racism, the crisis in Somalia, and support for Haitian refugees.

One of the most important milestones to happen, which has the potential to reshape Black community leadership, is the gang-truce movement involving Black and Latino gangs in inner cities around the nation. For years, local community leaders had attempted to convince warring gangs that their destructive behavior was harmful to themselves and to the community. In some instances, truces were created, but eventually succumbed to the politics of the streets, and the wars would begin again. Part of the reason many of the treaties fell apart was that the impetus behind them came from outside of the gang members themselves. What is distinct about the gang-truce movement of 1992-93 is its self-genesis nature.

Black former and current gang members in Los Angeles, tired of the carnage and war zone atmosphere, met in the late winter and spring of 1992, prior to the Los Angeles rebellion, to resolve long-standing differences and to fashion a treaty. Modeled on the 1949 United Nations-sponsored Arab-Israeli General Armistice Agreement, gangs from the Jordan Downs and Imperial Courts housing projects met and agreed to end the decade plus war that they had been waging against each other and the community.[42] They ended up fashioning a document titled the "Multi-Peace Treaty" that translated major provisions of the Arab-Israeli plan to their reality. For example, a section of the original document that banned "aggressive action by the armed forces" was changed to "no aggressive action by the leading influential gang members." Another section that referred to ending "attacks by land, sea or air" was reinterpreted to mean no "drive-by shootings and random slayings."[43]

An original section added by the gangs called for ending alcohol and drug abuse, a ban on the use of the "N-word [nigger] and B-word [bitch]," and the prohibition on throwing gang signs at rivals, a spark for many shootings and fights. The treaty supported "literacy programs, school attendance, voter registration, investment pools, cultural events, a food bank, and hardship funds created by annual dues of $100 per gang member."[44]

That truce and others that followed appeared to have a positive effect despite attempts by the Los Angeles Police Department to sabotage the effort. Black gang murders decreased significantly in the weeks after the treaties took hold. In the first quarter of 1993 in Los Angeles, "gang-related homicides were down 20 percent, gang-versus-gang murders were down 11 percent, and overall gang crime was down 2 percent."[45] Their truce movement would eventually become part of a national effort to bring peace to gang wars happening in cities around the country. Similar efforts had been started in Chicago and Minneapolis.

From April 30 to May 2, 1993, 164 gang and former gang members and more than sixty observers gathered in Kansas City, Missouri in what was billed as the "National Urban Peace and Justice Summit." Organized with help from the National Council of the Churches of Christ in the USA, the Summit set four goals for itself: "to strengthen the gang truces in cities across the country," "to extend the number of cities in which truces had been established," "to put in place a process to maintain peace," and "to discuss the means of achieving community economic development."[46] Though the gathering was overwhelmingly male, women also attended and, after some struggle, were able to have their voices heard. The women, Latina and Black, had complained about not being included in the planning of the event or being in the leadership of the Summit. The men apologized and women were brought into leadership positions and allowed a workshop. Participation overall was roughly split down the middle between Latinos and Blacks.

Among the "nations" present at the Summit were the Black Disciples, Black Souls, Bloods, Corbras, Crips, El Rukhns, Gangster Disciples, Latin Kings, Stones, and Vice Lords. Representatives came from Albuquerque, Atlanta, Boston, Chicago, Dallas, Lansing, Phoenix, San Antonio, San Francisco, Toledo, Washington, D.C., and several other cities. It's noteworthy that the only nationally known Black leader invited to the Summit was Rev. Benjamin Chavis, a longtime supporter of the gang peace movement and then freshly-selected Executive Director of the NAACP.

There were a number of recommendations coming out of the Summit. The chief demand was for economic development in the cities and poor communities. Along with long-term massive investments, Summit participants also advocated the immediate creation of 500,000 jobs for at-risk youth. To combat police brutality, they called on the community to institute community-based citizens' patrols. President Clinton was asked to appoint an independent national commission on police brutality.

The gang-truce movement is important for several reasons. First, if successful, it would go a long way in restoring the sense of security that has been lost in so many communities as a result of Black male youth violence, much of which is gang-driven. Second, it would also rescue a generation of Black males that the society has been ready to write off, incarcerate, and marginalize. Third, there is every possibility that new political leaders could emerge out of this process. It should be remembered that groups like the Black Panthers, the Student Non-Violent Coordinating Committee, and other radical groups were made up of teenagers and young people in their early twenties. One of the most significant problems plaguing the Black community is that leadership becomes rigid and new leaders are rarely cultivated. In most periods in Black history, new leaders and new organizations have risen to replace older organizations that would not or could not address the issues of their times.

Whither the gangs? One OG (Original Gangster) argues that the gangs are at a crossroads and will either mature into a social or political force or degenerate into a pseudo-underground urban guerrilla band. In any case, it is clear that they can no longer be ignored, contained, or crushed as long as the conditions that gave rise to their existence remain.

## Conclusion

In a general sense, these are the parameters that this book will examine. It seeks to critically analyze the behavior, dynamics, trends, and significance of Black leadership and Black politics in the current period. It is critical to re-emphasize here that Black politics is not simply defined by Black participation in national electoral campaigns or solely by the electoral arena. The grievances of the African American community occur at the community, local, and state levels as well as at the national level. And, it is at all these levels, collectively and individually, that people struggle daily.

It is not politically prudent, however, to ignore the role of the Black community and Black leadership in national elections. These elections serve as important barometers for gauging the political programs and strategies of activists and interest groups across the Black community. In the elections of 1992, a wide window was opened that allowed us to witness the response of Black leaders to issues of race as they affected the electoral arena, Black community life, and the relations among Black leaders themselves.

Finally, with the 1992 election of Bill Clinton, the Black community must address the issue of what can be gained from a Democratic administration and how to effectively get what is needed. Early warning signs indicate, in the words of Frederick Douglas, that without struggle, there will be no progress. Black politics in this era must address policy concerns with a new efficacy, clarity, and determination. We need to focus on identifying, building, and implementing the "Black agenda" and, in that context, speculate on what the Black community can expect from the Clinton administration.

# Chapter 2

# The Changing Structure of Black Leadership

[I]t becomes clear why there is such a lack of quality leadership in Black America today. This absence is primarily a symptom of Black distance from a vibrant tradition of resistance, from a vital community bonded by its ethical ideals, and from a credible sense of political struggle.

—Cornel West[1]

The often chaotic nature of Black politics has led many to believe that no coherent Black political leadership structure exists. In the atmosphere of the 1980s and 1990s, when Blacks have suffered numerous political and economic setbacks, it appears that any semblance of leadership has disappeared.

In fact, a highly structured leadership structure does exist. In the modern era, it has undergone important changes in the last three decades. In order to appreciate its current expression, it is critical to examine the nature of the transformation experienced by Black leadership in the post-civil rights period up to the present.

The period of the Civil Rights movement witnessed the emergence of new Black leadership, though not necessarily new categories of leaders. Many of the new leaders, particularly in the South, were still ministers and civic leaders, but with a new mission and political focus. The nodal point in the reconstruction of Black leadership was the passage of the 1965 Voting Rights Act. In the post-civil rights period leading up to the current era, traditional categories of leaders have been displaced, and this change has profound implications for the Black community. This change not only affects who determines the political agenda in the Black community, but also transforms the very nature of the debate around that agenda.

17

The transference of political leadership from religious leaders and professional Blacks (community-based leadership) to Black politicians (institutional leadership) has been given little examination by political scientists, observers, and activists. Yet, this transformation, more than any other trend, has been one of the chief factors in determining the character of modern-day Black politics.

## Definition of Black Leadership

What is Black leadership and who are Black leaders? African American political scientist Robert Smith argues that the current scholarly literature on the subject does not provide a universal and adequate definition of Black leadership or, for that matter, what it means to be a Black leader.[2] Smith's "consensus" definition, which states that Black leadership is that which "involves affecting the attitudes and behavior of [Blacks] insofar as social and political goals and/or methods are concerned,"[3] seems an appropriate starting point.

Using this definition, it is relatively easy to see that there is an identifiable Black leadership group within the Black community. What is perhaps more difficult to grasp is the structure of that leadership, the dynamics that shape its structure, and the manner in which that structure is transformed.

As Lewis Killian points out, it would be a mistake to assume that leadership structures are replicated regardless of the type and content of the community.[4] In other words, a Black leadership structure will not duplicate or emulate that of the White community. Leadership arises and takes shape in representing a specific community at a specific historic juncture. The leadership that has evolved within the Black community, and that functions as its representative to the dominant community, reflects the differences in how White and Black communities are defined. Killian argues that the Black community is distinct from the White community in three ways: first, it is a sub-community of the larger White community; second, it lacks a formal political organization; and third, its indigenous organizations are a result of exclusion from the larger community.[5]

The Black community, however, cannot be defined by what it is not, but rather has to be defined by what it is. In the view of Howard University's Ron Walters, the definition of the Black community has two aspects: first, the living, breathing neighborhoods where African Americans live and work; and second, the national "community" of racial membership that historically, socially, and culturally binds African Americans in an intricate web of group benefits and obligations.[6]

The development of the Black community does not then simply parallel the development of the White community. The function of the Black community has been to provide "a refuge," as E. Franklin Frazier put it, "in which Negroes could find protection against a hostile world."[7]

Thus, a Black leadership structure has evolved to meet the unique political needs of the Black community-needs that have changed over the years. A common framework for looking at the spectrum of political views of Black leadership is the integrationist-separatist model. Harold Cruse states, for example, that "American Negro history is basically a history of conflict between integrationist and nationalist forces in politics, economics, and culture, no matter what leaders are involved and what slogans are used."[8] Other writers, from Gunnar Myrdal[9] to Manning Marable,[10] have argued that Black leaders fall into the category of either accomodationist or reformist (or protest) leader. Whatever framework is used, Black leadership reflects a diversity of opinions and methods.

The roots of the Black community's leadership lie in the 500,000 Blacks who were "free" at the time of the Civil War. The advantage held by those Blacks who had not been enslaved or who had escaped slavery granted this group leadership of its newly freed kin by default. This leadership was overwhelmingly dominated by "preachers, teachers, undertakers, lodge leaders and those with light skin."[11] Also, as noted by Smith, they were "middle-aged, middle-class men."[12] It is critical to note that during the late 1800s and through the first half of this century, Black elected and appointed officials, of minuscule numbers in the North and virtually non-existent in the South, were the least influential of Black leaders. This structure, with its generally integrationist and accomodationist tendencies, remained intact until the modern civil rights era of the 1950s.

## Black Leadership in the Civil Rights Era

In the protest era of roughly 1945 to 1965, conservative Black leadership was both displaced and transformed. Increasingly dominated by a new generation of civil rights and religious leaders, whose separate qualities often blended together in leaders such as Martin Luther King, Jr., Ralph Abernathy, Wyatt T. Walker, and others, the old Black leadership structure began to crumble. Accused of being "more active in accommodating the masses to misery than in organizing them for an attack on the forces responsible for the misery,"[13] the older Black leadership structure came under increasing attack.

By the early 1960s, the leaders of the Civil Rights movement had supplanted the older religious and business leaders in the Black community. The dominance of the civil rights leaders was reflected in their perceived leadership role by both the Black community and the White community. The 1963 listing of *Ebony* magazine's 100 most influential Blacks, though highly subjective, gives an indication of the power of the civil rights groups vis-a-vis other categories of Black leaders.

In 1963, civil rights leaders represented the largest single category. Church leaders, according to the survey, represented only 5 percent of the national leadership of the time. This categorization of Black leadership is discussed in more detail in Chapter 3.

# Post-Voting Rights Act Era

The passage of the Voting Rights Act of 1965 was a watershed moment in Black political history. At that point, there were fewer than 500 Black elected officials in the nation.[14] Most of these politicians were located in the North and on the East Coast. Although about 60 percent of the Black population resided in the South, that region had only seventy-two Black elected officials.[15] Ten years later, that number would grow to over 2,000.

In 1965, Black leadership, at every level, was in the hands of preachers and civil rights leaders. Then the community experienced what A. Philip Randolph called a "crisis of victory."[16] The Civil Rights movement's inability to further build mass support for the civil rights agenda; the death of King, the movement's symbolic and real leader; and the huge growth in Black voter participation opened the door for a new generation and a new kind of Black leadership.

The effort to dilute and deny Black registration and voting had been unrelenting. Professor J. Morgan Kousser identifies at least sixteen tactics that had been used by southern Whites (and those in the North) to deny Blacks the right to vote and participate in the electoral process.[17] However, once unleashed, Black voting power exploded with hurricane force. In 1960, 1.5 million Blacks voted. By 1968, that number had more than doubled to 3.1 million. In the South, in particular, the Black vote grew by leaps and bounds. In Mississippi, Black voter turnout rose from 6 percent in 1960 to 59 percent by the early 1970s. Alabama saw an increase from 14 to 55 percent over this time period, while Arkansas' turnout rose from 38 percent to a whopping 81 percent.[18]

Black voting power and the possibility of electing large numbers of Blacks to office was also enhanced by demographic changes. As Smith notes,

"Between 1940 and 1970, the percentage of Negroes residing in urban areas increased from 49 percent to 81 percent. Between 1960 and 1970, the number of Negroes in central cities increased by 3.3 million, from 9.9 million to 13.2 million."[19]

This pull of African Americans to the cities by what economist Harold Baron termed the "demand for Black labor" had one other significant impact. Baron argues convincingly that the relocation of Blacks initiated "the formation of a distinct Black proletariat in the urban centers at the very heart of the corporate-capitalist process of production."[20] The collective consciousness that arose out of this process of change would be critical to the political behavior of Blacks both inside and outside of the electoral arena.

These two factors, the unleashing of the voting potential of Blacks and the concentration of Blacks in critical urban centers, were the foundations on which new leadership would emerge. That leadership would overwhelmingly, though not exclusively, consist of Black elected officials. It was also solidly middle-class, primarily male, and integrationist in its political outlook.

For a time, both the fading civil rights leaders and the infant Black elected leadership class were being challenged by Black activists to their left. From the Nation of Islam to the Black Panthers, young African Americans were being more militant, demanding, and confrontational than the Civil Rights movement could ever be. Malcolm X, who would eventually receive more fame and followers in his death than when he was alive, put pressure on Whites to make concessions by his mere presence on the Black political playing field. Malcolm X, who always chided the Black community for not standing up for its rights, fought the civil rights movement for most of his years as a leader of the Nation of Islam. During the last year of his life, however, his stance towards the civil rights movement changed considerably as he met with Fannie Lou Hamer, activists from SNCC, and even participated in some civil rights programs, including one in the South. In the Black agenda that he was constructing—essentially the text of the speech that he was going to deliver on the day he died—he called for voter registration and turnout as ways to put pressure on White politicians and to elect some Blacks to office. Malcolm's influence on the political consciousness of the Black community, and even on King himself, can be seen in King's later radical views opposing the Vietnam War and calling for economic restructuring of U.S. capitalism.

Following the demise of Malcolm, the Black Panthers rolled onto the scene. Calling for the revolutionary overthrow of the system, the Panthers grew into dozens of chapters around the country. Their advocacy of armed self-defense and the U.S. government's massive assault on the organization around the country served to increased their popularity among the young. The

Panthers criticized Black politicians for buying into the system of illusionary power, although it too would later unsuccessfully run candidates for office in Oakland, California. Other national Black groups calling for revolution at the time included the Revolutionary Action Movement (RAM), the Republic of New Africa, the League of Revolutionary Black Workers, the Congress of African People, United Slaves, and Student Organization for Black Unity, among others. Although all of these groups would eventually succumb to internal ideological and political struggles, along with deadly repression from local, state, and federal law enforcement agencies, their legacy would re-emerge in the aims and goals of the new radical reformers of the 1990s.

# Chapter 3

# The Organization of Black Leadership

Black people have no permanent friends, no permanent enemies, just permanent interests.

—the official motto of the Congressional Black Caucus[1]

## Overview

One of the most important organizations to develop out of the Black political restructuring that followed the assassination of Martin Luther King, Jr. was the Congressional Black Caucus, which was formally established in 1971. The original twelve members of the CBC saw themselves clearly as national leaders of the African American community. As they put it, they were the "representatives-at-large for 20 million Black people."[2]

Blacks also began to be elected in significant numbers at the local level, most importantly to the mayor's seat in major cities across the nation. In this regard, Black mayors of big cities, by virtue of their high visibility and powerful positions, assumed national stature. From the early period of Tom Bradley (Los Angeles), Kenneth Gibson (Newark), Richard Hatcher (Gary, IN), Carl Stokes (Cleveland), and Coleman Young (Detroit), to the more recent era of David Dinkins (New York), Wilson Goode (Philadelphia), Maynard Jackson (Atlanta), Sharon Pratt Kelly (Washington, D.C.), and Harold Washington (Chicago), Black mayors have become central to the national Black leadership core.

Of the hundreds of Black mayors around the nation, more than half are located in small, majority Black towns of less than 2,000 residents—towns that are dependent on White-controlled county and state government bodies.[3] Although mayors of towns such as Cotton Plant, Arkansas, Waterproof,

Louisiana, or Mount Bayou, Louisiana have virtually little local clout, they too reflect the shift of leadership to elected officials.

Table 3-1, which lists Black leaders by institution, shows that the influence of Black elected officials grew from 9 percent of the survey in 1963 to 42 percent by 1991, according to *Ebony Magazine*. This growth has been primarily at the expense of the civil rights establishment. Civil rights groups represented 18 percent of the survey in 1963, dropped to 11 percent in 1971, and, to be generous, represent 6 percent today.

Categorizing individuals is not as straightforward as it may seem. Some individuals, such as Jesse Jackson, fall into several categories. While, for our purposes, he is included in the category of civil rights, he could just as easily be classified as an elected official, religious leader, or a nationally known personality. In a similar way, Louis Farrakhan, who is included in the category of religious leaders, could also be classified as a nationalist.

In today's conservative political climate, civil rights organizations are having a difficult time maintaining their base in the Black community. Perhaps the most significant blow to civil rights organizations has been the increasing displeasure by the masses of Blacks with their agenda and strate-

---

### Table 3-1

### *Ebony Magazine's* List of 100 Most Influential Blacks by Institutional Affiliation 1963, 1971, 1980, 1991

| Affiliation | 1963 | 1971 | 1980 | 1991 |
|---|---|---|---|---|
| Elected Officials | 9% | 23% | 25% | 42% |
| Appointed Officials | 9 | 6 | 13 | 3 |
| Judges | 6 | 8 | 7 | 13 |
| Church | 5 | 3 | 7 | 8 |
| Business | 8 | 12 | 6 | 5 |
| Labor | 2 | 5 | 2 | 1 |
| Professional Assocs. | 0 | 1 | 4 | 3 |
| Publishers | 8 | 3 | 3 | 1 |
| Civil Rights Orgs. | 18 | 11 | 7 | 6 |
| Nationalists | 2 | 5 | 0 | 0 |
| Marxists | 0 | 3 | 0 | 0 |
| Personalities | 10 | 5 | 2 | 2 |

Source: *Ebony*, September 1963, pp. 22–23; April 1971, pp. 33–40; May 1980, pp. 45–52; and May 1991, pp. 48–54.

gies. A 1992 national survey of Black opinion of Black leadership, conducted jointly by the *Detroit Free Press* and *Detroit News*, contained mostly bad news for the civil rights groups.[4]

The survey interviewed 1,211 Blacks nationally and asked a wide range of questions principally concerned with the work of the National Association for the Advancement of Colored People (NAACP), the National Urban League (NUL), the Southern Christian Leadership Conference (SCLC), and the Congress of Racial Equality (CORE). While 86 percent thought that the organizations were useful, the majority of respondents felt that the civil rights groups were out of touch with the Black majority on many issues and concerns. For example, 55 percent of the respondents thought that Whites had too much influence over the civil rights groups.[5] Part of this perception is due to the erroneous belief that all of the groups are financially dependent on government grants or White philanthropy (see Table 3-2).

Only 40 percent felt that the groups were doing a good job of building unity within the Black community. More than half, 54 percent, thought the groups did a poor job in addressing the problem of Black unemployment. An even higher percentage, 64 percent, believed that the groups were doing a poor job of fighting crime in the Black community.[6]

When asked how effective particular groups were in representing the interests of Blacks, 87 percent felt that the NAACP was effective while 72 percent thought that the Urban League was effective.[7] It was unclear, how-

## Table 3-2

### Revenue Sources of Major Civil Rights Organizations, 1990

| Revenue Sources | CORE | NAACP Nat'l Office | National Urban League | SCLC |
|---|---|---|---|---|
| Direct Public Support | $5,430 | $2,110,496 | $5,926,095 | $287,276 |
| Indirect Public Support | 0 | 0 | 1,700 | 0 |
| Govt. Grants | 0 | 0 | 13,604,660 | 398,139 |
| Membership Dues | 9,442 | 3,939,561 | 1,246,165 | 15,907 |
| Other Revenue | 172,719 | 726,444 | 2,946,160 | 398,762 |
| Total | $187,591 | $6,776,501 | $23,724,780 | $1,100,084 |

Source: *Detroit News* and *Detroit Free Press*, February 23–24, 1992.

ever, whether respondents had a clear sense of what the organizations were actually doing. Some people were responding to the familiarity that the groups enjoy within the Black community.

Even many of those involved in the Civil Rights movement acknowledge that the distance between the traditional organizations and the community's issues has grown. Wade Henderson, the national legislative director of the NAACP's Washington, D.C. office, stated in an interview that, in terms of the non-civil rights issues facing African Americans, "These are among the most significant and disturbing problems currently confronting the Black community, and we have not yet been able to get a handle on [them] to determine how we're going to approach [them]. It's only recently that organizations like my own, for example, have tried to address that."[8]

The civil rights groups complained, in response, that their programs and work simply did not get the media attention that more sensationalistic events in the Black community did. Benjamin Hooks, then-NAACP president, stated that his organization had a wide range of programs, including those that address the needs of women, prison inmates, the religious community, youth, and the unemployed. He cited their Women in the NAACP (WIN) program, which seeks to empower women, for example, and their NAACP Economics Fair, which he states "has generated more than $45 billion in jobs, contracts, and services for minority people."[9]

Along with the fading support, some of the civil rights groups have had paralyzing internal dissension in recent years. In 1992, the NAACP, the largest of the major Civil Rights groups—500,000 members and about 2,200 chapters nationwide—went through an internal (and embarrassingly public) upheaval. The dramatic resignation of Executive Director Benjamin Hooks, despite his protests that the separation was amicable, was disquieting for many inside and outside of the organization. The public bickering and rushed denials reinforced the view held by many that the civil rights organizations are more concerned with their own maintenance than with advancing the cause of Black rights.

At the annual board meeting, a major dispute erupted over term limits for top officers of the organization. Board Chairman William Gibson opposed a resolution that would have limited official service to two three-year terms. Gibson was in the middle of his second term at the time. When the smoke had cleared, a number of longtime board members had been ousted or had their power reduced, including former NAACP National President Hazel Dukes and civil rights legend Julian Bond.[10]

In the midst of these battles, it was also revealed that the NAACP was struggling with a $500,000 deficit, according to *USA Today*.[11] These financial difficulties reportedly lead to some staff layoffs and one-day-per-pay-period furloughs for some of the remaining staff.

Hooks, while not forced out, apparently grew frustrated with his and the organization's inability to overcome these problems. He also had to withstand criticism inside and outside of the NAACP for his support for D.C. Mayor Marion Barry during his trial on drug charges and his initial public support for Clarence Thomas. The 67-year-old Hooks said that he was retiring because "I recognize that I'll be pushing up roses pretty soon. I'd like to smell a few of them before I start pushing them up."[12]

In the spring of 1993, the selection process to bring in a new executive director to succeed Hooks became quite public and quite controversial as the list of front-runners leaked out. In the end, four names emerged as the top candidates: Ben Chavis, Jesse Jackson, Jewell Jackson-McCabe, and Earl Shinhouser. Jackson's quest for the position surprised many. Jackson's politics are considerably to the left of the NAACP leadership and much more rainbowish.

Yet, at a more sublime level, Jackson's desire to run the NAACP was logical. The NRC took a lot of hits during the 1992 elections. Marginalized by the new administration in the White House, the 500,000-member NAACP would have provided Jackson with a potential escape from the crisis of program and strategy that he had appeared to be in. The organization would also have provided Jackson with the relatively institutional stability that has been sorely lacking in his career. If his strengths and the organization's resources could have achieved a meld, a powerful revitalization of Black grassroots activity could have been in the making.

Chavis also saw the potential of heading the NAACP and developed a strategy for winning the job that included work with a public relations firm, personally visiting chapters and officials of the organization, and even producing a biographical videotape that was sent to all the board members. As Chavis presented his case, he began to win over those who did not know him or knew very little about him. Although a number of newspapers published misleading reports stating that the NAACP search committee had ranked Chavis behind Jackson on a numerical scale developed by the search committee, Chavis actually had the support of the majority of that body. The contest became more controversial when the search committee decided not to recommend any one member and to send the names of all four applicants back to the board for a decision.

Jackson, according to a number of reports, was upset over not winning the position from the search committee. Supporters of Jackson hoped, at that point, that he would avoid the embarrassment of potentially not getting the position by withdrawing his name. Some had felt that for Jackson to even seek the position was a diminution of his stature and had the appearance of his groping for a job. For others, it looked as though the NAACP was becoming more concerned with finding a way to tell Jackson that he didn't have the position than with making a decision. In the end, three days before the board met, Jackson held a press conference and announced that he was withdrawing his name. He stated that while he was honored that someone had submitted his name for the position, and that he had discussed seeking the position with board Chairman William Gibson, he believed that the internal conflicts within the organization were harmful. In a five-page letter sent to Gibson and the board, he specifically opposed a proposal by Gibson that would give the chairperson substantial control over the officers and employees of the NAACP. Jackson argued that the changes being proposed would greatly weaken the executive director, leaving the office of the executive director less able to effectively lead the day-to-day activities of the NAACP. He wrote, "A strong director—with meaningful powers and duties—is essential to a strong NAACP."[13] Jackson concluded that the changes being proposed by Gibson were not acceptable.

In response to what they felt were attacks on the organization by Jackson, some board members wrote a letter of their own. They said that it was "highly likely" that Jackson would not have won the position and that his withdrawal was, "at best, a misunderstanding of the NAACP history of governing, or, at worst, purely self-serving."[14] The authors of the statement claimed that members from around the country had expressed concerns about Jackson's administrative skills and "freelance" style. In the end, the board chose Chavis.

Chavis first came to national attention as a member of the Wilmington 10 in the early 1970s. Chavis, eight Black male high school students, and a White woman were charged with the firebombing of a White-owned grocery store in Wilmington, North Carolina. The retaliatory charges stemmed from anti-segregation protest efforts by Chavis and local civil rights leaders. In a textbook case of southern racial injustice, Chavis and the others were railroaded to jail. Although evidence was fabricated, witnesses bribed, and testimony recanted, the ten were convicted and sent to prison. A national and international movement emerged to free the ten that included support from Amnesty International, petitions to the governor, a film by African director Haili Gerima, and other efforts. In 1980, after having spent four and a half years in prison writing and working on a doctorate degree, Chavis and those who were still in jail were released after their convictions were overturned by the 4th U.S. Circuit Court of Appeals.

As a staffer and director of the United Church of Christ, Chavis earned leadership accolades for his work exposing to the world the brutal mutilations occurring in Angola and organizing against "environmental racism." Jonas Savimbe's UNITA, a renegade army of mercenaries backed by South Africa and U.S. conservatives, was unable to legitimately come to power in Angola and resorted to terrorizing the population by murder and mayhem. As a result of their terrorist activities, principally aimed at civilians, Angola has the highest amputee rate in the world. Domestically, Chavis stood out front in demonstrating how corporations targeted poor Black communities as dumping sites for hazardous wastes and other deadly products.

A longtime advocate of Black independent politics, Chavis had for many years called on Black leftists and radicals to work with and in the civil rights groups. Although he had led a call for a Black independent party, at one point, Chavis had always seen himself as part of the radical wing of the Civil Rights movement. Through his weekly column in mainly Black newspapers, "Civil Rights Journal," he built a following in the Black community.

## Today's Black Leadership Structure

Despite the shakeups noted above, a fairly structured Black leadership construct continues to exist. The Black leadership structure has essentially five tiers: The top level consists of organizations that try to unite Black leadership under one umbrella; the next level includes organizations trying to promote an agenda; the middle level represents Black community investment in Black elected officials; the next level includes national church organizations; and at the bottom level are local leaders who exert immediate influence. What separates the various levels is their ability to influence policymakers (Whites) and maintain legitimacy and power within the African American community. The leadership itself is characteristically liberal, primarily male, dominated by personalities, and politically oscillates between pragmatic and ideological goals.

Defining a structure of Black leadership is complicated by the fact that there are individuals who rise above organizational or categorical definition. As scholar Robert Smith states, "There is still in Black politics a place for the charismatic-individualistic leader."[15] Though Jesse Jackson's National Rainbow Coalition and Operation PUSH rank below other national groups in terms of real influence, resources, and power, Jackson himself certainly ranks in the first tier of national Black leadership. Similarly, though the Nation of Islam's efforts are confined to the fringes of the Black community, its leader, the controversial Minister Louis Farrakhan, exerts an inordinate amount of stature, visibility, and sway.

The first tier of the structure consists logically of those organizations that attempt to unite the national Black leadership under one political umbrella. At present, the only ongoing organization making this effort is the Black Leadership Forum. The barely known BLF is composed of the leaders of thirteen national Black organizations. It serves mainly as a clearinghouse on issues of national concern to the Black community. Unlike some Black leadership institutions, the BLF is explicitly tied to the interests of the Black community, although how much loyalty it has won from that community is highly questionable. Ron Walters remarks that the BLF is "attempting to function in a national leadership capacity with an uncertain basis of legitimacy."[16]

The second tier of national Black leadership is the Congressional Black Caucus (CBC). Due to its national recognition by Blacks and Whites, its ability to wield influence within the Black community, and its capacity to promote (if not implement) an agenda, the CBC exerts more power than any other individual Black organization. To some degree, however, the perceived power of the CBC is greater than its real power. In Congress, the CBC has rarely advanced a united agenda and often unites more as a defensive posture than as an aggressive proponent of a given set of legislative goals. While central to the coalitions that have come together in the past to sponsor national mobilizations of Blacks, such as the March on Washington and the marches to make Martin Luther King, Jr.'s birthday a national holiday, the CBC has yet to demonstrate an ability to mobilize on its own.

Perhaps more importantly, the CBC must confront the contradictory objectives of, on the one hand, maintaining symbolic representation, while on the other, continuing to gain legitimacy within a governmental institution that many within the Black community view as built on interests counter to Black development. To quote political scientist Marguerite Ross Barnett, "The Congressional Black Caucus, in order to be effective within the electoral context, would have to understand and directly attack the structural conditions of Black subordination."[17] It's unlikely that such an assault will make it on the CBC's strategic agenda.

Also, the CBC became a victim of its own success. As the number of Blacks in Congress has grown, there appears to be decreasing unity among its members on critical Black and non-Black issues, such as who to support in a presidential election, or even whether to promote its own alternative budget. And there is every reason to think that the situation will continue along this trend as the CBC expands. By the beginning of the 103rd Congress in 1993, the CBC had grown to forty Black members, primarily due to redistricting following the 1990 census. As the largest single political bloc in Congress, the CBC potentially exerts a significant amount of influence over the passage of legislation. This power is tempered, however, by the political differences internal to the Caucus. While the majority of its members will probably not deviate too far from center, the CBC already houses politicians who are straining just to be civil with each other. Ideological orientations range from the extreme conservatism of Republican Rep. Gary Franks to the leftist orientations of Reps. John Conyers and Ronald Dellums.

In 1993, under the leadership of Kweisi Mfume (D-MD), the CBC became much more visible and outspoken on a wide range of issues concerning the Black community. The Caucus has also taken steps to strengthen its links with other groups in Congress, particularly the Congressional Hispanic Caucus. If the CBC can maintain even minimal unity—not a small "if"—its leadership role in the Congress and the broader Black community will be enhanced considerably. External to Congress, perhaps the biggest test of the power and politics of the Caucus will be manifested in the role, if any, it decides to play as a bloc in the 1996 presidential elections.

The third tier of national Black leadership also reflects the political investment that the Black community has made in elected officials. Groups such as the National Black Caucus of Local Elected Officials, National Black Caucus of State Legislatures, and National Conference of Black Mayors are the organized expressions of Black elected power. Although the leaders of these groups, for the most part, are not well known, their sway with policymakers and legislators at the local, county, and state levels is critical. Much of the influence vested in elected officials is rooted in their potential ability to deliver material benefits to the Black community. Unlike many in the civil rights and nationalist communities, whose objectives are sometimes more symbolic than concrete, elected officials tend to focus on pragmatic issues and concerns.

The fourth level of leadership would appear to be national church organizations, such as the Progressive National Baptist Convention and the National Baptist Convention, U.S.A., and policy institutions, such as TransAfrica and the Joint Center for Political and Economic Studies. These groups have important and wide constituencies within the Black working-class and middle-class communities. They also have the resources to activate and push those constituencies in a certain direction. Finally, they are able to gain the ear of policymakers because of their demonstrated ability to mobilize and influence large and critical sectors of the African American community around specific policy issues and concerns.

At the fifth and final level of the leadership structure in the Black community are various community activists, local Democratic party leaders, local elected officials, civil rights organizations, radical organizations, nationalist groups, and individuals. For the most part, this grouping exerts more immediate leadership over clusters of local Black communities, but has relatively little influence over Whites in the community or the local power structure.

Many leaders who have been delegitimated by Whites and by system-oriented Blacks find a base among significant sectors of Blacks in local areas. The District of Columbia's Marion Barry, Milwaukee's Michael McGee, and New York's Al Sharpton are only three of many individuals who have had little legitimacy with Whites and may even alienate many Blacks, yet clearly must be seen as part of the Black community's leadership.

No discussion of Black leadership in the 1990s can avoid dealing with the role of Min. Louis Farrakhan and the reconstituted Nation of Islam. Without a doubt, Farrakhan remains one of the most popular Black leaders in this period. The Nation's limited but undeniable success in ridding some Black communities of drug dealers, and Farrakhan's unyielding critique of racism is perceived as a last line of resistance by many who believe that other Black leaders have "sold out." In the face of this popularity, some liberal Black leaders have reached out to Farrakhan and the Nation of Islam.

Efforts to reunite Black radical liberals and Black nationalists is a common theme in Black political history. However, from Marcus Garvey and W.E.B. DuBois to Malcolm X and Martin Luther King, the hope of forging a trans-ideological working unity has often crashed against the hard rock reality of fundamental programmatic, strategic, and philosophical differences. Nowhere has the contemporary effort been more evident than at the 1993 Annual Congressional Black Caucus Legislative Weekend affair in Washington, D.C.

On September 16, 1993 at "Race in America" forum the speakers included Jesse Jackson, President of the National Rainbow Coalition; Ben Chavis, Executive Director of the NAACP, Kweisi Mfume, Chairman of the Congressional Black Caucus, and Min. Louis Farrakhan. Rep. Maxine Waters was added to the panel at the last minute when it was belatedly realized that all the scheduled participants were men. Tension dominated the meeting because of the controversy surrounding Farrakhan's exclusion from the 30th Anniversary March on Washington event held only three weeks earlier. According to the organizers of the march, there was never any intention of inviting Farrakhan to speak. However, Farrakhan's followers and others close to the march contend that Farrakhan was to be invited, but that the invitation was held back due to pressure from Rabbi David Saperstein, Executive Director of the Union of American Hebrew Congregation. Those supporting Farrakhan backed up their charges with a copy of a letter sent by Saperstein, published in the Nation's newspaper, *The Final Call*, and in other Black publications, to leaders of the march including Jackson, Chavis, Coretta Scott King, and march coordinator Walter Fauntroy. The letter stated that if Farrakhan was invited to speak, then Jewish groups who were supporting the event would pull out.

Although Farrakhan was not at the march, his followers were there distributing copies of the Saperstein letter and clearly angry that march organizers had appeared to capitulate to Saperstein and excluded a popular, though controversial, Black leader. Black-Jewish relations during the time were already frayed by revelations of spying by the Anti-Defamation League, and by the ADL and American Jewish Congress support of conservative efforts to jettison Lani Guinier.

At the forum, which CBC members had hoped would focus on strategies for change, all attention zeroed in on Farrakhan. In response to his criticism about Black leaders' backing down to those outside of the Black community, Chavis and Mfume issued apologies to Farrakhan. Chavis stated that it was a mistake not to invite Farrakhan to speak at the Anniversary march. In his closing remarks, which in subsequent days fueled even more controversy, Mfume pledged to enter into a "covenant with the nation of Islam" similar to the CBC's relation with the NAACP and other groups. To the cheering crowd, the coming together of Farrakhan and the CBC seemed a remarkable achievement and a necessary bonding in this age when disillusionment and disappointment with traditional Black leadership is at its zenith.

This event was remarkable given the tendency of many in the Black leadership elite to distance themselves from Farrakhan. When given the choice between White liberal and moderate support and association with Farrakhan, most have chosen the former. While some truly believe that accusations that Farrakhan is anti-Semitic are accurate, others are simply protecting what they perceive is their non-racial image and political ambitions.

Those who feared a backlash from the meeting's rapprochement did not have to wait long. Within the CBC itself, members began to disassociate themselves from Mfume's words and actions. Some stated, generally off-the-record, that Mfume acted on his own volition and did not represent the views of all the members. Congresswoman Eleanor Holmes Norton, the day after the forum, did a television interview where she was critical of Farrakhan and questioned Mfume's judgement. According to one Capitol Hill newsletter, *Congress Daily*, some Jewish members of Congress called Black Members to express their "concern" and "surprise" about the budding CBC-NOI alliance.[18] The response of many of the Black members, it was reported, was to state the Mfume acted as an individual and that, in this instance, did not speak for CBC as a whole.

The truce was also attacked in the mainstream press. A *New York Times* editorial said that Mfume "seems not to understand the uses of power" and that he "behaved like a novice." Ominously, the *Times* stated that "his conduct suggests a misconception about what constitutes genuine leadership and whence its power flows."[19] While some Black reporters, such as the *Washington Post*'s Dorothy Gilliam, celebrated the alliance, others raised doubts.[20] William Raspberry, also with the *Post*, argued that "Farrakhan brings with him the baggage of anti-Semitism" and that he has an "obsession with Jews."[21] Raspberry felt that Black leaders reaching out to Farrakhan would drive away critical White allies.

Attacks on Mfume became so intense that he was forced to reply with a statement on *CNC* letterhead. In a three-paragraph missile, that did not once mention Farrakhan by name, Mfume highlighted the Nation's efforts around drugs and violence, he wrote that the CBC will "continue to seek a dialogue and to work where possible with those who we feel are committed as we are to real and meaningful social change for our people, including the Nation of Islam."[22]

As in the past, prospects for the liberal-nationalist alliance are probably slim. Interests disengage fairly quickly. Efforts to construct what Jackson termed "operational unity" between Black liberal and nationalists remain important, however. These alliances, however, as Jackson vainly attempted to discuss at the meeting, must be built around a concrete program and around concrete issues. There must be a unifying strategy and program—a guide to measure the commitment, clarity, and capabilities of Black leadership.

Black nationalism has never completely disappeared from Black political life. Particularly in periods of increased dispossession and abandonment by government, group solidarity rises and a circle-the-wagons attitude appears. In the 1990s, frustration with the federal and local governments and with liberal Black leadership, many of whom themselves may bend toward a less integrationalist stance, will likely create new political leaders whose first (and last) instinct will be toward one of the many varieties of nationalism that have always existed in Black America.

This overall structure is built on a house of cards. The escalating social crisis within the African American community has not yielded to any sector of Black leadership. Indeed, it would appear that the alienation of many Blacks from Black leadership, particularly those most trapped in poverty and dysfunctionality, is expanding exponentially. If we return to our definition that Black leadership implies the ability to affect the attitudes and behavior of Blacks, then the term "endangered species" gains new relevance for the current Black leadership structure. In other words, the situation is ripe for new leadership models and strategies to emerge.

# The Future of Black Leadership

A number of challenges, both internal and external, confront Black leadership in the immediate future. At the top of the agenda is the issue of how Black leadership can maintain legitimacy at a time when a large section of the Black community is facing one of the most severe social crises in its history. Cynicism toward Black leaders is probably at an all-time high and is reinforced by the negative images of Black leadership in the mass media in recent years, e.g., the arrest and jailing of Marion Barry, turmoil within the NAACP, and disunity in response to the Clarence Thomas nomination. Under these circumstances, the ability of Black leadership to sustain and reproduce itself is severely undermined.

This limit will be even more profoundly felt in the period ahead as the demands for more resourceful and talented leadership grows. Black leadership in the future, whether in the form of an organization or a movement, must be capable of an organizational efficacy unlike any of the past. Leadership will be required to raise funds, administrate, manage, mobilize, inspire, develop strategies, and win concrete victories all at the same time. All of this must happen in the face of systemic resistance that will be greater than at any point in recent memory.

For the traditional leaders, the strategy of voter registration and voter turnout will likely remain predominant for the foreseeable future for two reasons. First, the advocates and implementers of this strategy are also its chief beneficiaries. Certainly, Black elected officials have a vested interest in the continued growth of the Black electorate. Second, the level of community development necessary to implement an alternative strategy is still maturing. The human and material resources that aided in the proliferation of an array of strategies in the protest era have dissipated, declined, or disappeared. As critical as the Black vote has been for the expansion of Black political power, merely voting must not become an end unto itself. As far back as 1944, Ralph Bunche warned of the danger of fascination with the vote. He wrote, "The vote has become a fetish with many Negroes, but there is little evidence that social problems anywhere in the world are solved by fetishism."[23]

The disproportionate and growing investment of leadership in Black elected officials must also be examined critically. Some critics of this trend believe that even under the best circumstances, Black elected officials have a marginal usefulness. Marable argues that "Black politicians in any real sense do not 'govern'—they merely seek to participate in the system as marginal adjuncts to a long-standing process."[24] Whatever one's views on these elected and appointed officials, the conditions of the masses of Blacks make it clear that just putting African Americans in office is no guarantee of social progress. Indeed, it can be argued that to just focus on electing Blacks diverts financial resources, time, leadership skills, and energy from developing strategies that, in the end, will be more beneficial to the Black community in the long run.

Still others call more explicitly for a return to strategies of mobilization and protest. If Black grievances are to be addressed, they reason, it will come from a program of planned social disequilibrium. Along these lines, social critics Frances Fox Piven and Richard Cloward state that "whatever influence lower-class groups occasionally exert in American politics does not result from organization, but from mass protest and the disruptive consequences of protest."[25] As King and the earlier civil rights leaders recognized, it was the in-your-face confrontational politics of protest that moved the nation to reform.

A growing local Black leadership argues for a return to non-electoral modes of struggle, including protests, civil disobedience, a focus on internal community development, and separatist Black cultural practices. While not dismissing struggles in the electoral arena, they are critical of a misplaced priority on that strategy. Many contend, including some elected officials, that without a mass movement and mass-based organizations challenging the system, gains in the electoral and legislative arenas will be minor.

# Chapter 4

# The New Black Politics

Blessed are those who struggle
Oppression is worse than the grave
Better to die for a noble cause
Than to live and die a slave

—The Last Poets[1]

To become the instruments of a great idea is a privilege that
history only gives occasionally.

—Martin Luther King, Jr.[2]

## Emerging Political Trends in the Black Community

A political Perestroika of sorts has occurred in Black America. A quiet, but undeniable restructuring has unfolded in the past decade that has seen a challenge of the liberal Black leadership structure by two emerging strains of Black political activists and thinkers.

Both of these developing strains reject traditional liberalism as well as the neoconservatism that has attracted some Blacks. These strains or tendencies emerged out of two different political orientations and, more important, hold vastly different notions of what constitutes and will achieve Black liberation.

One strain, whose presence and position grew during the 1992 presidential campaign, can be termed the "new politics of accommodation." This group is made up disproportionately of elected officials, but includes business leaders, entertainers, a few religious leaders, and heads of some professional organizations. Some writers have termed their politics as "post-Black." Political writer Manning Marable, in applying the term to Black elected officials, defines post-Black politicians as "elected officials, recruited from the professional classes, who are racially and ethnically 'Black' but who favor programs with little kinship to the traditional agendas of the civil rights movement...[they] generally favor the death penalty, oppose new taxes, and support corporate interests."[3] Other terms that have been used to describe the politics of this group are "cross-over"[4] and "deracialization."[5]

While moderate in political perspective, this trend is distinct from the conservative yelpings of the Shelby Steeles and Thomas Sowells, who essentially argue that racism has disappeared and that discussion of race and racism (let alone attacking the problem) is fruitless and counterproductive. The post-Black tendency acknowledges the continuing legacy of racialized differences within the United States.

Yet, they are also distinct from the old civil rights crowd in a number of ways. First, they are less community-based than the civil rights leaders of the past. As civil rights scholar Clayborne Carson has argued, most of the civil rights leaders in the 1950s and 1960s were locally based and accountable to the Black community.[6] They could often wield more influence than national figures, including Rev. Martin Luther King, Jr., in many situations. The new Black accomodationists, in many cases, have weak local bases despite many being elected officials. Furthermore, these elected and appointed officials represent not only a broader racial constituency, but also a wider class constituency. They must deal not only with the interests of their poor and working-class residents of all races, but also with those of the corporate, real estate, banking, and commercial sectors of their districts or wards. This latter set contributes heavily to campaign coffers as well as employing skilled lobbyists to ensure that their concerns are presented in the most effective and aggressive manner possible.

The second difference concerns their relationship with the Democratic Party. While many Black leaders of the past saw the relationship as primarily tactical, for many Black politicians today it has strategic value. In other words, in their estimation the party has a long-term significance to securing equal rights and opportunities for African Americans. This means not only that they dismiss any idea of a third party, but also that they are willing to defend the Democratic Party first and foremost even if some of its individual leaders come under criticism. Unlike leaders of other social and political groups, such as women's organizations and gay and lesbian groups, who advocate a quid pro quo relationship with the major parties and are prepared to electorally punish those who do not address their concerns, these moderate Black leaders are generally mute in promoting any new strategies.

# The New Radicals and Electoral Politics

The other political trend to strongly emerge in the Black community can be termed the "new politics of resistance," i.e., the new generation of radical reformers. For this group, the battle for civil rights has reached a strategic end. While acknowledging that the civil rights struggle is not over, they advocate a wider agenda that includes economic and political concerns that have been ignored (or at least are perceived to have been) by the major parties and the established Black leadership. Expansion of human rights, building multi-racial coalitions, ending environmental racism, and implementing strong legislation against corporate crime are seen as just as critical to a Black agenda as are stopping racist violence, strengthening affirmative action, and easing access to voting. More sophisticated than the militants of the past, the new radicals struggle for community, political, and economic empowerment rather than just mere access. In addition, the demand for more democracy both in society and in the movement is central to their politics.

Unlike many Black radicals in the 1960s, the current group sees political and tactical value in electoral politics. Although, like more moderate Black leaders, they tend to support Democrats over Republicans, on occasion support for an Independent is given. Overall, however, they are unwilling to concede control over public policy and public resources to White or Black officials of any party whose interests are other than those of the Black community. Thus, the new radicals have seen the necessity of participating in insurgent electoral movements even while engaging in non-electoral campaigns.

The new radical leaders recognize that to engage in electoral politics does not mean an abandonment of non-electoral struggles and strategies. While the historic record shows that many former civil rights activists and newly elected Black officials appear to make that separation, it is unnecessary and unwise. Building community institutions, engaging in protest politics, creating grassroots economic development plans, initiating alternative cultural organizations, and fighting for new intellectual and scholarly discourses must go hand-in-hand with the battle for political empowerment in all its various forms, including electoral. Radical reformers argue that, indeed, for the Black community to be effective electorally and in other arenas implies a willingness and a capacity to engage in protest activities. In many cases, this will mean confronting not just intractable White officials and White corporate power, but also Black elected and appointed officials.

A second point that is considered by the radical leaders is that economic development and power in the United States, as well as the distribution of social and cultural norms, is rooted in political power and public policy. The development of capitalism in the United States did not proceed outside of the public policy arena. It was the political power to meet the needs, limits, resources, military backing, ideological atmosphere, educational, and socialization interests of capital that allowed the present economic system to take shape. It is through public policy that the nation's tax system is progressive or regressive, that trade policy is expansive or curtailed, that investments in the developing world are exploitative or balanced, or that federal resources and revenues are wasted on military spending, or investment in communities in need. To disengage from this process is to surrender a key sphere of power relations to the forces that least have the Black community's interests at stake.

It has become essential for those who seek to understand the dynamics of African American life and politics to analyze the role that electoral politics plays in the Black community. Virtually every ideological strain across Black America's political landscape has become engaged at some level in the electoral area. Recent election cycles, for example, have seen the involvement, indeed, the candidacies of nationalists and even members of the Nation of Islam. This participation reflects the fact that electoral politics has moved from the back burner of Black struggle, where it was less than two decades ago, to a critical, if not central role in Black politics.

The tracking of these emerging radical Black voices has perhaps been best articulated in James Jennings' groundbreaking *The Politics of Black Empowerment: The Transformation of Black Activism in Urban America.*[7] Jennings argues effectively that the struggle in the 1950s and 1960s was to implement a progressive Black electoral and community agenda, and did not end with merely getting access to the ballot and to elected office. In the 1980s, a much broader grouping of Black activists than the traditional Left began to conclude that progressives, rather than just their liberal allies, must obtain political and economic power if a progressive agenda were to be realized. They found comradeship with many of the older activists and thinkers who had broken with the Civil Rights movement many years before. Many of the activists involved in those early efforts of the Civil Rights movement melded into the insurgent electoral efforts of Jesse Jackson's 1984 and 1988 presidential campaigns, Harold Washington's 1983 mayoral race and administration in Chicago, Mel King's 1983 mayoral race in Boston, and other historic electoral challenges by progressive African Americans.

These campaigns reinvigorated activists, intellectuals, and many heretofore apolitical forces in many Black communities across ideological and class lines. At the core of these campaigns was a vigorous and committed struggle against racism. In practice, however, these campaigns went beyond just racial identity politics because they confronted not only traditional White power structures, but also old-line Black politicians who hesitated to get with the program of challenge that these confrontations represented. For example, support for Jackson at the national level or support for Harold Washington's campaigns at the local level became lines of demarcation between the new radicals and those unwilling to challenge the status quo. For Jackson, this line was more taut in 1984, when his campaign more truly represented an insurgency, than in 1988, when a more mainstream campaign was conducted and lots of political room was made for many of the Black politicians and leaders who had not supported him in the first campaign.

Jennings argues that a "new Black political activism" emerged out of these crusades. This new politics moves beyond just seeking access to power to seeking power itself. In dozens of interviews conducted around the nation, Jennings talked with Black grassroots organizers who have spent the last decade and a half challenging the power structures of White and Black elected officials and local corporate barons by fusing electoral campaign savvy with classical protest tactics.

The political arrival of this generation of Black moderates and radicals represents less a paradigmatic shift than a paradigmatic flowering. These trends have always existed in the Black community, but have evolved with each generation with new dynamics, alliances, purposes, and effectiveness. Liberalism still remains the dominate political ideology of the Black leadership elite. However, the ideology of liberalism is increasingly being criticized as unable to resolve the spiraling crisis of deterioration faced by many, if not most, sectors of the Black community.

## Conclusion

The growth in elected officials, over 8,000, has changed not only the notions of Black leadership, but also the practice of Black politics. It would be erroneous, however, to conclude that non-electoral concerns have lost their saliency or relevance. Radical Black activists have demonstrated in practice that such a bifurcation will not be tolerated.

As argued below, not only radical Black leaders and activists have seen the value of using the electoral arena in different ways. Black voters have also become more sophisticated and strategic in their voting patterns and more likely to confound conventional wisdom as they define their interests distinct from how others would like to define them.

# Chapter 5

# Independent and Alternative Challenges

Things fall apart. The center can not hold.

—William Butler Yeats
"The Second Coming"

In numerous venues across the nation, grassroots leaders have risen up to challenge the political hegemony of liberal and traditional Black leadership. In the first decade after the passage of the Voting Rights Act, the Black community supported wholeheartedly the "first" Black mayor, council member, school board member, county official, or state representative or senator. Although often these first-time elected officials were more moderate than the political movement that put them in power, their symbolic meaning and, relative to most of the previous White officials, their willingness to effect changes that would benefit the Black community endeared them to the community and generally assured Black support in future elections. Early big-city mayors, such as Detroit's Coleman Young, Los Angeles' Tom Bradley, and Newark's Kenneth Gibson, fit this model.

But what a difference an era makes. By the mid-1980s, after a decade or so of experience with Black leadership in managerial and administrative political power, a new generation of activists feel little nostalgia for—or even remember—the era before Blacks were increasingly elected to leadership roles. This generation is not only willing to challenge the power of Black leaders, but has effectively organized to do so. One area where this has been the most apparent is in electoral politics. At the national electoral level, the first wave of this insurgency at a mass level was the historic Jesse Jackson campaign of 1984, followed, with some moderation, by the 1988 Jackson effort. Much of the energy of those campaigns came from the activists who had taken on Black leaders at the local and state levels and were now prepared to struggle with those national Black leaders who were perceived to be unwilling to join the Jackson campaign. By 1992, with Jackson out of the race, a number of Black radical urgings within the national electoral arena took shape. While these campaigns generated relatively few votes and limited support, and, to some degree, were unknown to many in the Black community, they underscored a new phase in the African American movement for political power.

Jackson's entrance into the 1984 and 1988 races confronted not only the moderates and conservatives in the Democratic Party, but also directly affronted the hegemonic political position of traditional Black leadership within the Black community. In 1993, it was the hope of Black presidential candidates Ron Daniels and Lenora Fulani to repeat this struggle. Determined to break up the two-party system, Daniels and Fulani entered the race early and stayed until the very end. Other Black progressives, nationalists, and conservatives below the presidential level also ran as outsiders as either radical Democrats, Republicans, third-party candidates, or Independents. These efforts, though garnering few votes, not only put on notice the major parties that they would be challenged, but also sought to wedge Black leadership either away from the major parties or away from the Black masses.

The 1992 political campaigns of Fulani, Gwen Patton, and the many Black women who ran for Congress also sought to break open the male-dominated sphere of Black electoral politics. Several studies have indicated that, across the board, Black women tend to be more progressive on issues than Black men. In one study, in virtually every category of opinion about Reagan, Black women were less charitable than Black men. Women viewed Reagan as more prejudiced (74 percent to 69 percent) and disapproved of his job performance more strongly (85 percent to 78 percent). Overall, more women stated that they would prefer a Democratic administration to a Republican one (74 percent to 65 percent).[1]

Outside of electoral politics, a number of Black women were also becoming more visible as national leaders in the Black community. Spelman College President Johnnetta Cole, Children's Defense Fund head Marian Wright Edelman, Civil Rights Commissioner Mary Frances Berry, and others were more and more being relied upon to provide leadership around the many issues confronting the Black community.

# Ron Daniels and the Struggle for Black Independent Politics

Ron Daniels, a longtime advocate and organizer for Independent Black politics, symbolically announced his candidacy on Columbus Day, October 14, 1991, in Washington, D.C. Daniels stated:

> While this nation prepares to settle in for yet another season of politics as usual, I believe that the progressive movement should launch a massive human rights crusade to place America's injustices against African people, Native Americans, Latinos, Asian Americans, and poor and working people before the world. As a part of that crusade, an Independent presidential campaign should be seen as a vehicle to intensify the fight for power. Those who have been the historical victims of a racist and exploitative system must amass the power to govern and create a new society.[2]

Daniels' only experience at running for office happened in 1977 when he ran for mayor of Youngstown, Ohio. He captured 18 percent of the vote in a three-way race, a record for an Independent. He has taught at Youngstown State University, Hiram College, and Kent State, all in Ohio, and at Cornell University in Ithaca, New York.

From 1974 to 1980, Daniels was president of the National Black Political Assembly (NBPA). The NBPA played a key role in expounding the idea of Black politics Independent of the two major political parties. Formed in March 1972 in Gary, Indiana, the gathering was attended by over 12,000 people.[3] In keeping with the idea of Black unity across ideological spectrums, the convention was chaired by Gary Mayor Richard Hatcher, Imamu Amiri Baraka, the leading nationalist of the time, and Rep. Charles Diggs from Detroit. The NBPA was the most significant effort at Black unity since the days of the Black Power conferences in the mid-60s and the 1970 Atlanta Congress of African People, which brought together 3,500 including Julian Bond, Louis Farrakhan, Whitney Young, and Amiri Baraka.[4] The Atlanta gathering passed a resolution that boldly stated: "Now is the time for a Black political party."[5]

The notion of a Black political party surfaced again at the NBPA convention. A number of individuals who spoke at the convention, including Jesse Jackson, called for building a Black political party. Jackson stated "that the water had already broken and that ready or not the Black party was on its way."[6] Calling for a Black liberation party, Jackson stated, "Without the option of a Black political party, we are doomed to remain in the hip pocket of the Democratic party and the rumble seat of the Republican Party."[7] Jackson would later back off this position.

Also, the idea of running an African American candidate for president outside of the major parties was discussed. The seeds of this notion had been around for at least a year and had been discussed extensively by Black political leaders and activists such as Jackson, Rep. John Conyers, Cleveland's mayor Carl Stokes, New York's Percy Sutton, and others.[8] It is important to note here that Black male leadership, both inside the CBC and outside of it, dismissed the candidacy of Rep. Shirley Chisholm who was running for president at the time.

The militant call of the convention stated in no uncertain terms that the United States was "built on the twin foundations of White racism and White capitalism."[9] In what has become known as the Gary Statement, it was written:

> We come to Gary in an hour of great crisis and tremendous promise for Black America. While the White nation hovers on the brink of chaos, while its politicians offer no hope of real change, we stand on the edge of history and are faced with an amazing and frightening choice: We may choose in 1972 to slip back into the decadent White politics of American life, or we may press forward, moving relentlessly from Gary to the creation of our own Black life...None of the Democratic candidates and none of the Republican candidates—regardless of their vague promises to us or to their White constituencies—can solve our problems or the problems of this country without radically changing the systems by which it operates.[10]

However, the dream of Black political and ideological unity began to unravel even before the convention opened. For the most part, members of the CBC and many other Black elected officials were reluctant to sign on to the radical statements emanating from NBPA activists. Many had already joined or were about to join the campaigns of either Hubert H. Humphrey or George McGovern. A number of the moderate elected officials were clearly uncomfortable with the radical message of the nationalists and various socialists who were involved in both the leadership and general membership of the NBPA. Furthermore, the presidential campaign of Shirley Chisholm also raised some issues that created divisions. At the root of the tensions was the refusal by male members of the CBC to support her decision to run as a Democrat.

The main split in the NBPA occurred between the nationalists and the Black elected officials. Ideological differences over support for the Democrats and resolutions concerning busing and the Palestine cause divided the NBPA beyond repair. Although Daniels, who was the leader of the Ohio delegation, and others sought to maintain unity, most of the Black elected officials did not participate beyond Gary.

The NBPA met in Little Rock, Arkansas in 1974. Soon after Daniels was elected chair of the struggling organization at a meeting in Columbus, Ohio. The Assembly met again in Cincinnati, Ohio in 1976. At that gathering, the focus was on launching the candidacy of an Independent Black candidate. Unfortunately, the leaders of the NBPA did not discover until he was actually speaking that their preferred choice of Rep. Ron Dellums was rejecting the offer to run. He stated, "It is not my moment; it's not my time."[11]

Although its bi-annual gatherings grew smaller and smaller, its core activists continued to call for African Americans to move away from being locked into the Democratic and Republican parties. At its meeting in New Orleans in 1980, activist Rev. Benjamin Chavis put forth a resolution that called for the creation of a Black independent political party within 100 days.[12] The resolution was passed and work began both on planning the logistics of organizing a convention and constructing a charter for the impending body.

The National Black Independent Political Party (NBIPP) was founded in Philadelphia in November 1980, only days after the election of Ronald Reagan, at a convention attended by 1,500 to 2,000 Black activists, organizers, and intellectuals. The gathering spanned the political spectrum from nationalists to socialists to Democratic Party operatives. Eventually, Daniels was elected chairperson. NBIPP ultimately succumbed to internal ideological squabbles and became peripheral to other political activities occurring within the Black community, most notably, the 1984 Jackson for President campaign. The NBIPP charter prevented the organization from endorsing or working for Democrats or Republicans. Although individual members were naturally free to do as they pleased, the organization itself could not and would not support Jackson's action. Daniels understood and, as an individual, supported Jackson's challenge to the Democrats. However, as head of the organization, he did not deem it politically appropriate to play any kind of leading role in the campaign.

By the time of Jackson's 1988 run, Daniels had left NBIPP and had become a part of Jackson's staff as executive director of the National Rainbow Coalition (NRC) in 1987. As the Jackson operations began to turn toward the campaign, Daniels was tapped to become deputy campaign manager and southern regional coordinator for the Jackson team. Although

Daniels' work on the campaign was exceptional and productive by all accounts, he did not rejoin the Jackson staff after 1988.

Dating back to as early as 1990, Daniels had contemplated running for president as an Independent. He argued that the NRC was virtually inactive and that a void existed in Black and progressive politics. Under the banner of Campaign for a New Tomorrow, Daniels articulated the goals and objectives of his efforts to bring a new politics to the nation. Among the goals that he outlined were to:

- utilize an Independent presidential campaign as a vehicle for massive political education;
- develop a progressive platform and agenda with the "Black Agenda" and the issues of other people of color, the poor, and working people as the core;
- launch an Independent multi-racial campaign led by African Americans and people of color;
- project an Independent presidential candidate with a Native American woman as the vice presidential choice;
- convene a national progressive convention after the Democratic and Republican conventions; and
- build an independent political organization.

His progressive platform called for elimination of racism and all forms of discrimination; complete equality for women; creation of a socially responsible economy with sustainable development; enactment of a domestic Marshall Plan; demilitarization of the economy and at least a 50 percent cut in the military budget; quality, equal education for all; respect for the sovereignty and treaty rights of Native Americans; reparations for African Americans; and a peace and development foreign policy.

As he promised at the outset of his campaign, Daniels also recruited a Native American woman, Asiba Tupahache, to be his running mate. Articulate and clear-sighted, she became the first Indian woman to run for the office of the vice president and helped Daniels make the case that multi-racial leadership must be the wave of the future.

Initially, 14 states and the District of Columbia were targeted for the building of local and state campaign committees. He hoped to raise at least $5,000 each in those states, which would then qualify him for federal matching funds. These states included California, Florida, Georgia, Illinois, Louisiana, Maryland, Massachusetts, Michigan, Missouri, New Jersey, New York, Ohio, Pennsylvania, and South Carolina. The next level of states targeted for organizing included Alabama, Indiana, Minnesota, Mississippi, North Carolina, Virginia, and Wisconsin.

Daniels' campaign generated enthusiasm among a number of groups and individuals in the progressive movement and on the Left. Individuals affiliated with the National Committee for Independent Political Action (NCIPA) worked on Daniels' campaign, as they felt that he was putting into practice their belief that progressives should run for office outside of the major political parties. While not going as far as an endorsement, James Vann wrote in the *NCIPA Discussion Bulletin* that "[t]he goals being sought by Ron and his Campaign for a New Tomorrow are precisely the same goals advocated by the general community of the left."[13]

He also received encouragement and support from other journalists. One scribe in the *Pittsburgh Post-Gazette* wrote, "The Daniels candidacy is valid if for no other reason than it will encourage activism, organization, self-determination and unity among society's most oppressed groups."[14] One of the most important endorsements that Daniels won was from Matthew Rothschild, publisher of *The Progressive*. After criticizing Clinton, Bush, and Jackson, Rothschild contended that progressives should stand on principle and vote for one of their own. Stating that he hoped Bush lost, he ended by saying he would "not vote for Bill Clinton. I'll be casting my ballot for Ron Daniels."[15] Daniels also received the endorsement of Rev. Calvin Butts of the Abyssinian Baptist Church in New York's Harlem. Butts, a nationally known black church leader, had earlier supported Ross Perot. But after Perot initially dropped out of the race in July 1992, he gave his enthusiastic embrace to Daniels. The Butts endorsement was widely publicized and certainly influenced a number of voters to consider Daniels' progressive proposals and policy positions.

In the end, several weaknesses hurt Daniels' effort. His campaign lacked the material resources, political support, and organizational infrastructure that is required to operate even a third-party campaign. Many activists who agreed with Daniels' politics nonetheless felt that the campaign standards set by Jackson—albeit within the political space of the Democratic Party—must be approached if a third-party candidate is to be considered seriously.

A second related problem had to do with the genesis of the campaign. Many felt that to launch a national campaign outside of the major parties, there must be significant grassroots support. The Daniels' run did not start with this support and was unable to build it through the campaign season.

It was argued by some that, given these conditions, it would have been best for Daniels to run in only a few cities or states, using 1992 as a preparation and recruitment effort for a larger campaign in 1996. By running only in a few places, it was contended, he could build support, secure resources, and more readily challenge the major parties.

# Other Progressive Black Challengers

Below the presidential level, there were other progressive Black challengers to high office. In Alabama, activist Gwen Patton ran as an Independent candidate for the U.S. Senate while in California, political scientist Gerald Horne ran for the U.S. Senate on the Peace and Freedom Party ticket. Patton is a longtime civil rights activist who worked with the Student Non-Violent Coordinating Committee and, most recently, with the Southern Rainbow Coalition.

Patton discovered early on in her challenge against incumbent Democratic candidate Richard Shelby and Republican candidate Richard Sellers the formidable obstacles placed in front of an Independent candidacy. The difficulties of ballot access in Alabama undermined the notion of democratic fair play. State law mandates that an Independent candidate obtain signatures from 1 percent of all registered voters, about 25,000 to 26,000 names, in order to get on the ballot. A minor party, however, needs to collect signatures only from 1 percent of those who voted in the last governor's election, about 12,000; an Independent presidential candidate needs only 5,000.[16] Due to the unfairness of this ballot access provision, Patton filed a lawsuit against Alabama Secretary of State Billy Joe Camp to change the law and prevent the printing of the November ballots.

The suit stated that the signature requirement for Independent candidates "serves no compelling state interest" and is "excessively burdensome and discriminatory."[17] In a victory for Independents everywhere, Patton won the suit and had the petition threshold for Independents reduced to the same requirement as for minor parties. She received support on her lawsuit from a number of newspapers from around the state.[18]

In her signature-gathering effort, she collected 12,876 valid signatures, 717 more than the 12,159 needed, from 195 cities in fifty-four out of the sixty-seven counties in Alabama. On August 31, 1992, she turned in her petitions to the Election Division office. What should have then been the end of her ballot-access battle was just the beginning of another sabotage on her campaign.

Patton made repeated phone calls to the Election Division office to find out the status of her petitions; her calls were not returned. She was finally informed, nine days later on September 8 by Election Division Director Jerry Henderson, that her signature count was only 11,788 and that she was not going to be on the ballot. He also told her that he had already given probate judges throughout Alabama the go-ahead to print ballots without her name on them. Apparently, the official petition counters, who had first received the signatures on August 31, did not see them again after they were taken to Henderson's office until September 3.[19]

She filed another lawsuit to have the ballots printed again. On October 6, following a seven-hour hearing, U.S. District Judge Robert Varner ruled against Patton essentially claiming that although she probably had been wronged, the $2 million to reprint the ballots was too high. Varner noted that "the state had control of these documents for some time when, really, their sanctity was not safeguarded."[20]

Shelby won the race, but Patton's struggle was a critical battle for the Independent movement. Her victory in changing the petition requirement was important while her experience with the "lost" petitions underscores the roughness of the path to electoral success that Black and other progressive Independents must tread.

Gerald Horne, a former head of the National Black Lawyers Guild, has been a political analyst, scholar, and activist for many years. He ran for the Senate on California's Peace and Freedom Party. The party grew out of the radical social movement of the 1960s and first got on the ballot in 1968. In 1992, it had a registered base of 68,182 members—about 0.48 percent of the total California electorate.[21] Its progressive program called for ending racism, massive cuts in the military, conversion of the military industry to socially productive civilian use, taxing the rich, gender equality, environmental reform, and raising the minimum wage.

Horne, who is chairman of the Black Studies Department at the University of California, Santa Barbara, ran against Democrat Dianne Feinstein and Republican John Seymour. His program included opposition to the death penalty, cutting the military and intelligence-gathering agencies by 85 percent, expanding affirmative action, and increasing taxes on the wealthy. Like other Independents and third-party candidates, Horne harbored few illusions that he could beat his better-financed and media-anointed major-party opponents, but he felt that his role and campaign were important in many other ways. He stated, "The historical function of certain third parties...is to raise cutting-edge ideas that are not now on the immediate horizon."[22]

# A League of Their Own

Beyond the individual campaigns, a number of gatherings occurred, some Black and some multi-racial, whose purpose was to analyze the racial and class dynamics of the 1992 races. In February, for example, a "National Emergency Conference on Black Independent Politics" was held in Wash-

ington, D.C. at Howard University's Howard Inn. Organized by New York
WLIB talk-show host Bob Law, activist Damu Smith, youth organizer Kathy
Flewellen, and others, the two-day meeting discussed electoral and non-elec-
toral strategies available to the Black community in 1992 and beyond.

In June, a different group of Black activists and intellectuals met at the
same site, to discuss the theme, "Democracy and its Discontents: An African
American Perspective." Organized by writer Manning Marable and political
activist Greg Moore, the meeting sought to identify the most urgent issues
facing African Americans in the effort to build a multicultural democratic
movement for fundamental reform in the United States. Although the one-
and-one-half-day conference was almost all Black, it was sponsored by the
Center for a New Democracy which is affiliated with the primarily White
New Party. The New Party is one of a number of third-party efforts initiated
in the past few years. The primary commitment coming out of that gathering
was to make an effort to establish a progressive African American think tank
and research center.

In the summer of 1992, while the Democrats and Republicans plotted
their strategies for the remaining days of the campaign, the Independents also
made moves. From the Left, Ron Daniels made good on his promise to use
his campaign as a spark to gather together progressives to attempt to forge
unity and develop an alternative platform.

A little more than 300 progressive grassroots and political activists met
in Ypsilanti, Michigan from August 21 to 23 in what was billed as a "People's
Progressive Convention"(PPC). Called by Daniels and his Campaign for a
New Tomorrow along with the National African American Network, the
National Committee for Independent Political Action, and others, it sought
to bring together those who abhorred the two-party structure of U.S. politics,
and to build unity around a common program and strategy for progressive
change.

The national call to a Progressive People's Convention stated,

It has become clear to a majority of people in the United States
that no matter which establishment party candidate for President
wins, we will get at best the "lesser of two evils." We don't get
what our country desperately needs. We need fundamental
change in the economic and political structures of our society. A
flawed Presidential sweepstakes is a much too narrow prescrip-
tion for solving our nation's ills. For no matter who wins, the
quality of our lives continues to deteriorate. We cannot depend
upon those in power to solve the problems of our society and

promote policies which are in the best interests of the American people. We must do it ourselves.[23]

The call took great pains to make it clear that people of color were key to the convention's success and implementation of its goals. It stated, "We must hold high the principle that the most oppressed segments of our society, the Native and African Americans, Latinos, and Asian American peoples, must be at the center of the leadership core of any new political formation that seeks to compete for power and represent the people who have been most abused by the current two-party system...Therefore, our goal is that the People's Progressive Convention will be truly 50 percent people of color."[24]

By most estimations, the convention did not achieve its goal of 50 percent people of color representation. Estimates vary that between 15 and 30 percent of the convention was Black, Latino, Asian, and Native American. Underfunded, inadequately advertised, and held in an inconvenient venue in a month when vacations are usually taken, many well-known activists of color did not attend. About half of those in attendance were women. Activists from labor unions, women's organizations, community groups, anti-racist groups, and peace groups were there. Members of the Green Party, the Peace & Freedom Party, the Labor Party, the Wisconsin Farm Labor Party, and other third-party groups were in attendance. The initial goal of the convention was 1,000 participants—which it did not meet.

Although Daniels played a central role in organizing the conference, he explicitly stated that it was not convened to endorse his campaign. Many of those attending, however, were supporters and campaign workers for Daniels. In his keynote speech, Daniels reiterated many of the themes he had been articulating across the country. He criticized both the Republicans and the Democrats and, in a rhetorical flourish, declared, "We're not talking about changing masters, we're talking about overturning the plantation system."[25]

The convention received a broad array of endorsements from leftist, progressive, labor, student, women, Asian, Black, Latino, and academic activists. Thes included Rep. Ronald Dellums (D-CA), lawyer Arthur Kinoy, writer Manning Marable, and long-time southern activist Gwen Patton, among others.[26]

Out of the convention came the National People's Progressive Network (NPPN). Its role is to continue to broaden the outreach and put in place an organizational structure for the Network. A nine-member steering committee was established, consisting of Rich Adams, Amy Belanger, Rona Carter, Ron Daniels, Carl Edelman, Kathy Flewellen, Ted Glick, Nancy Randolph, and Sandra Rivers.

In terms of the 1992 election, the convention pretty much decided to bow out. Given that some of the participants were resolutely opposed to supporting Clinton, Bush, or Perot, while others belonged to organizations that had made commitments to back the Democrats, and still others were supporters of Ron Daniels, there was little room for compromise on the election. This tension was captured in a resolution proposing that the national organization would never support a Democrat or a Republican. After some debate, the resolution was passed with an amendment added that excluded local, regional, and constituent organizations from the proposal.[27]

Overall, discussion was lively, and activists made serious attempts to assess the state of the nation and of the movement for social change. The leaders and participants of the gathering engaged in a critical and vigorous dialogue about how to rebuild a progressive and left base—thundered by the end of the Cold War, the decline of the National Rainbow Coalition, the closing of several progressive publications, and an ebb in progressive political activity in general. The fact that people could be brought together from around the nation under these circumstances was testimony to the hard work and sober approach of the convention organizers.

There were a number of troubling aspects to the convention and the politics that led it. One of the earlier objectives of the convention was to develop an alternative progressive platform. The fact that that did not occur reflects not only problems in planning, but also a political tendency to evade the difficult issue of consolidating a broad movement around a given set of principles and programmatic ideas. A platform unites as well as demarcates and the organizers of the convention felt a need for unity at all costs. In 1992, that evasion exacerbated the problem of political meandering that left progressives with no leadership role in the election process. The opportunity to codify progressives' differences (perhaps even some points of convergence) with the Democrats was missed. It was important for progressive and left activists to address the concerns of the nation, and advocate a strategy for involvement with the national and local elections. A progressive voice needed to be heard that gave leadership on how to maximize the benefits that could be gained from the electoral arena even as a critical perspective was developed and alternatives are constructed.

Political writer James Vann notes, the NPPN views itself as coordinating and networking the various third-party efforts occurring on the Left. Beyond the dubious proposition that a new, small, and ill-defined formation could accomplish such a task, the fragmentation of progressives and the progressive movement's distance from the social, cultural, and political life of people in society—particularly people of color—are not just a function of poor logistics and shoddy mailing lists. Progressives' disunity and distance from people of color are directly related to their lack of clarity regarding such key issues as principles, program, and strategy—issues which have yet to be addressed in the post-Cold War, post-National Rainbow Coalition world.

Despite the valuable and important mass work of those who attended the convention, the lack of a broad and rigorous progressive vision with the capacity to institutionalize and reproduce itself continues to marginalize the movement.

For many activists who had participated in the Jesse Jackson presidential campaigns of 1984 and 1988, some of whom played leading roles at the PPC, they found themselves wanting in terms of the 1992 election. Many were unwilling to support or work for Clinton, yet most overwhelmingly felt getting rid of Bush would be a step in the right direction. The PPC failed to address this quandary. Vann also pondered whether the PPC was an attempt to replace the National Rainbow Coalition, whose glorious mission and high hopes way back in 1983 seemed like a lifetime ago, but was now lost in the muddy waters of Washington, D.C.'s inside-the-beltway politics. Despite its flaws, the NRC was and remains influential because it has deep roots in Black political culture, i.e., the behavior and social patterns of Black political participation and leadership styles.

The convention was an important gathering because it was a sign of life within the progressive movement and an effort to challenge the rightward drift of national politics. Organizers correctly recognized the timely need to step back and reflect upon the state of the progressive movement. Along these lines, another important meeting, held June 1992, was that of the Committees of Correspondence (COC).

The COC is comprised of many former members of the Communist Party USA (CPUSA) and other leftist and marxist organizations and progressive individuals, a great many of whom are Black, Asian, and Latino, who are struggling to move past the ideological turf fights that previously existed among various socialist and communist groups. The five co-chairs of the COC, all people of color, include the late northern California activist Kendra Alexander, journalist Carl Bloice, prolific scholar Manning Marable, former CPUSA leader Charlene Mitchell, and labor organizer Rafael Pizarro. Its National Coordinating Committee includes a number of stellar activists such as journalist Frances Beal, internationally known activist and scholar Angela Davis, labor writer Geoffrey Jacques, the well-respected radical lawyer Arthur Kinoy, California State Assemblywoman Barbara Lee, and former Berkeley Mayor Gus Newport.

The COC stated in its declaration of principles, "We are motivated by the profound conviction that our country needs a humane alternative to the anti-human system of capitalism. For the majority of working people, and especially racially and nationally oppressed people, this system does not work."[28] The organization urged the defeat of Bush and Perot in the election, begrudgingly giving support to Clinton; called for "a lobbying campaign for a progressive economic agenda"; and voted to join the efforts to end the U.S. economic and cultural blockade of Cuba.[29]

# Somewhere Over the Rainbow: The New Alliance Party

One the most controversial political forces on the American scene in recent times has been the New Alliance Party and its perpetual candidate, Dr. Lenora Fulani. In 1992, the combative NAP leader, who holds a Ph.D. from City University of New York in developmental psychology, made her second effort at running for president as the candidate of the controversial New Alliance Party. In 1988, when she had also run as a NAP candidate, she had won 128,678 votes.[30] As the sole Black woman presidential aspirant, Fulani made headlines during the 1992 campaign by shouting down Bill Clinton and Jerry Brown in Harlem and Brooklyn, respectively while they gave speeches in the brutal battle over the New York primary.

Progressive, civil rights, Jewish, Black, and grassroots activists have long-standing criticisms of NAP as a White-controlled cult that falsely postures as a Black, gay, and women-led progressive party. Indeed, Fulani readily admits that Fred Newman—who is White, holds a doctorate in the Philosophy of Science from Stanford, and was once an ally of right-wing extremist Lyndon Larouche[31]—is the brains behind the NAP.

The organization began around 1970 on Manhattan's Upper West Side formally becoming the NAP in 1979.[32] In 1974, for a brief period, it worked in concert with ultra-right extremist Lyndon Larouche. NAP argues that, during that period, Larouche was operating as a leftist. However, many Black and progressive activists had long dismissed Larouche and his brutal Labor Committee cadre as either police agents, right-wing fanatics, or both. At the time, Larouche's followers were physically attacking Black and leftist activists on campuses and at meetings around the country.

In the 1984 presidential race, NAP ran Black activist Dennis Serrette as its candidate on thirty-three ballots. He garnered 35,000 votes.[33] Serrette eventually became critical of the NAP, had a falling out with the organization, denounced its tactics and operations as cultist, and left the group. In turn, he was denounced by NAP and called a traitor and other names. He would later play a key role in Ron Daniels' 1992 presidential campaign.

Up until that point, for the most part, NAP was little known outside of New York City, its home base. One of the things that the NAP did in 1984 was to create a front organization called the Rainbow Alliance. This obvious effort to capitalize on the recognition that the term "Rainbow" had in the

Black community, due to its association with the insurgent campaign and movement by Jesse Jackson in the 1984 race, was immediately criticized by a number of activists. Jackson himself, on a number of occasions, has had to make it painfully clear that there is no relationship between the National Rainbow Coalition and the Rainbow Alliance, the NAP's lobby operation (the Rainbow Lobby), and the NAP itself.[34] In some circumstances, the NAP has claimed that it supported Jackson's 1984 and 1988 runs; in other circumstances Jackson is called "a complete sell-out."[35]

By 1988, Fulani had replaced Serrette as the party's main Black leader. She launched her 1988 campaign under the theme of "two roads are better than one," which she said meant if Jackson did not win the Democratic nomination (the first road), then her campaign would be in place for those progressives who wanted to flee the major parties (the second road). Promoting itself as a "Black-led" party, the NAP fielded organizers who had mastered the intricacies of third-party and Independent ballot access and began to run candidates at every level of the electoral spectrum. These campaigns had not only a political purpose, but also a profound economic imperative.

To the surprise and concern of many, within the first few months of the 1992 campaign season, Fulani raised more than $600,000 in campaign matching funds. In the January 1992 Federal Election Commission listing of distributed matching funds, Fulani was trailing only President George Bush and Senator Tom Harkin. This was a great leap over her 1988 total of $922,106.34 in matching funds.[36] In 1992, according to the FEC, Bush got $2,629,365, Harkin $1,075,188, and Fulani $624,497. Gov. Bill Clinton, then the perceived Democratic front-runner, got $579,364. Virginia Governor Douglas Wilder, the only other Black candidate to qualify prior to his quitting the race, had raised only $198,315. In order to qualify, Fulani had had to raise $5,000 in at least twenty states, which she did in California, Connecticut, the District of Columbia, Georgia, Illinois, Indiana, Massachusetts, Maryland, Michigan, Minnesota, North Carolina, Ohio, Oregon, Pennsylvania, Rhode Island, Texas, Virginia, Vermont, Washington, and Wisconsin.[37]

Research by a number of journalists has shed light on the sources and means of Fulani's phenomenal fundraising. According to Fulani herself, a key source of her funds has come from people in treatment at the NAP's social therapy sessions, who have made donations to her campaign. While technically legal, such practices raised serious questions about whether NAP's therapy patients, many of whom are Black, were being exploited.

The NAP's financial acumen, however, is much too sophisticated to resort simply to its patients. The organization has become extremely proficient at legally exploiting the federal election system. The NAP has been able more than any other activist group and as well as the major parties, to get the maximum mileage out of reaping federal matching funds. The NAP's members, volunteers, patients, and employees make donations to the campaigns of NAP candidates, which in turn are eventually matched by the government. Those campaign funds are then funneled back to businesses created and owned by the NAP. These expanded dollars are then paid to employees and the process starts over again. In the last half of 1991, 35 percent of Fulani's expenditures went to NAP-related businesses.[38] None of these activities is illegal and, for that matter, unusual, in that the major parties also play the same game.

Among the businesses owned by or affiliated to the NAP are an advertising agency, a law firm, a publishing house, a theater company, an accounting firm, and a music agency. Some of these enterprises are Fred Newman Associates; East Side Center for Short-Term Psychotherapy; Washington Center for Crisis Normalization; Newman and Braun; Fulani, Silverman and Young; the Institute(s) for Social Therapy; Barbara Taylor School; Castillo Communications, Inc.; Castillo International Inc.; Ilene Advertising Inc.; Castillo Cultural Center, Inc.; and Fred Newman Productions—Budweiser Musicruise; New Alliance Productions; All Star Talent Show Network; International People's Law Center; and Automated Business Services.[39] The party also puts out a number of publications including the *National Alliance* newspaper, *Practice*, and *Probe*. NAP's businesses employ more than fifty people and bring in roughly $3.5 million a year. The Rainbow Lobby alone brings in $1.5 million a year.[40]

The Washington, D.C.-based Rainbow Lobby has spent much of its time actively organizing around H.R. 791, the Democracy in Presidential Debates Act of 1991.[41] One sore point with the NAP (and other Independents and third parties) is the ability of groups like the League of Women Voters and others to exclude those outside of the two-party system from the major nationally televised presidential debates. The NAP argues correctly that such exclusion actually stifles debate and limits democracy. The arbitrariness of this rejection was highlighted in 1992 when H. Ross Perot was allowed to participate in debates although he had not run in any primaries and entered the race at the very last minute. H.R. 791 was drafted by the Rainbow Lobby, introduced in Congress by Rep. Timothy Penny, and had a number of co-sponsors including several Black congresspersons such as Reps. John Conyers, John Lewis, Eleanor Holmes Norton, and Major Owens.[42]

In 1992, Fulani initially sought to get on the ballot as a Democrat in some states and on a third-party candidate in others. Her name appeared as a Democrat in the New Hampshire primary, where she won only 402 votes.[43] In addition to running under the New Alliance Party, she also sought the nomination of the Peace & Freedom Party in California, the Liberty Union

Party in Vermont, the United Citizens Party in South Carolina, and the Illinois Solidarity Party.[44]

In California in June, Fulani won the Peace & Freedom Party primary (51 percent) over Ron Daniels (33 percent) and R. Alison Star-Martinez (17 percent).[45] At the Peace & Freedom Party convention, however, the delegates gave the nomination to Ron Daniels after a contentious fight over the negative role of New Alliance Party activists in the Peace & Freedom Party.

# Transcendental Leadership:
# The Political Reaches of James Bevel

The Civil Rights movement produced a number of inspiring and heroic individuals. From Fannie Lou Hamer and Robert Moses to Rosa Parks and H. Rap Brown and thousands of unsung warriors, these individuals will go down in history as unyielding fighters who did not surrender their integrity and beliefs despite the odds. Some of those who led that movement, however, got lost along the way. Instead of history judging them as humanity's champions, they became tragic figures whose most recent years have been obscured and lost in whimsical and sometimes reactionary causes. James Bevel, an outsider even during his days as a close associate of Martin Luther King, Jr., is such a figure.

Bevel's decision to run as a vice presidential candidate under Lyndon Larouche in 1992 reflects not so much a challenge to Black leadership as an echo of the problem of leadership transition in the Black freedom movement. The fact that Bevel could align himself with individuals who so dramatically operate against the interests of the Black community is a triple tragedy, for it tarnishes Bevel's genuine contribution to the movement in another place and time, attempts to legitimize the racist practices and utterances of Larouche, and confuses the activist and ideological inclinations of the young who seek to link the movement of the past with that of today.

Bevel had joined King's Southern Christian Leadership Conference (SCLC) in 1961 and quickly became one of King's most valued strategists. He was involved in nearly all of the key civil rights actions of that era, including the brutal Birmingham campaign, the sit-ins, and the Freedom Rides movement. As a minister who had attended seminary school with then-SNCC leader and current U.S. Congressman John Lewis, he was also an inspiring though often frenzied orator. He was referred to by one observer as a "spiritual kamikaze."[46]

After King was killed, Bevel claims that the FBI took over the SCLC (and still runs it), so he left.[47] With the end of the civil rights era, unable or unwilling to make the transition to the new period, Bevel disappeared into relative obscurity. He pastored several churches and ran an organic farm in Virginia in those years. His association with the religious right and other conservatives grew during this time. Without question, his most dangerous alliance has been with jailed cult leader Lyndon Larouche.

Larouche, who has run for president on numerous occasions, put Bevel on the ticket as his vice presidential choice. Larouche's motivation for selecting Bevel is clear: he seeks, for the purpose of recruitment, to make inroads in the Black community. Once a self-proclaimed (though doubtful) leftist, Larouche swerved his rhetoric and politics sharply to the far Right and now espouses some of the most crackpot conspiracy theories going.

Larouche's Schiller Institute, ostensibly an institute to promote American-German friendship, has become Larouche's principle vehicle for recruiting in the Black community. The Institute was headed by Helga Zepp-Larouche, Lyndon's wife, but a Black man, Allan Salsbury, was given the position of assistant director. A march and rally was sponsored by the Institute in Washington, D.C. on Martin Luther King's birthday, January 15, 1985. It attracted 5,000 to 10,000 people. The purpose of the march was not to celebrate King's birthday, but to win Black support for Reagan's Strategic Defense Initiative (SDI), better known as Star Wars. Reportedly, some blacks were convinced to come to the rally because they thought it was in support of ending hunger in Africa. Banners were passed out with the bizarre slogan, "I Have a Dream, Feed Africa, and Build the Beam." The beam referred to Larouche's techno-fantasies of new weaponry systems to combat mythical but powerful enemies. Larouche has had some success at winning over Black clergy. According to the Atlanta-based radical right watchdog, the Center for Democratic Renewal, Black ministers such as Pine Bluff's Rev. Laman Keels, New York City's Rev. James Cokley, and McAlester, Oklahoma's Rev. Wade Watts were all present at the march and rally.

Larouche is anything but a friend of African Americans. He has used racist images and language and extremist theories to attack Black leaders. He accused Randall Robinson of the Washington, D.C.-based Black lobby group, TransAfrica, of being an agent of the International Monetary Fund (IMF), and a stool of communists and terrorists. He charged that Jesse Jackson was being controlled by Israel's secret service agency, Mossad. In an attack on Andrew Young in the April 26, 1985 edition of Larouche's newspaper, *New Solidarity*, he declared in a front-page headline, "Mayor Young Backs Genocide Against Blacks." He called former Congressman Walter Fauntroy an agent of the IMF and an advocate of policies that "will murder 300 million Africans."

He has worked in coalition with the enemies of African Americans for many years. Larouche aligned with the apartheid regime in South Africa, for example. According to the October 7, 1979 *New York Times*, Larouche was paid by South Africa's former Bureau of State Security, which tortured and terrorized the nation's Black population, to produce reports on the U.S. anti-apartheid movement.

In the United States, Larouche has worked closely with leaders of U.S. apartheid movements: the Ku Klux Klan and the American Nazi Party. Klan members have often served as his bodyguards and traveled as his security. Roy Frankhouser, an activist with the American Nazi Party, became a part of Larouche's inner circle.[48]

Bevel failed to acknowledge these associations and the racist and fascist character of the Larouche movement during his campaign. He spent most of his time discussing the Larouche campaign effort to remove the statue of Albert Pike, a founder of the Ku Klux Klan, which stands in front of the courthouse in Washington, D.C. and is maintained by the National Park Service with taxpayers' dollars.[49] Despite the fact that the removal of the statue is a legitimate issue, Bevel's alliance with the far Right has closed most doors in the Black community and, for many, he is generally dismissed as tainted by his relationship with Larouche. His and Larouche's ability to capitalize on Bevel's association with King will fade over time.

# Conclusion

Although the Independents would have a negligible impact on the outcome of the 1992 election, their efforts continued to remind Black voters of the contradictory nature of U.S. electoral politics. They also reminded people of the limits of a two-party system in terms of the national political discourse and the arenas of debate. While the traditional liberal Black leadership was generally unmoved by the activities to its left, it still found itself facing a number of political events and incidents that highlighted its weaknesses and inability to shape events in the present period.

Black voters, for instance, in a number of instances rejected the electoral choices offered by traditional Black leaders. As described in the next chapter, Black voters will often perceive their interests in a different light from that of Black leaders and support candidates who have been ostracized by the status quo political system.

# Chapter 6

# Black Voters and the Struggle for Political Power

The message to White Democrats is that Black voters can no longer be taken for granted because they have "nowhere else to go." We had to break the dependency syndrome. We moved from a relationship born of paternalism to one born of power.

—Jesse Jackson[1]

## The Sleeping Giant Stirs: The Black Vote Distinguishes Itself

Driving down Martin Luther King, Jr. Avenue in Southeast Washington, D.C., it is easy to understand why urban rebellions happen. Overwhelmingly and majestically Black, the area houses one of the nation's largest mental hospitals and the city's sewage disposal facility. Along with the bus stops where working people wait to catch the bus each morning and the small convenience stores that sell sodas to the children are broken streets and broken street people. Seniors sit on porches braving Washington's notorious August humidity while homeboys secure corners for marketing their illegal wares. Lack of an official city presence, such as regular garbage pickup and road repair, is stark.

In the United States, every city has its "Southeast." In these communities, although residents work hard and struggle daily to persevere against the odds—pervasive drug trafficking, a growing homeless population, vanishing social services, street crime, and political apathy—they are more often than not abandoned by local and national leaders. Their misery serves as background for photo-ops from politicians who, like voting booths, appear only around election time. Partially out of sheer frustration and partially out of exercising a conscious political decision, voter registration and turnout in low-income Black communities are often severely depressed.

This has led many pundits and political operatives to assume that the Black poor care little about participating in the system when, in fact, their not voting is "protest participation" in a system that has little legitimacy in their eyes. While the Black vote, in 1992, generally went as expected, in a number of cases it broke with media and pundit assumptions as Blacks voted radically different from White voters.

On the pavements of Martin Luther King, Jr. Avenue and surrounding neighborhoods, the protest power of the Black vote was dramatically enacted in the September 1992 primary election for the D.C. City Council. Perhaps the most stunning vote in the nation was the election of Marion Barry to a seat on that august body. The former mayor of Washington, D.C., whose videotaped arrest, then conviction and imprisonment on drug charges seemed to be the epitome of his political career, rebuilt his base in the city's Ward 8 area and solidly defeated a twelve-year incumbent in the election. Adopting an African name, Anwar Amal, and African-designed clothing, Barry was reborn as he tapped into the deep-felt grievances of the Ward and the residents' frustration with the city's leadership. Only six months out of jail, Barry embarked on his political comeback campaign by going door-to-door in the ward and to the churches preaching redemption and hardcore truths. While it was true that Barry had not done much for the Ward during his twelve years as mayor, he was able to effectively convince Ward 8 voters that he had reconstructed himself and that the incumbent, Wilhelmina Rolark, would not meet their needs. Rolark was seen as tied into the city's established Black leadership and viewed as either elitist, incompetent, or uncaring.

As the poorest and least-serviced area of the city, there was also deep resentment toward Mayor Sharon Pratt Kelly and other city leaders by the ward's residents. In the 1990 election that brought her to power, Kelly had received her fewest votes from Ward 8 and had to combat an image of being elitist and too tied to the city's White establishment. She had also been Barry's harshest critic during his last days in office. Barry would later use that criticism in his comeback to distinguish himself from the mayor. When Kelly and every member of the City Council, other city leaders, and all of the city's newspapers endorsed Rolark, they pretty much solidified Barry's posturing as an anti-establishment candidate and sealed his victory. Despite their revulsion of the prospects of a Barry return, as one reporter observed, "not a single member of the Council dared travel to the neighborhood to help win [Rolark] votes for fear of a confrontation with Barry."[2] In the election, Barry won 69.5 percent of the vote, more than three times Rolark's margin.[3]

Speaking in populist tones, Barry stated to his new constituents, "You have made Ward 8 the most famous place in America...People now know where you live. You have empowered yourselves...You are a sleeping giant that has risen."[4]

Black voters in the nation's capital, who have historically been progressive on a wide range of issues, also rejected a congressionally imposed ballot initiative to bring the death penalty to the city. The measure was soundly defeated by a margin of 3-1, 67 percent to 33 percent.[5] In many areas of the city where homicide and other crimes are rampant, Blacks voted overwhelmingly to defeat the measure and did not buy into the conservative argument that the death penalty would help the crime and violence problems. District of Columbia voters also voted 3-1, 64 percent to 36 percent, to limit campaign donations in city elections to $100. Although opposed by virtually every elected official and city leader, community support for campaign finance reform was high and expressed at the ballot box.[6]

In other areas of the country, similar Black voter revolt occurred. In November 1992 in Florida, Alcee Hastings was elected to Congress to represent the 23rd Congressional District. As a U.S. District Judge, Hastings had achieved national prominence in 1989 when he was charged with bribery and impeached by the U.S. House of Representatives. The Judiciary Committee in the U.S. Senate then convicted him and he was removed from the bench. Although that decision was later overturned by the U.S. Supreme Court in 1992, many thought that his reputation was irreparably damaged. He won a solid victory in the election, however, by garnering 65 percent of the vote in his election.

Finally, one of the most interesting races was the New York Senate, in which radical nationalist minister Al Sharpton came in third in the Democratic primary. By all accounts, Sharpton ran a serious and thoughtful campaign and won over many who had previously dismissed him as a charlatan and self-promoter. He won 166,665 votes (15 percent) statewide.[7] Overall, he won 67 percent of the Black vote, 20 percent of the union vote, and 16 percent of the Latino vote.[8] Reflecting upon his decision to run for office and the new "legitimacy" that he gained as a result, Sharpton said, "It was time to bring down the volume and bring up the program."[9] These days Sharpton regularly meets with New York Mayor David Dinkins, Rev. Jesse Jackson, members of Congress, and even New York Governor Mario Cuomo.

Support for Barry, Hastings, and Sharpton is significant in demonstrating the way in which the African American community defines its interests and refuses to swallow wholesale the political judgement of the media and conventional political analysts. When it is genuinely thought that a particular candidate will address the concerns of the Black community, whether supported by the local power wielders or not, that candidate will generally find a base among African Americans.

This does not mean that the Black community is simply willing to waste its votes. For instance, while many did not think that Jesse Jackson could win the presidency, victory was measured in other terms. It was broadly understood that Jackson's campaign was a bargaining tool on behalf of the Black and progressive communities. At the same time, the African American community is extremely practical and will not simply, in most cases, vote for a candidate just because he or she is Black or is able to articulate the community's interests. Independent Black candidates Ron Daniels and Lenora Fulani discovered this truth. So did conservative Black challengers, such as former Virginian Republican U.S. Senate candidate Alan Keyes and former Maryland Republican U.S. House candidate Michelle Dyson. In Keyes' case, the Black community made it quite clear that it would prefer a liberal White Democrat, in this instance Sen. Barbara Mikulski, to a reactionary Black, Reaganist Republican conservative.

## The Struggle for Theory

Although most theorists would agree that, in the modern era, there is very little chance of a Black stampede toward the Republican Party, the examples cited above indicate that the motivation and practice of the Black voter are more complex and layered than generally acknowledged. In national terms, this means that the level of Black participation in Democratic politics has the potential to flux in ways that critically affect the outcome of close presidential races. That factor alone shaped the Jimmy Carter, Walter Mondale, and Michael Dukakis campaigns and their postures toward the African American electorate and community.

It has been equally clear to many Black political activists and thinkers that a passive go-along-to-get-along strategy is limited, at best, and, at worst, misguided and dysfunctional. To the degree that the Black vote is locked into the Democratic Party, it is also in danger of being taken for granted and undermined as a bargaining tool. Thus, these dilemmas have given rise to theoretical efforts to guide the strategy of the Black community in presidential politics.

This field of study is relatively new. Although Blacks have been voting in presidential elections since the middle of the last century, it wasn't until the passage of the Voting Rights Act (VRA) of 1965 that the majority of Blacks were enfranchised. Gaining the capacity to vote was particularly critical in the South, where the majority of Blacks resided, then and now. In many instances throughout the region, whites held elected office in cities and counties where Blacks were either a majority or a significant proportion of the population. Both coercive and legal tactics prevented the Black community from assuming electoral power, although in a number of southern states, Blacks were, and still remain, significant proportions of the state's voting-age population.

Yet, even with the passage of the VRA, significant barriers existed, primarily though not exclusively in the South, that depressed Black voter registration and participation. The U.S. Commission on Civil Rights, for example, reported ten years after the VRA was passed that "There is still hostility and resistance to the free and effective political participation of Blacks, Native Americans, Puerto Ricans, and Mexican Americans."[10]

Despite the passage of the VRA and other local remedies, Chandler Davidson's *Minority Vote Dilution* identifies a number of barriers that still impact on Black voter participation. These include purges of "registration rolls, changing polling places on short notice (or without any notice at all), the establishment of difficult registration procedures, decreasing the number of voting machines in minority areas, and the threat of reprisals."[11] Other tactics that are employed that dilute the power of the Black vote include holding at-large elections, requiring runoffs, decreasing the size of a particular government body, and gerrymandering.

The Black community has taken on all these obstacles and maintained at least a modicum of participation in all presidential elections. Following the Civil War, most Blacks supported Abraham Lincoln's Republican Party. This was not only due to the symbolic acknowledgement that Lincoln had signed the Emancipation Proclamation. Despite the overthrow of the Republican Party in presidential elections until 1936 when Roosevelt's New Deal held more sway than Republican austerity in addressing the impact of the Depression on African Americans. However, it wasn't until the 1948 election of Harry Truman that Blacks solidly lined up in the Democratic camp where they remain to this day (see Chapter Thirteen for more discussion of Blacks and the 1948 campaign).

Black political scientists, such as Lucius Barker, Mack Jones, Lorenzo Morris, Adolph Reed, Robert Smith, Katherine Tate, Ron Walters, Linda Williams, and Hanes Walton among others, have attempted to construct various theories of modern Black participation in local and national elections.[12] This work becomes more critical as Black voter participation increases (potentially), more experience is gained by African Americans who choose to run for president, and dissatisfaction with the two-party system ebbs and flows. The early 1972 run by former Congresswoman Shirley Chisholm, who competed in ten primaries and won only thirty-five delegates, and challenges by Rev. Jesse Jackson in 1984 and 1988 furthered the theory and analysis.[13] The 1992 election provides even more fruitful and wide-ranging phenomena and events that must now be factored into that evolving field of study.

Essentially, two main ideas have unfolded concerning Black participation in electoral politics: exercising leverage through the strategic or tactical use of the Black vote on either the Republican or Democratic party to secure commitment toward a Black agenda; or initiating an independent race outside of the major party structures. There are various elaborations on those themes with varying degrees of intensity along the ideological continuum, but in essence they constitute the strategic options, other than not voting, available to the Black voter.

One of the analysts in this realm is political scientist Ron Walters, author of *Black Presidential Politics*, one of the few extensive theoretical studies on the subject. He argues that given the reality that Blacks are a permanent minority in the United States, Black political power can come from the barrel of a ballot box only if that potential voting power is leveraged. The ability of Blacks to use their vote strategically, i.e., to reward or punish politicians, requires a unity of purpose and ability to implement the threat. This leverage, argues Walters, can come from either inside of one of the parties ("dependent leverage") or outside of the major party structures ("independent leverage"). Jackson's presidential campaigns are an example of the former while the motion of organization and mobilization started by H. Ross Perot is an example of the latter.

Walters sees the distinction between dependent leverage and independent leverage as crucial. He defines dependent leverage as "the attempt by Blacks (or any other such group) to achieve political influence by both seeking institutional integration into the party's administrative and political structure, and by seeking to become a 'balance of power' factor in the voting coalition through contributing dependable and substantial electoral support to party candidates."[14] This approach has severe weaknesses, he contends, in that it is dependent upon promises and trust. Independent leverage, i.e., the exercise of electoral power external to the major parties is preferable, Walters argues, and requires Black leadership to meet "the challenge of disciplining the Black vote through organization."[15]

Walter's notion of independent leverage melds somewhat into the repeated call for a third-party that many progressives and leftists have sought for decades. Efforts at building third parties have taken numerous forms, including multi-racial, all Black, communist and socialist, and labor-based. In 1992, with the ascendancy of Perot, conditions seemed more favorable than ever. While there have been incessant calls for third parties and Black parties over the years, for a number of reasons most Black voters—58 percent to 38 percent according to a recent poll[16]—have been unreceptive to that option although they, like the majority of Americans (see Table 6-1), report high displeasure with both the Republicans and the Democrats. Those Blacks who prefer staying in the two-party system have felt that most candidates representing third-party or independent efforts have not had the resources to spread their message and image in the way that the major parties do. Expensive media advertising has been out of the reach of financially strapped third-party campaigns. Jackson accumulated the resources to run a campaign more or less comparable to the other Democratic candidates. Most third-party and Independent candidates simply don't have the resources to effectively compete with the major-party candidates in terms of staff, media buys, and candidate promotion.

When featured by the mainstream media, third-party and Independent candidates are deliberately ridiculed. Media coverage is usually derisive, scornful, or misinformed. Generally, however, these candidates are ignored. For the most part, only the major-party candidates' press conferences and campaign events are attended by the media. These two factors affect the Black community in particular, as Blacks are overly influenced by the mass media.[17]

In 1992, there were a number of serious efforts to expand or launch third parties in the United States. The major attempts were the New Party based in the Midwest; the National Organization for Women's (NOW) 21st Century Party; the Labor Party, spearheaded by progressive trade unionists;

---

### Table 6-1

### Respondents That Agree That Both Major Parties are Out-of-Touch

| | |
|---|---|
| Agree | 82% |
| Disagree | 15% |
| No Opinion | 3% |

### Respondents That Believe It Would Be Good for Country If There Were a New Major Party

| | |
|---|---|
| Good | 66% |
| Bad | 24% |
| No Opinion | 10% |

Source: *The Polling Report*, June 6, 1992, p. 7.

the Green Party, the oldest of the group, whose support is primarily rooted in the environmental movement; and Ron Daniels' Campaign for a New Tomorrow. In addition, there are many state-level efforts, from California to Alabama to Vermont, to build and widen third-party and progressive electoral activities. Most of these efforts, with the exceptions of the Alabama New South Coalition and Campaign for a New Tomorrow, are overwhelmingly White, although they seek participation by people of color. The leadership of these groups has minimal Black or Latino representation and generally has not rooted in inner-city communities to any significant level.

Another theoretical issue that deserves attention is the rise and prominence of the politics of "deracialization," which claims to transcend racial politics. While this process has received more attention recently, as some observe s have pointed out that this phenomenon actually dates back a number of years. Walters notes, "...it is possible to dismiss the fact that 'mainstream/crossover' politics is a new phenomenon, since even a cursory look at the data...clearly shows that since at least 1968 Blacks have represented a variety of political jurisdictions where Blacks constituted a minority of the population."[18]

However, a distinction must be made between those Black politicians who by circumstance find themselves in political jurisdictions that are not majority Black and those who by ideological choice promote a politics of deracialization, i.e., they "seek to deemphasize those issues that may be viewed in explicitly racial terms...while emphasizing those issues that appear to transcend the racial question."[19]

Political scientists Charles Hamilton and Stokely Carmichael penned the influential *Black Power: The Politics of Liberation in America,* which "advised the Democrats to pursue a deracialized strategy" as far back as the mid-1970s.[20] By the mid-1980s, a number of Black political theorists and elected officials advocated that the Democratic Party, if it were to break its presidential losing streak, would have to adopt a non-racial approach. Sociologist William Julius Wilson offered similar advice to the Democrats. He wrote, "An emphasis on coalition politics that features progressive, race-neutral policies could have two positive effects. It could help the Democratic party to regain political support, and it could lead to programs that would especially benefit the more disadvantaged members of minority groups—without being minority [i.e., race-specific] policies."[21]

Using the term "hidden agenda," Wilson elaborated on this theme in *The Truly Disadvantaged: The Inner City, the Underclass, and Public Policy.* He wrote passionately:

> I am convinced that, in the last few years of the twentieth century,
> the problems of the truly disadvantaged in the United States will

have to be attacked primarily through universal programs that enjoy the support and commitment of a broad constituency. Under this approach, targeted programs (whether based on the principle of equality of group opportunity or that of equality of life chances) would not necessarily be eliminated, but would rather be deemphasized—considered only as offshoots of, and indeed secondary to, the universal programs. *The hidden agenda is to improve the life chances of groups such as the ghetto underclass by emphasizing programs in which the more advantaged groups of all races can positively relate* (emphasis in the original).[22]

Wilson contends that he is not a conservative or neoconservative. In defending himself against that charge, he states that "...unlike neoconservatives whose antipathy toward activist government policies is the fundamental basis for criticizing race-specific programs, my article calls for activist government policies that would focus more on race-neutral programs to address some of the most troubling domestic problems in the late twentieth century."[23] In other words, Wilson argues that he is not opposed to race-specific programs, but rather believes that priority emphasis should be given to race-neutral programs.

Yet, as economist Thomas Boston notes, Wilson's difference with the neoconservatives does not erase the fact that there is convergence on fundamental questions regarding race and racism. Boston rightfully argues that Wilson's view and that of the neoconservatives "contends that racial discrimination has all but vanished and can no longer be blamed for impeding the progress of Black society."[24]

A number of events and incidents underscored Boston's criticism of Wilson and those who prefer to view racism as only a bygone era with little contemporary relevance. The nomination and seating of Clarence Thomas on the U.S. Supreme Court, the national prominence and legitimizing of racist David Duke, the spring 1992 uprising in Los Angeles, and the impact of urban Hip Hop culture on U.S. politics all dramatically demonstrate that racism and racial politics live on. These political moments highlighted the unfinished agenda of democracy and equality in the United States. They also exposed the crisis of strategy and program within Black leadership as it divided on how to respond to these situations.

# Part II

# Critical Moments and Issues in Contemporary Black Politics

# Chapter 7

# Doubting Thomas

A judge must be fair and impartial. A judge must not bring to his
job, to the Court, the baggage of preconceived notions, of ideology, and certainly not an agenda.

—Judge Clarence Thomas[1]

In a number of cases, race-based agendas were effectively used to
fracture the Black community. The Bush administration calculated correctly
that its nomination of Clarence Thomas to the U.S. Supreme Court would
initiate a debate among African Americans over the value of having a Black
on the Court and perhaps create a space just wide enough for Thomas to slip
through. With the nomination of Thomas, George Bush found himself in a
win-win situation: if the nomination succeeded, then Bush would have the
ultra-conservative that he desired, and if the nomination failed, Bush could
then justify putting virtually anyone up for nomination without regard to
throwing a political bone to the Black community.

Confronted with the 1991 Supreme Court nomination of Clarence
Thomas, who is ideologically opposed to the legacy of civil rights, Black
leadership and the Black community fragmented politically. The Thomas
battle exposed a fragility within the Black community whose repercussions
will be felt for years to come and much of whose meaning has been left
dangerously unexamined.

Supreme Court nominations have immense relevance to African
Americans. Critical Supreme Court decisions in the last century, most notably
the Dred Scott decision (1857) and *Plessey v. Ferguson* (1896), determined
the destiny of millions of African Americans and codified into law and policy
the mass repression and neo-enslavement of blacks.[2]

Prior to the 20th century, other than Black media outlets, African
Americans had little political or social capital to impact on Supreme Court

decisions or on those who did the deciding. Beginning in 1912, through the vehicle of the three-year-old NAACP, blacks as an organized political force were able to intervene in the Supreme Court nomination process. In that year, the NAACP opposed President Taft's nomination of Judge Hook because of his racist views. Based on their organized and vigorous opposition, Hook's name was withdrawn by Taft.[3] From that point on, Black and civil rights organizations would consistently, and in a unified fashion, challenge nominees deemed to be antagonistic to the interests of blacks, the poor, and others locked out of the mainstream.

The nomination of Thomas raised new questions for the civil rights and civil liberties communities, as a whole, and for the Black community, in particular. The race of the nominee had never been an issue in previous campaigns against Reagan and Bush nominees. All had been White; therefore, groups could focus solely on questions of qualifications and ideological orientation. The previous victories against Reagan left the coalition of groups who united in opposition to the conservative packing of the Court unprepared for the racial and ideological issues that Thomas' nomination generated. Black groups, in particular, found themselves in a quandary, as a confrontation between racial solidarity and ideological principle seemed imminent.

A wide range of statements and articles were issued by Black interest groups in the period between Bush's July 1, 1991 nomination of Thomas and the opening of the first round of hearings in mid-September. From Black members of Congress to the more traditional civil rights leadership, questions concerning the meaning of race, ideological differences among African Americans, and qualifications of the nominee were raised time and time again.

In the period between Bush's nomination of Thomas and the first round of hearings, a sharp political debate erupted among blacks over the significance of Thomas' race. The debate polarized in two ways: one, between Black liberals and Black conservatives tied to the Reagan and Bush administrations; and, two, within the civil rights community itself. The confusion over whether race should override ideology and competency grew sharper as the days passed and contributed significantly to the lack of unity among blacks needed to undermine Thomas' support.

Justice Thurgood Marshall's presence on the Court, even in the face of Reaganism, meant for many African Americans that a "Black" viewpoint would be rendered in the Court's decisions. To African Americans, the importance of having this perspective on the Court was a critical reason why opinion polls taken immediately after Thomas was nominated indicated that the majority of blacks supported the nomination. A poll taken of 402 blacks found that 54 percent approved of the nomination, while 17 percent disapproved.[4]

Supporters of Thomas cited this poll and similar ones[5] often to indicate that civil rights groups who opposed Thomas were out of touch with the perspectives and goals of the Black masses. What they failed to mention was that the same poll also indicated that the majority—52 percent— of blacks questioned did not think that Thomas represented the views of most blacks on issues concerning civil rights. When broken down by income groups, 67 percent of Black households earning above $50,000 held that view while only 41 percent earning below $30,000 thought that Thomas did not represent their perspective.[6] When compared with Justice Marshall, only 7 percent of those polled felt that Thomas would be more effective than Marshall. Nineteen percent felt that Thomas would be just as effective, while 29 percent thought that he would much less effective. Finally, the poll also found that only 36 percent believed Thomas would do a good job ensuring equal rights.

The split in the Black community over Thomas had several roots. The importance of maintaining a Black presence on the Court, even if symbolic, was powerfully persuasive. Many of Thomas' supporters used this argument when it was clear that his ideological stands and poor qualifications would otherwise be disqualifying factors for many, if not most, blacks. Evidence also seemed to indicate that income was a critical factor among blacks in whether they supported Thomas. Given that education generally corresponds positively with income, it is probable that the more informed someone became, the less likely it is that he or she would support Thomas. Perhaps the most critical factor leading to confusion in the Black community was the split among Black leadership. For many who would look to take their lead from civil rights leaders or elected officials, they found strong support and strong opposition from all sides—a situation that was unprecedented.

## Ideology and Thomas

As conservative supporters attempted to selectively use poll data to build support for Thomas, some Black civil rights leaders acted cautiously. Joseph Lowery, SCLC president, advised his followers to hold off on any criticism of Thomas. He noted his hesitancy to go against what seemed to be a wave of popular Black support for Thomas. Lowery stated, "Blacks are very reluctant to say, 'Hold him back.'[7] Lowery, who would eventually decide to back Thomas, went on further to state, "We need to give the guy the benefit of the doubt for the time being."[8]

While many Black groups agreed that one's race was important, there were clearly differences in the nature and priority of that importance. It appeared that many blacks who supported Thomas did so merely because he was Black. Washington, D.C. newspaper publisher Calvin Rolark, for example, argued, "The best interests of Black America would be served by at least having Thomas as a justice of the Supreme Court, rather than not having an African American at all."[9] Rolark's perspective was that it was better to have a Black conservative if a conservative was to be had. He wrote, "If the nominee had not been Thomas, it would have been a conservative White woman or White man."[10]

Rolark's views were echoed by former NAACP Board Chair Margaret Bush Wilson, who had once housed Thomas when he was a college student. Arguing that Thomas "knows the struggle and hardship blacks and the impoverished of every race grapple with daily,"[11] she defended him solely on racial grounds and expressed her indignation at blacks who opposed him. "When the history of these times is written," she wrote, "it will be interesting to see how historians view the position of the National Board of the NAACP—an organization committed to advancing colored people, which is opposed, on ideological grounds, to this nomination of a Black man to the U.S. Supreme Court."[12]

Wilson and others argued that Thomas' life experiences gave him a racial perspective that was sorely needed on the high court. She argued, "Throughout the history of the U.S. Supreme Court, I don't believe any other nominee can claim to have come so far. In point of fact, Judge Thomas' unique perspective belongs not only on the Supreme Court, but in the legislature, in the work place, at city hall and on our campuses."[13]

Robert Woodson, a former official with the National Urban League and an outspoken leader among the current generation of Black conservatives, held similar views. Woodson, who organized a coalition of conservative blacks to support Thomas, stated, "There's a tremendous outpouring [from blacks], and I think this Thomas nomination demonstrates that it is the [Congressional] Black Caucus that is out of step with Black America. Clarence Thomas represents the new mainstream of Black thinking in America, and he should be on the Court."[14]

For those who opposed Thomas, these arguments were fallacious and dangerous. "With Justice Marshall's departure, it is imperative that a Black join the Court—but not any Black, at any cost,"[15] declared the Congressional Black Caucus Foundation (CBCF) in one of the sharpest rebuttals to the argument put forth by Wilson and others. The statement issued by the CBCF made it clear in no uncertain terms that "Clarence Thomas is not our champion. He is the President's gesture."[16] As one of the first critics of the nomination, the CBCF wrote:

> It is said that a Black on the Court, no matter the ideology, brings
> to the Court's deliberations the perspective of those who have

been called "nigger"...There is some truth in all this, but much of it is romantic nonsense. The record demonstrates that what Clarence Thomas has drawn from his experience in order to shape his perspective and views is idiosyncratic and far outside the mainstream of African American perspectives.[17]

The Foundation focused its criticism on the manipulative tactics of the White House and the administration's media campaign to win support for Thomas by highlighting his poor upbringing. The Foundation declared:

> If some African Americans have seemed to approve of this nomination, it must also be noted that few members of the public have studied Clarence Thomas' record. Instead, they have been introduced for the first time to a Black man and told his life story in order to deflect attention from his record. And, they have heard and seen a public relations campaign waged by the President with all the resources of the Administration at his disposal.[18]

Other civil rights leaders also criticized the hypocrisy of the White House in selecting Thomas because of his race despite its protestations to the contrary. The National Urban League's Jacobs stated, "When you have one seat vacant, if you select an African American, it is not because you've run out of smart White boys."[19] "Clarence Thomas is really an affirmative action nominee," Jacobs said sarcastically.[20] Jacobs, however, would decline to oppose Thomas.

The debate over the significance of Thomas' race did not subside when it came time for the hearings. Testimony from CBC members, in particular, made the point that Black leadership had a responsibility to see beyond race to the more important issues of ideology and competence.

With the sole exception of one member, conservative Republican Rep. Gary Franks, CBC members felt that being Black was not enough. Rep. Louis Stokes, for example, stated with strong conviction, "As African Americans we not only wanted to see another worthy person replace [Marshall], we wanted to see another qualified Black American replace him." However, he continued, "We would not be credible if we had a standard built upon the race of the nominee. We believe that the same standard must be applied to Thomas that we applied to Robert Bork when we opposed his nomination."[21] Stokes testified, "We are pained because as much as we would like to see the diversity that another Black American would bring to the Court, Judge Thomas is not the man."[22]

Rep. John Lewis, one of the most active CBC members in the opposition to Thomas, spoke in a similar vein. Lewis, who hails from Thomas' home state of Georgia, was under special pressure to support Thomas. Yet, he refused to back Thomas and stated firmly, "I have been advised by some that I should not testify against Clarence Thomas because he is Black. The color of Clarence Thomas' skin is not relevant; the person, his views and his qualifications are."[23]

Other Black groups outside of the CBC also made the point that it was important to have a Black on the Court. Adjoa Aiyetoro, national director of the National Conference of Black Lawyers (NCBL) echoed the CBC members in her testimony. Speaking for her organization, Aiyetoro said, "The NCBL believes that it is extremely important to confirm a person of African descent to serve on this country's highest court. However, of greater importance to NCBL and its members is the confirmation of a candidate whose record demonstrates a clear respect for the law combined with a compassion to securing political, economic, and social justice for millions of people in this country excluded from the 'American dream.'"[24]

Among the Black judges that President Bush could have nominated were Harry T. Edwards, A. Leon Higginbotham, Jr., Damon J. Keith, and Amalya L. Kearse. Edwards, who sat on the federal bench in the District of Columbia Circuit Court, has written four books on legal questions, published more than fifty articles, and currently teaches at the New York University Law School. Higginbotham, a well-known jurist, sits on the Third Circuit Court in Philadelphia. Keith sat on the U.S. Eastern District of Michigan where he was the chief judge, and had been appointed by Bush in 1990 to the Commission on the Bicentennial of the U.S. Constitution. Kearse, whom many felt had a better chance of being nominated than Thomas, is on the Second Circuit Court in New York. Her impressive record includes work on the Executive Committee of the Lawyers for Civil Rights Under the Law and on the President's Committee for Selection of Federal Judicial Officers. She is also active in many community and social organizations including Big Sisters, the Legal Aid Society, and the National Urban League. Kearse is considered politically moderate and would probably have been acceptable to both Black conservatives and liberals.[25]

Another example of reluctance to accept Thomas just because he is Black can be found in the testimony of William Lucy, president of the Coalition of Black Trade Unionists. Stated Lucy: "We believe that the content of his character is of grave importance—not the color of his skin or the numerous barriers he has overcome to reach his current status in life. All of this is of little consequence in determining his qualifications to sit on the Supreme Court."[26]

Some observers who were questioned not only saw Bush's selection of Thomas as racial manipulation, but also raised questions about Thomas' own views of Blackness. On racial issues, Thomas himself was often duplicitous.

He demanded that society be viewed from a "colorblind" perspective that virtually did not acknowledge racial differences. Yet, he repeatedly highlighted his rise through segregation to justify a notion of Black self-help that embodied the racial differences that he sought to deny. While insisting that blacks should not be given any special treatment because they are Black, Thomas accepted admission to Yale's School of Law through the school's affirmative action program. As Reagan's chief Black loyalist, he accepted the chairpersonship of the Equal Employment Opportunity Commission (EEOC), although he had once went on the record stating that, "If I ever went to work for the EEOC or did anything connected with blacks, my career would be irreparably ruined."[27] He also relaxed this principle in accepting Bush's nomination which was clearly to fulfill the "Black" seat on the Court.

For Thomas, being Black is reduced to an individual physical identity that is almost incidental. He refuses to see, as Howard University Professor Ronald Walters wrote, that being Black "ultimately means more than color; it also means a set of values—values from which Thomas is apparently estranged."[28]

Few, if any, believed that Bush's selection of Thomas was ideologically-free. Indeed, Thomas' supporters and opponents alike saw the nomination as a reward for a decade of service. Thomas' broadsides against the Civil Rights movement had endeared him to Reagan and Bush and made him one the few high-profile blacks in their administrations. Even Thomas referred to himself as a "designated Black/conservative/Republican/Reagan appointee" in his oft-quoted speech, "Why Black Americans Should Look to Conservative Policies."[29]

Some of Thomas' defenders attempted to downplay the extremeness of his views. Margaret Bush Wilson made a strained effort to place Thomas in the civil rights arena. Wilson wrote, "Judge Thomas reflects the diversity and complexity of African American thinking, but his views are not nearly as radical as his critics suggest. He has pushed for a new frontier in civil rights."[30] It is doubtful that anyone, other than Wilson, believes that Thomas' frontier had anything to do with advancing the cause of civil rights.

Other supporters of Thomas were more honest in presenting Thomas' views. Black conservative economist Thomas Sowell became a strong advocate for Thomas and the positions that he had staked out. Sowell, like most Reagan-era conservatives, argued that liberal justices, such as Thurgood Marshall and John Paul Stevens, have manipulated the law and moved away from the "original intent" of the nation's founding fathers. According to Sowell, "Judge Thomas is one of the people who believes that the role of a judge is to carry out the law as it is written, not to strain and twist the law to mean what he wants it to mean. Most Americans share this belief in 'judicial restraint'—but not the elite of the political left."[31] By the Left, of course, he meant the civil rights groups, civil liberties organizations, women activists, labor and other groups labeled leftist by conservatives.

For his part, Thomas' opposition to affirmative action, flexible inter-pretations of the Constitution, minority set-asides, and other political icons of the liberal community was well established in the public record. On affirmative action, for example, he stated, "During my first year in the Administration...we began to argue against affirmative action. We attacked welfare and the welfare mentality. These are positions with which I agree."[32] His attacks on affirmative action were relentless and infuriated civil rights advocates. He once stated: "[It] is just as insane for blacks to expect relief from the federal government for years of discrimination as it is to expect a mugger to nurse his victims back to health. Ultimately, the burden of your being mugged falls on you."[33]

Eminent Black historian John Hope Franklin penned the most eloquent response to Thomas' and other Black conservatives' view of "self-help." Franklin wrote:

> Self-help is admirable so long as it encourages initiative and achievement in a society that gives all its members an opportu-nity to develop in the manner best suited to their talents. It must not be confused with or used as a substitute for society's obliga-tion to deal equitably with all its members and to assume the responsibility for promoting their well-being. This involves equal educational, economic and political opportunity regardless of age, gender or race. Judge Thomas, in failing in his utterances and policies to subscribe to this basic principle, has placed himself in the unseemly position of denying to others the very opportunities and the kind of assistance from public and private quarters that have placed him where he is today.[34]

Franklin refused to testify at the Thomas hearings. Although he had testified at nominee hearings in the past, he viewed the Thomas hearings as a sham. He said, "I saw that they were going to let him back off anything he had ever said. I decided if they weren't going to do their part, I couldn't run with the ball for them. I didn't think those White men had the nerve to speak out courageously against a Black man...I gave up on it."[35]

In one last area of ideological differences, the National Conference of Black Lawyers discussed Thomas' questionable alliance with individuals who had close ties to the hated White apartheid government of South Africa. NCBL National Director Adjoa Aiyetoro testified:

NCBL is deeply troubled by Thomas' apparent support for the current South African government and his lending of the prestige of his office to efforts supporting the racist regime in South Africa. For the past ten years, Mr. Thomas has served as a member of the Editorial Advisory Board of the *Lincoln Review,* the quarterly publication of the Lincoln Institute for Research and Education, founded by J. A. Parker, who is a paid agent of the racist government of South Africa and who has been described as Thomas' political mentor.[36]

Parker not only is tied into the apartheid regime, but is also an activist in the global fascist movement. He served for many years on the Board of Directors of the U.S. branch of the World Anti-Communist League, which is comprised of fascists, neo-Nazis, death-squad leaders, racists, and anti-Semites.[37]

# Unqualified

While the focus of most Black opposition to Thomas was on President Bush's exploitation of race and ideological issues, a number of groups also argued that Thomas was not qualified for the position of associate justice. Black interest groups argued that although no specific legal criteria exists, historic precedent on nominees has set certain standards that Thomas did not meet. For example, the Senate Judiciary Committee relies upon the rating of nominees by the American Bar Association (ABA) for its initial assessment of a particular nominee's judicial skills and competence. The ABA's Standing Committee on the Federal Judiciary has three rating levels: well-qualified, qualified, and not qualified. On August 28, 1991, the ABA rated Thomas "qualified."[38] Twelve of the fifteen-member committee voted Thomas "qualified," two voted him "unqualified," and one member did not vote.[39] No sitting Supreme Court Justice had received a "not qualified" vote since 1970.[40] Though "qualified" is not the lowest ranking, no nominee since Sandra Day O'Connor joined the Court in 1981 has received that rating and been confirmed.

This was only the beginning of the challenges to Thomas' qualifications. Many opponents highlighted Thomas' tenure as head of the Equal Employment Opportunity Commission (EEOC) as riddled with incompetence and negligence. Cases involving race or age discrimination, many of which involved Black seniors, were backlogged by the thousands. As the CBC pointed out, "Because of his mismanagement and indifference, more than 13,000 age discrimination claims missed the statutory deadline for action and had to be revived by a special statute."[41] Overall, between 1983 and 1987, the backlog of complaints to EEOC grew from 31,500 to 62,000.[42]

# The Anita Hill Charges

Anita Hill's allegation that Thomas sexually harassed her did not fundamentally change the alliances or support by Black leadership of his nomination. Those who supported him continued to and those who opposed continued to fight against the nomination. The sensationalism of the charges, however, turned the whole process into grand spectacle and raised the intensity of the debate to its peak. Thomas' defenders bluntly refused to entertain any notion that Thomas was guilty, although they had no proof whatsoever that Hill was lying. Instead, they resorted to character attacks and rumor-mongering about Hill. She was accused of either fantasizing, being in cahoots with the Democrats and radical feminists groups, or seeking revenge as a "scorned" woman. The suppression of other female witnesses who would have testified that Thomas also harassed them contributed to the conclusion that the Senate Judiciary Committee was less interested in the truth than in getting through what was a humiliating process for all.

Few made note of the fact that both Thomas and Hill had been loyal Reagan Republicans and had participated fully and knowingly in that Administration's assault against the Black community and other dispossessed sectors of society. As Cornel West wrote, "Both Thomas and Hill supported an unprecedented redistribution of wealth from working people to well-to-do people in the form of regressive taxation, deregulation policies, cutbacks and slowdowns in public service programs, take-backs at the negotiation table between workers and management, and military buildups at the Pentagon. Both Thomas and Hill supported the unleashing of unbridled capitalist market forces on a level never witnessed in the United Stated before that have devastated Black working and poor communities."[43]

Beyond the disputed facts of the Hill and Thomas allegations and counter-allegations, it is fairly clear what motivated Hill's earlier silence, Thomas' unbelievable defense, and the behavior of other Black Republicans who came to Thomas' defense: The motivation in each case was naked careerism. For none of these Reaganists were the interests of blacks, women, the poor, or working people in general paramount. Hill admitted freely that she did not go public—though she mentioned her charges about Thomas to friends privately—because she wanted and enjoyed her career-climbing with Thomas at the Department of Education and the EEOC. Likewise, Thomas' ever changing stories and incredulous denials were also career-building tactics.

# Black Leadership and the Campaign Against Thomas

As noted above, many of the key civil rights leaders came out in support of Thomas. Although the NAACP went on the record against Thomas, then-Executive Director Benjamin Hooks had expressed reluctance to oppose the nomination. Reportedly, Hooks had responded positively to White House overtures and had even supplied the Bush White House names of Black leaders who might be sympathetic to Thomas.[44] It was mainly the persistence and commitment of NAACP Washington Office Executive Director Wade Henderson that eventually forced Hooks to go along with the majority opinion of the NAACP board that the Thomas nomination needed to be defeated.

While the CBC was strong on the record against Thomas, it failed to mobilize the necessary mass pressure to defeat him. Although the Caucus had come out in opposition in July 1991, most of August was lost as a mobilizing period since most members of Congress were away on vacation during the congressional recess. Delays in hiring or putting together a media team to field anti-Thomas op-ed articles were key factors in failing to gain the momentum in the Black community to stop the nomination. In September, the first round of the Thomas hearings occurred at the same time as the Congressional Black Caucus's Annual Legislative Weekend. With thousands of politically active and concerned blacks in town for the CBC activities, a golden opportunity to demonstrate a show of force against the nominee was squandered as members of the CBC vetoed a call for a protest down at the Supreme Court.

A number of Black women scholars and activists noted that many of the already muted protests against Thomas seemed to shrink even further after the Hill allegations. Many stated that not only did the issue of sexual harassment by powerful men have a ring of familiarity, but that the issue was also valid within the movement for social change. More broadly, it was noted that the serious questions concerning how Black women are treated and portrayed in business and professional situations, everyday work, and in popular culture underscored the second-class position that Black women had been relegated to even in the Black community. Although many Black women's organizations came out against Thomas, a few prominent Black women—notably poet Maya Angelou— supported him.

Thomas since has accumulated one of the worst anti-Black records in recent Supreme Court history. Time and time again, he has been the deciding vote in cases that have gone against the interests of the black community as seen by even Black moderate leaders. Ninety percent of the time, Thomas has voted with Justice Antonio Scalia, widely considered to be the most conservative of the present Court. Whether driven by a profound self-hate or psychologically-addicted to retrograde conservatism or both, Thomas has voted with a vengeance to limit civil and human rights.

In *Shaw v. Reno,* Thomas was the deciding vote in allowing whites in North Carolina to object to two newly-created black majority congressional districts. Blacks are 22 percent of the state's population, but had not been able to elect a representative to Congress since the end of the last century. Thomas was also the deciding vote in *St. Mary's Honor Center v. Hicks* which held that even if an employer blatantly lied in a bias suit, that still did not entitle the aggrieved employee an automatic win. In one outrageous dissent, *Hudson v. McMillian,* Thomas and Scalia stood alone. The majority ruled that an Eighth Amendment violation against cruel and unusual punishment had occured in a case where an inmate in Louisiana had been tied to the floor and severely beaten by prison guards. Thomas wrote that the inmates injuries "were not significant enough" to be a constitutional violation.

Those Black leaders who supported Thomas failed on the most elementary level. They did not take Thomas at his word. He stated that he would support conservative policies, and his recorded statements and actions backed up that assertion, yet Black leaders defending his nomination faithfully believed that he would change or that because he was Black that he would not betray them. The lesson from the Thomas experience is clear: ideological and political views can not be dismissed in the name of a hopeful racial unity.

The political themes debated in the fight over Thomas' nomination have meaning beyond that particular campaign. As blacks face an uncertain future, questions concerning the efficacy of Black leadership remain critical. If the Thomas fight is any indication, these questions remain unresolved.

# Chapter 8

# The Hazards of Duke

His positions are my positions.

— James Meredith[1]

One episode that highlighted the unease that African Americans felt in the 1990s was the declaration by White supremacist and former Ku Klux Klan leader David Duke that he was entering the 1992 race for president. Duke's election to the Louisiana House of Representatives, his serious run for governor of that state, and his decision to run as a Republican gave his campaign a qualitatively new significance.

The Duke phenomenon was the child of twelve years of racism, intolerance, and class privilege gushing from the Reagan and Bush administrations. His decision to run as a Republican was neither illogical nor careless. If Duke had a chance of winning, it would be by implementing a strategy that mixed the conservative Republican program with overt racist signals and an appeal to the economic frustrations of working-class and middle-class Whites—in essence, the strategy that had put Reagan and Bush in the White House.

By the time he was seventeen, Duke had joined the Klan. In 1969, while attending Louisiana State University, he formed the White Youth Alliance. Six years later, the nation's best-known avowed racist formed his own version of the Knights of the KKK in Louisiana; he soon became the Grand Wizard of the organization. Duke's efforts to put a clean-shave, respectable veneer on the Klan gained him national recognition by other racist groups and the media. Internal squabbles and his competition with other Klan members, however, eventually forced him out of the KKK.[2]

In 1980, Duke formed the National Association for the Advancement of White People, whose purpose as to advocate racial separation and linkups with other White supremacist groups.[3] But, unlike other Klan leaders, Duke also had political ambitions and set his sights on winning elected office. In 1988, he ran for president, first as a Democrat in some of the southern primaries and then in the general election on the ticket of the ultra-Right-wing Populist Party. He won 48,000 votes. [4] His campaign manager for this race was Ralph P. Forbes, who had been a leader of George Lincoln Rockwell's American Nazi Party in the 1960s[5]

Building on the resources, contacts, and media attention made during his first presidential campaign, Duke ran and won a seat in the Louisiana state legislature where he represented the 99.6 percent White suburban community of Metairie outside of New Orleans. In that race, the turnout was extremely high, 78 percent, of which he won a convincing majority.[6] Duke's support was not limited just to the backwaters of Metairie, however. When he was sworn-in, he received a standing ovation from the other state legislators.[7]

No sooner had Duke won the state race, than he set his sights on the U.S. Senate seat held by Sen. J. Bennett Johnston. Duke raised at least $700,000 for his campaign and polled a quarter of the vote statewide. In the race, Duke won 44 percent of the vote and 60 percent of the White vote.[8]

Duke's rapid rise and growing prominence as a Republican sent shudders throughout the party's national leadership. Reagan and Bush made efforts to disassociate Duke from the national party during his various campaigns. Then Republican National Committee (RNC) chairperson, Lee Atwater, had dismissed Duke as a "charlatan."

Yet, for the Republicans, Duke was hard to dismiss. His program—characterized by his criticizing the poor for the deterioration unfolding in the nation and attacking welfare—while advocating harsher criminal penalties, curbs on immigration, higher tariffs on imports was virtually identical to the program of the Republican Party, and the Reagan and Bush administrations.

In addition, Duke's rise was the logical result of the racial maneuvers of Louisiana's Republican Party since the passage of the 1960s Civil Rights and Voting Rights acts. David Treen, former Congressperson, who had been elected, in 1980, as the first Republican governor of the state since Reconstruction, had built his career earlier as chairperson of Louisiana's States' Rights Party, which advocated racial segregation. Although Treen recanted his earlier segregationist views, he and the state's Republicans engaged in ongoing anti-Black tactics such as attempting to purge blacks from the voter's rolls.[9] Duke defeated David Treen's brother, John, who, as one reporter noted, "agreed on almost everything" that Duke stood for.[10] The party's 140-member central committee could not even come up with the votes to censure Duke, as proposed by some members, even as Duke's racist activities—such as bringing a Klan Grand Wizard on to his staff—continued.[11]

Duke's admonition that he was a loyal and true member of the Republican Party—some have called it the RepubliKlan Party—had a solid ring of truth to it. Duke's populism reached beyond the borders of Louisiana. Almost half of the 14,000 individual contributors to his gubernatorial campaign came from outside of the state.[12] His conservative populism existed side-by-side with his hardline racist views. Duke continued his associations with Nazis and Klan members and even sold racist and anti-Semitic materials from his legislative office.

Duke's infamy would reach its peak in 1991 when he announced that he was seeking the office of governor for the state of Louisiana. While some in the national party snickered at Duke's ambitions, it was no longer a laughing matter when he managed to come in second in the non-partisan primary race and forced a runoff between himself and Democratic candidate Edwin Edwards, a former governor who had left office in 1987 in disgrace. Edwards had been indicted twice on corruption charges, but acquitted, and had been accused of gambling and womanizing during his time in office.

Duke beat Democrat-turned-Republican Governor Buddy Roemer, who had the backing of virtually every national Republican honcho. Duke came in second with 484,923 votes (32 percent) behind Edwin Edwards' 516,119 (34 percent). Roemer followed in third place with 408,904 (27 percent).[13] Suddenly, the very real possibility that Duke could become governor created a new dynamic in the Republican calculations for retaining the White House in 1992. First, Duke could shrivel the already low Black support that Bush enjoyed, boosted by the Clarence Thomas Supreme Court nomination, simply by having his name linked with Bush's. More important, from the vantage point of the Republicans, Duke's presidential aims could seriously threaten Bush in the south if a Governor Duke were to enter the primaries. At that moment, the one fact that was absolutely clear, in the words of Loyola University political scientist Ed Renwick, was that "Duke had become the voice of a majority of White voters in Louisiana."[14]

The desperation of the Republicans was demonstrated in their flurry of endorsements for the Democrat, Edwards. President Bush, defeated Governor Roemer, Republican ex-Governor David Treen, and other prominent Republicans found themselves in the embarrassing position of having to support a Democrat, one who had a record of disgrace and scandal at that. Polls taken right before the election showed that a significant number of Whites were backing Duke. When Whites were asked which of the two had the worst past, Duke or Edwards, 29 percent said Duke did, while a whopping 48 percent said Edwards did.[15]

What was frightening about the Duke phenomenon was that Duke received support not only because of his past, but also in spite of his past. His Republican platform won over many middle-class and working-class Whites who tended to view themselves as not racist. However, three Republican administrations in a row had consciously and frequently employed racial signals to push their agenda of tax cuts, law-and-order, welfare reform, and U.S. global hegemony. Those policies and statements gave birth to the David Duke of the late 1980s. As *USA Today* stated, "The White House is hard-pressed to explain how Duke's message on the economy differs from President Bush's."[16] In fact, Republican National Party Chairman Clayton Yeutter stated, that in terms of Duke's advocacy of basically the Republican economic program, Republicans "would be on similar ground with Duke on fundamental economic policy questions."[17]

African Americans constitute 27 percent of the Louisiana's electorate. It was estimated that even if Black turnout reached 100 percent and every vote went to Edwards, he would still need more than one-third of the White vote to win.[18] Duke had already proven that he could win more than 50 percent of the White vote. The race began to turn Edwards' way when the state's business community joined the battle on his side out of a fear that a Duke governorship would destroy the state's economy, and as mobilization by the Black community and other groups, particularly Jewish and civil liberties organizations, reached a fever pitch. These groups also launched widely publicized stop-Duke campaigns.

In previous campaigns, pollsters had underestimated Duke's support primarily because many of his supporters tended to lie. In this election, however, polls taken right before the election underestimated the support for Edwards. A Mason-Dixon poll released three days before the election showed Edwards with 49 percent, Duke with 42 percent, and 9 percent undecided.[19] Theoretically, Duke had a chance if the undecideds broke his way. In fact, the opposite happened. On election day, Edwards decisively beat Duke by 61 percent to 39 percent.[20]

Although Edwards was the victor, it was Duke who dominated the airwaves in the hours and days immediately following the election. To a great degree, Duke was legitimized by the media in its greed to capitalize from the Duke phenomenon. This put Duke in a strong position to set the terms of his free public relations. Phil Donahue, for example, agreed not to play tapes of Duke's past Klan activities or display racist quotes that he had made. "Nightline" agreed not to have a representative of the Louisiana Coalition Against Racism and Nazism who could dispute Duke's version of the situation in the state.[21]

On December 4, 1991, one month after losing to Edwards, Duke announced that he was entering the Republican presidential race. He indeed articulated a program that called for opposition to "quotas," affirmative action, immigration, and welfare. Using racist language, he also explicitly attacked the Japanese as economic enemies of the United States, much as Hitler had attacked the Jews as economic enemies of Germany.[22]

Once in the race, vigorous and sometimes successful efforts were made by Republicans to keep him off of the ballot. A U.S. district judge in Georgia, for example, ruled that state GOP leaders had the right to exclude him from the ballot and that to allow Duke on the ballot against their wishes would be an infringement on their "freedom of association" rights as a private organization.[23] Duke found similar successful Republican opposition in other states such as Wisconsin and Florida. He managed to get on the ballot in Massachusetts, Connecticut, Michigan, South Carolina, Tennessee, Mississippi, Texas, Oklahoma, Kansas, Oregon, and Louisiana.[24] The American Civil Liberties Union, in a move that generated criticism from a number of quarters, took up Duke's case and filed a number of lawsuits on Duke's behalf.

In the primaries that he did participate in, Duke was trounced. In the South Carolina race, he received 7 percent of the vote compared to Bush's 67 percent and Patrick Buchanan's 26 percent.[25] Duke would fade rather quickly and eventually disappear from the media's sensationalism radar. Duke's politics and dreams of an American Fourth Reich did not disappear, however; they metamorphosed into the campaign of Patrick Buchanan. Throughout the election season, Republican candidate Buchanan, an ultra right-wing journalist, echoed Duke's message of blaming people of color for the nation's woes, xenophobic slanders against the Third World, and calling for a return to conservative traditional values. Buchanan's extreme right positions would serve to pull George Bush even further away from the Republican political center, his natural base.

Black leaders around the nation denounced Duke. Most spoke also of the relationship between the rise of Duke and Republican policies and politics. Most of the problem with Duke, however, arose from the ease with which he was able to tap into the racial and class fears of Whites from across a spectrum of socio-economic backgrounds. The difficulty facing Black leaders was how to deal with Whites who didn't support Duke, but supported Duke-like proposals. These whites were clearly willing to go with the more sophisticated appeals to race, such as articulated by George Bush and company and even some Democrats. Thinly-covered racially based appeals dressed up in rhetoric such as "new mainstream" influenced many white voters.

This complicated amalgamation of class and racial politics was not so easy to dismiss. Reaganist attacks on the standard of living of all working people had been vicious, but many working-class Whites had a racial blindspot that looked right past Reagan and only saw racial minorities as the root of the nation's decline. During twelve years of Republican reign, the divide between the haves, have-some, and have-nots expanded greatly. The economic desperation caused by the collapse of middle-class and working-class jobs and wages, opened the door for race-based appeals, in the absence of a strong and broad movement for class unity in the face of a common enemy.

Although Reagan and Bush touted the Republican Party commitment to advancement for all Americans—i.e., opposition to Black racial preference, but not to White—class-based politics were at the heart of the new conservatism. For many Whites, and to the panic of White leaders in the Republican Party, a vote for Duke was seen as a revolt against a system that no longer represented their interests. On the other side, for many blacks who felt the same way, revolt took on a more expressive character.

# Chapter 9

# The Fire Once More

What happens to a dream deferred?
Does it dry up like a raisin in the sun?
Or fester like a sore and then run?
Does it stink like rotten meat?
Or crust and sugar over like a syrupy sweet?
Maybe it just sags like a heavy load.
Or does it explode?

—Langston Hughes, "Dream Deferred"[1]

During the 1992 elections, the candidates had studiously avoided discussion of the issue of race and the plight of the cities. While many Black grassroots activists complained that the campaigns were ignoring the concerns of the inner-cities, many of the African American politicians supporting various candidates rationalized that being mute on these issues was a necessary tactic to win the White suburban and middle-class vote. The shortsighted and misguided judgment of twelve jurors in the small southern California community of Simi Valley changed all of that.

As shocking as was the original broadcast of the amateur videotape of three White Los Angeles police officers brutally beating an unarmed Black man, while more officers stood by and watched, the acquittal of those same officers and their sergeant a year later was even more stunning. The subsequent uprising in Los Angeles, the costliest in U.S. history, occurred in the middle of the campaign season and appeared to be a divine intervention. If the candidates were not going to voluntarily raise and address the issues of racism and despair, discuss growing frustration and cruel poverty, reject the politics of intolerance and abandonment, then those concerns would, with hurricane-level force, inject themselves into the debate.

The videotaped beating of Black motorist Rodney King startled a nation that had blinded itself to rampant police brutality against the African

American community and to the deteriorating social circumstances of the nation's inner-city poor. Virtually alone, rappers in Los Angeles, Oakland, Houston, New York, and other cities had been rapping for years to a deaf nation about unchecked murders by police and the beatings of young Black males. Buying into the conservative argument that street crime was a greater security concern than police brutality, few Black leaders heeded the call of the rappers.

In Los Angeles, where grassroots activists and others called incessantly for censoring and dismissing the overzealous Police Chief Daryl Gates, Mayor Tom Bradley conceded to Gates' threats and power more than he resisted. It took the awkward and poorly shot, but riveting video by plumbing-supply store manager George Holliday to expose to the nation and the world the reality of Los Angeles, shatter forever the pristine and fabricated police images portrayed in *Columbo, Adam 12,* and *Dragnet,* and raise anew the American specter of racism.

# L.A. and the Crisis of the Cities

Through the prism of what happened in Los Angeles, insight is provided into the current national crisis of Black and White leadership and the lack of an ameliorative vision and strategy for addressing the conditions destroying inner-city Black communities. The abandonment of the cities by the federal government, state governments, and leadership of all colors is, in effect, the abandonment of a large sector of the African American community. The cities, which house 58 percent of all Blacks, have become the line in the sand for social policy reform. Since the 1950s, out-migration from the cities has had several waves. In the first wave in the 1950s, Whites left the cities in droves following the urban rebellions and Black Power initiatives of that period. As Blacks became majorities or near majorities in major cities, Whites were willing to concede political management (though ultimately not power) to Blacks while retaining economic dominance. From Detroit to Cleveland, the city became the epicenter of African American life and culture.

The second wave of out-migration has been more recent, in the 1980s, and has mainly been an outpouring of middle-class and affluent Blacks to the near suburbs. In cities, such as Washington, D.C., New York, Los Angeles, and Detroit, middle-class Blacks have become the new suburbanites living on the edges of the major cities in which they work, go to universities, and enjoy its cultural life. Yet, frustrated, frightened, or alienated with growing crime, homelessness, joblessness, and increasing taxes, they have built their personal lives and their future in enclaves that are away from what is perceived to be the urban crisis. Many middle-class Blacks have felt not so much pulled out of the cities as pushed.

What the cities have been left with is a structural and political contradiction that transcends race, but has a racial edge. In the post-industrial era of the 1990s, a shrinking tax base and an exponentially expanding social crisis have handed city managers and administrators, who are increasingly Black, a skimpy menu of strategies from which they attempt to function and survive. White taxpayers and businesses that remain in the cities demand more laws and tax relief.

Ideologically influenced by Reaganism, the overarching concern of these middle-class taxpayers is personal and property security. Just as Reagan and Bush gave disproportionate weight to the military at the expense of domestic programs, cities are funding police department operations at the expense of city services, social programs, and economic development plans. What this has meant is that the new housing program for the poor is a jail cell and the only expansion in local jobs is in the fields of law enforcement and security.

What does it mean for Black leadership that repressive authority is now in the hands of Black city mayors and managers? It is ironic that many of those now in positions to call out the police to repress protesters and urban rebellions are, of course, in those very positions because of Black protests from years past. Black protests for responsive government are likely to be met with resistance in an ever escalating war of nerves between the poor, their allies, and city government. These developments have precipitated a duel "crisis of legitimacy" for Black elected leadership and the governmental bureaucracy it represents.

While the presence of Black elected officials has been important, and they have had a positive impact on the lives of Blacks at a local level, the continuing deterioration of conditions in the inner-cities, more often than not, has pitted those officials against the Black poor. The willingness of many Black city leaders to make peace with capital, generally at the expense of poor and working-class interests, evaporates the sense of solidarity and racial unity that was the basis for electing many of the Black officials in the first place. Arising out of this situation is a new set of Black activists and advocates who must reignite an insurgency of the masses to once again wrestle concessions from those in power.

That insurgency has taken the forms of both traditional street protests and electoral activism. This duel approach has generated more resistance than mere protests alone. In fact, it can be assumed that electoral activism is a form of protest politics when it challenges the status quo and the assumptions that it rests upon. While traditional Black protest politics have reached a certain accommodation with local power structures, electoral activism affords no such recourse. In the past, for Black activists to be seen as legitimate in the eyes of the corporate state has meant that they had to make the transformation from protest to politics, i.e., to seek and be satisfied with access to the negotiating table and the trappings that come with that position. White political analysts (along with many Black ones) expected the protest form of struggle to come to an end. They assumed, often correctly, that protest could be bought off and that with political maturity, militant Black activists would become a part of the system. Nothing captures better the frustration of many conservatives because some Black leaders have not met this expectation than the remarks of George Will, who bemoaned, "Why can't Jesse Jackson be like Tom Bradley? "[2] Indeed, it was Bradley's city that shook the 1992 campaign season to its rafters and, lit by the fires of rage, illuminated the unspoken convergence of racial politics and presidential quests.

# Background To Revolt

Los Angeles is the nation's second-largest city. Home to the professional-image construction industry, it has projected itself as a people-friendly, laid-back isle of sun and leisure. It is perceived by millions around the globe as a Shangra La of suntanned Anglos with colorful Black and brown street gangs. This, of course, is sheer fantasy.

The city of Los Angeles is located in Los Angeles County, which is home to nine million people. This includes the city of Los Angeles, population 3,485,000, plus eighty-seven smaller cities and towns. The county is 13 percent African American, 10 percent Asian and Pacific Islander, 40 percent Latino, and 37 percent White. Los Angeles, the city, is 13 percent African American, 39 percent Latino, 9 percent Asian/Pacific Islander, and 37 percent White.[3]

Although it boasts a diversity unmatched by most cities in the United States, it is also, as one analyst described it, "one of the two or three most segregated major cities in America."[4] African Americans tend to be disproportionately concentrated in South Central, Los Angeles, Mexican Americans in East Los Angeles, Whites on the West Side, and Asians in Koreatown. Newer Latino immigrants, principally from Central America, are located either in South Central or Koreatown. South Central is 55.5 percent Black, 10.5 percent White, 1.1 percent Asian, and 45.1 percent Latino (Black or White); Koreatown is 5 percent Black, 25.4 percent White, 26.5 percent Asian, and 67.9 percent Latino (Black or White).[5] Race and class crossover in the city is accidental and incidental. These fulcrums of isolation have been exacerbated by the increasingly dismal economic and social picture confronting poor Black, Asian, and Latino communities in the city, particularly in South Central and Koreatown, where both communities have poverty rates that exceed 30 percent.[6]

The collapse of the Black community's social and economic safety nets in the Los Angeles area is reflective of what's happened to African Americans across the nation, yet is distinctive in important ways. More than most areas, Los Angeles city and county is segregated in ways and in a seeming permanence that the segregationists of the Old South would salivate over. This segregation represents a profound, positive correlation of race, nationality, and class. At the bottom of every social and economic indicator, notwithstanding a spate of Black elected officials, is the African American community.

The mayoral administration of former South Central policeperson Thomas Bradley translated into few gains for the Black community. Elected to mayor in 1973 on the strength of L.A's West Side liberals and the eagerness of the Black community to position one of its own, it became clear fairly early on that Bradley had ambitions and political views that would limit his contact and commitment to the Black community. His tendency to modulate politically between liberal views (on many social issues), moderate views (on many political issues) and conservative views (on virtually all economic issues) alienated him from the community out of which he rose. Bradley became one of the first Black mayors elected in the post-Voting Rights Act period to advocate and practice the politics of deracialization.

This perspective was most sharply represented in his two unsuccessful runs for governor in 1982 and 1986. Operating what some analysts have called a "color-free" campaign, Bradley failed to inspire Black voters to turn out and lost the 1982 race by the closest margin in California's history for a gubernatorial race, 49.3 percent to 48.1 percent. The mere 93,000-vote difference was mostly made up of Black voters who chose to stay home rather than go to the polls to vote for a candidate who they felt did not address their concerns in his campaign and did not even open a campaign headquarters in their communities.[7]

During Bradley's twenty-year tenure misery grew in Los Angeles and in the counties for the dispossessed. In Los Angeles County, 40 percent of the children live under or at the poverty level.[8] Job growth in the areas where the Black population is most concentrated expanded by less than 1 percent.[9] Black youth in the area, in particular, have been unable to find work. Unemployment for Black youth hovered at around 45 percent.[10]

Part of the problem is the lack of Black-owned businesses in the Black community, especially South Central. Prior to the 1965 Watts riot, most of the small shops and stores were owned by Whites or Jews. In the last twenty-five years, they were replaced not by Blacks, but by Korean immigrants, who were able to get loans and credit from banks while Black city residents could not. Also, Korean immigrants were permitted by the South Korean government to take up to $100,000 from the country as startup capital for new businesses in the United States. U.S. Korean banks and credit associations, operating what is known as the *kye* system, also facilitated the ease by which Korean merchants moved into South Central. Most of these businesses are family-run and, prior to the 1992 uprising, rarely employed community residents.[11]

Jobs disappeared in California, and particularly in Los Angeles, during the Reagan and Bush years like wisps of smoke from southern California's long-closed factories. In the period 1978–1989, about 200,000 well-paying manufacturing jobs vanished from Los Angeles.[12] More than 100 plants closed during this period, many of them fleeing to Mexico or other developing nations. The situation worsened during the latter half of the Bush administration. According to the *Washington Post*, while the United States lost two million jobs between June 1990 and December 1992, about 27 percent of that job loss occurred in the five-county Los Angeles metropolitan area. That translates into roughly 540,000 jobs![13] Overall, the state accounted for 38 percent of the nation's vanishing jobs (See Table 9-1).

·Latinos also suffered from the economic dislocations of Reaganism. Many new, mostly undocumented Latino immigrants were able to find work in the new service industries where job creation was occurring. Hired at minimum wage or less in most instances, Latinos were preferred over Blacks because their undocumented status made them more exploitable and less able to fight unsafe and unjust working conditions.

While southern California was taking hits from the disinvestment of the private sector, the federal government was doing its version of a fire sale on the cities. Federal aid to Los Angeles was cut back, going from $370 million in 1977, when such aid accounted for 18 percent of the city's budget, to $60 million in 1990, accounting for less than 2 percent of the budget.[14]

How did Bradley and the Los Angeles City Council respond to this economic crisis? For the most part, Bradley caved-in to the reactionaries on the Council who believed that it was more important to protect property and contain the growing rage of the underclass, than to provide opportunities and service. The decision to choose cops over community was demonstrated most vividly in the budget priorities of Bradley and the Council. In 1987, they allocated a paltry $30,000 for recreation equipment for 150 centers across the city serving hundreds of thousands of Los Angeles citizens.[15] The city also provided $500,000 for jobs for 100 high-risk youth. This was for a region where the low estimate of just Black youth gang members is about 50,000. When citizens complained, the city cried "budget crunch." However, in the 1987–1988 budget, the city whimpered and gave the Los Angeles Police

**Table 9-1**

**Plant Closures in Los Angeles Since 1965**

| Company | City | Year Closed | Jobs Lost |
|---|---|---|---|
| American Bridge | Commerce | 1979 | 700 |
| Bethlehem Steel | Vernon | 1982 | 1,600 |
| Chrysler | Commerce | 1971 | 2,000 |
| Discovision | Carson | 1982 | 1,000 |
| Fibreboard | South Gate | 1978 | 250 |
| Firestone | South Gate | 1980 | 1,400 |
| Ford | Pico Rivera | 1980 | 2,300 |
| GM | South Gate | 1982 | 4,500 |
| Goodrich | Commerce | 1976 | 1,000 |
| Goodyear | Los Angeles | 1980 | 1,600 |
| Johns Manville | Vernon | 1982 | 200 |
| Lure Meat Packing | Vernon | 1978 | 500 |
| Max Factor | Hawthorne | 1982 | 1,000 |
| Uniroyal | Commerce | 1978 | 1,450 |
| Weiser Lock | South Gate | 1981 | 2,100 |

Source: *Inside the L.A. Riots*

Department $436.1 million, 17.6 percent of the city's overall budget, without a moment's hesitation.[16]

Los Angeles reflected the new law enforcement priorities of the state as the California penal system experienced unprecedented expansion. Spending on criminal justice grew by 70 percent as the state "expanded the capacity of seven of its existing prisons and built thirteen new facilities to bring the current total to twenty-five."[17] In addition, six more facilities were in the planning stage or being constructed. California's hardening line on crime resulted in the state's prison population, two-thirds of which is Black or Latino, leaping from 22,000 in 1980 to over 106,000 by 1992.[18] Many of these prisoners are high school dropouts from the Los Angeles area, where the dropout rate is nearly 40 percent. In South Central, however, the rate is between 63 and 79 percent, and about 25 percent in the junior high schools.[19]

It was these conditions which fed escalating tensions in the city between different racial and class groups. Relations between Black community residents and Korean store owners deteriorated badly in 1991. In one six-month period, at least two Koreans and three African Americans were killed in disputes between individuals. In one situation, a Black man was killed by a store owner in a disagreement over a wine cooler.[20]

On March 15, 1991, tensions between the Black and Korean communities escalated considerably following the killing of a fifteen-year-old Black high school honor student, Latasha Harlins, by a Korean store owner. The incident began when store owner Soon Ja Du accused Harlins of attempting to steal a $1.79 bottle of orange juice from her store. Reportedly, Du shouted, "You bitch, you're trying to steal my orange juice," and attacked Harlins.[21] After a brief scuffle, Harlins put the juice on the counter and began to walk out of the store. Du, at this point, pulled a gun and coldly shot Harlins in the back of the head. Harlins died with two $1 bills clutched in her fist. The money was obviously to pay for the juice, that is, until her assaulted dignity compelled her to make the fateful decision to walk away.

The details of the event were never in question because the entire encounter, in these security-driven times, was videotaped by the store's security camera. Du faced a maximum of sixteen years in prison after being convicted of voluntary manslaughter. At her sentencing on November 15, 1991, Judge Joyce Karlin sentenced Du to five years probation, a $500 fine and community service.[22] That action—which one writer noted essentially said to the Black community that murdering a Black youngster "was scarcely more serious than drunk driving"[23]—prompted more Black community outrage and protests.

The sense of siege felt by the Black community continued. Five days after Du received probation, Brendan Sheen, a twenty-six-year-old Black man who lived in the Glendale area, was sentenced to thirty days in jail for beating his cocker spaniel.[24] Many Blacks made the comparison between the harsh treatment given a Black man for hitting his dog and the Harlan murder. Unfortunately for the Black community, these insults, incidents, and indignities were just another day in the 'hood.

# L.A. Law

In Los Angeles county, there are forty-three separate police departments, including the infamous Los Angeles Police Department (LAPD) and its closest relative, the Los Angeles Sheriff's Department. Notorious for its brutality, shameless for its arrogance, peacock proud of its reputation for efficiency, the 8,300-member LAPD was seen by many as an out-of-control gang in blue. The city's "thin blue line" was truly an occupation army, given that most of its force, if not the overwhelming majority, lived outside of the city; 2,000 members of the LAPD lived in Ventura county, where Simi Valley is located. In the last survey of the L.A. Police Department taken in 1986, the unrepresentative composition of the LAPD was 67 percent White, 12.4 percent Black (13.6 percent in 1992), and 16.5 percent Latino.[25]

The Los Angeles Sheriff's Department (LASD) has about 8,000 officers who police the unincorporated areas of Los Angeles county as well as, by contract, the jurisdictions of forty-two cities.[26] Like the LAPD, the Sheriff's Department has had hundreds of lawsuits filed against it for brutality and terrorism, particularly its reprehensible Lynwood substation located near South Central Los Angeles. It was accused by the NAACP and others in civil suits of "unwarranted beatings, racial abuse, destruction of property, and unjustified shootings."[27]

For years, the LAPD had truly gotten away with murder. According to the report issued by the Independent Commission on the Los Angeles Police Department—known as the Christopher Commission after its chairperson, Warren Christopher—"the LAPD shot dead or wounded more people in relation to the size of the police force than in any other of the six largest U.S. cities."[28] In 1990, this bloodletting by the LAPD resulted in eighteen dead and forty-four wounded. In that same year, the LASD murdered twenty-six and wounded thirty-two.[29]

Among the most egregious killings were:

- In March 1988, Hong Pyo Lee, a twenty-one-year-old unarmed Korean was shot nine times in the back and head by four Sheriff's deputies. The county was forced to pay $1 million to Lee's family.
- In September 1988, an unarmed Black man, James Earl Bailey, was shot by a deputy from the Lynwood station. His family was awarded $525,000.
- In March 1987, an unarmed Latino man, Pascual Solis, was shot nine times by a deputy from the Lynwood station who first emptied his gun into Solis and then reloaded and shot him four more times while he lay on the ground. His family was awarded $520,000.
- In October 1985, Danny Smith, an unarmed Black man, was shot by four LAPD officers repeatedly in the back. The city was forced to pay $625,000 to his family.[30]

Lawsuits associated with these and other police murders grew over the years and cost the city plenty. In 1971, the city paid $11,000 in suits against the LAPD. By 1991, the price of paying off the homicidal tendencies of L.A.'s official death squads had risen to $11.3 million with complaints flooding in at a rate of 600 calls annually.[31]

The LAPD also gained infamy for its use of the deadly choke-hold. At least fifteen suspects, all people of color, died from this police procedure. Gate's response to the community's outcry against these tortuous deaths was obdurate and typically racist. He stated ignorantly: "We may be finding in some Blacks when [the carotid choke-hold] is applied the veins or arteries do not open up as fast as they do on normal people."[32]

Gates made other racist remarks publicly that infuriated the community. According to the *Wall Street Journal*, he stated that the reasons that Latino officers had not been promoted was because they were "lazy" and that many immigrant Jews were KGB agents sent to Los Angeles to sabotage the 1984 Olympics.[33]

Long denied by the police, mildly addressed by most local Black political leaders, raging in the voices of the rappers, invisible to L.A.'s Anglos, the police-community civil war needed an icon, its ordinary individual elevated to historic symbolism. That catalytic moment arrived on the night of March 3, 1991.

Shortly after midnight, Rodney Glenn King, an unemployed father of three and recent parolee, and his two passengers were involved in a high-speed chase with the LAPD and other area police. King was fleeing from a beating that had played in his head long before his actual beating would be viewed by millions. After the vehicle was finally stopped, King and the other two were ordered out of the car. LAPD officers immediately set upon the large-bodied King, who they claimed refused their orders to submit to arrest, and beat him mercilessly. While twenty-one LAPD officers and other area police stood around watching, three White LAPD officers, Laurence Powell, Timothy Wind, and Theodore Briseno, beat, punch, kick, and hit King repeatedly. He was stunned twice with 50,000 volts of electricity from a laser gun and whacked 56 times by the three cops and their commanding officer, Sgt. Stacey Koon. One of the passengers in King's car said that as the beating went on he heard "bones being cracked...loud thumps, gushy sounds."[34] According to King, he was also called "nigger" and other names during the beating. Koon supervised the entire episode, fired the Taser gun, and gave the orders to beat King.

Unbeknownst to the officers as they flailed away at their victim, what writer Cedric Robinson called their "pavement lynching" of King, was being recorded by a brand new video camera. The eighty-one-second video, which would later be shown around the nation and the world, was shot by George Holliday, a White plumbing company manager who had arisen from his bed to see what all the commotion was about outside of his window. Holliday had attempted to report what he had seen to the proper police authorities, but was rebuffed. That's when he made the fateful decision to sell his cinema verité to local television station KTLA, which then sold the tape to CNN.

Those repeated broadcasts would be picked up by the networks and eventually make it one of the most nationally watched filmed events ever.

King's injuries, some permanent, were gruesome. He had a broken cheek bone and fractures in his skull. His ankle was broken and he had been beaten so severely around the face that he required twenty stitches to his face and mouth. The force of the blows to his head had been so strong that fillings from his teeth had been knocked out.

The officers involved reflected the reputation for brutality and racism that the LAPD was known for throughout the Black community. Reportedly, Wind was so exhausted after the beating that he fell asleep for a few minutes when it was over. Powell, who, in a frenzy, delivered the majority of the blows, often used racist language over the police communication equipment, including referring to Blacks as "Gorillas in the Mist" earlier in the evening. It would later be revealed that racist and sexist statements over the police communications equipment were quite normal. Koon attempted to cover up the beating and protect Powell by making false statements on the police report. Gates' response was typically demented and crude. He stated that King was a criminal and that he hoped that this incident would "be the vehicle to move him down the road to a good life."[35]

It was only after this incident, which led to the four officers being charged with assault with a deadly weapon and use of excessive force, that Bradley finally joined the public cry of others who felt unequivocally that Gates had to go. Bradley's fear of losing his liberal and Black support, on the one hand, and his business allies, on the other, grew as it became clear that the trial of the officers charged in the beating would be one of the most watched trials in recent memory. Bradley benefitted almost immediately after calling for Gates' resignation. Around the time of King's beating, Bradley's approval rating among Blacks was 66 percent. After the beating, but before he called for the resignation, his approval rating had fallen to 54 percent. Soon after his statement, it rose up to 64 percent.[36] It was, therefore, critical for his political standing in the Black community that Bradley join with the demand of most L.A. Blacks that Gates must go.

Overall, however, Bradley's standing across the city dropped. His approval ratings went from 61 percent before the beating, to 53 percent after calling for Gates' resignation, to 48 percent after the Christopher Commission study criticizing LAPD performance was released, to 38 percent after the 1992 rebellion. Whites and Latinos in the city became increasingly dissatisfied with Bradley's leadership. After the rebellion, however, less than half of the Black community, 47 percent, approved favorably of Bradley.[37]

# Decisions, Decisions—The Simi Valley Lynching

The lawyers for the officers had argued successfully for a change of venue, which the city prosecutors had only meekly opposed. Although moving the trial to the nearly all-White Simi Valley community, northwest of Los Angeles, seemed highly unreasonable, the widely broadcast video appeared to most to be compelling evidence that the LAPD had acted brutally and illegally and most felt that convictions were assured. Even when the jury of ten Whites, one Asian, and one Latino was selected,[38] few believed that the four officers would be found innocent.

How very wrong this belief would turn out to be! Grasping the racial predilections of the Simi Valley-based jury, the defense successfully implemented a strategy of putting Rodney King on trial in absentia. In an area where the Black population is only 2 percent, the defense did not have to drill very deep to tap into the prejudices of the White jurors. The sentiments of many Whites in the area toward Blacks is captured in the remarks of one resident, who did not wish to be viewed as a racist, who stated: "There's a Black person up our street and we say 'Hi,' like he's a normal person."[39] While few Blacks could be found in Simi Valley, it was overrun with LAPD officers. According to one report, "Of the 8,300 officers on the LAPD, a staggering 2,000 of them live in Simi."[40] The defense gave the jurors the rationale they needed and found acceptable to make their inevitable decision: Rodney King was in charge of the whole situation! Though King did not testify, for the Simi Valleys jurors, it was King who was on trial and not the officers charged with beating him.

On April 29, 1992, the jury returned its verdict on the eleven charges: not guilty for all four officers on ten of the charges and a hung jury on one charge facing Powell. Like a small pebble thrown into a large ocean, the word rippled out to those outside of the courtroom, to the L.A. community, and to the rest of the nation. Response was immediate and unequivocal. From Hollywood to South Central to police headquarters at Parker Center, the inferno commenced. As millions watched across the nation, Los Angeles began to go up in flames. Gangs of youth—of all races—launched a war in the streets of the city. Whites (and some White-looking Latinos) unfortunate enough to be in the path of the tidal wave of fury that the verdict unleashed were dragged from cars and beaten. Small stores, especially liquor stores and Korean-owned markets, provided the illumination for the rebellion as they burned through the night and were systematically destroyed with a military game plan similar to the way the U.S. attacked Baghdad during the Persian Gulf war.

Much of the city's leadership, especially Bradley, was embarrassingly powerless as the uprising spread, with some notable exceptions. As the insurrection grew on that first evening, Bradley's aides, and presumably Bradley, were more concerned with how to get him safely out of the First A.M.E. Church in South Central. He had come to the church to discuss with community and church activists how to peacefully respond to the verdict, but now discovered that he had to deal with the anger raging throughout the city, some of it directed at him. Eventually, he had no choice but to crouch low, dash to his limo in the church's parking lot under the protection of his aides, and speedily escape the wrath of the community as angry residents beat on his car.

Two of Los Angeles' Black leaders, Congressperson Maxine Waters and City Councilperson Mark Ridley-Thomas, who both represent South Central, were stellar articulators of the grievances and needs of their constituents and of the community. On talk shows, in the streets, and in community meetings, they strongly condemned the verdict, the Reagan-Bush assaults on the cities, the nation's persistent racism, and the failure of the candidates and parties to address the concerns of the poor. Both Waters and Ridley-Thomas had been on the front-lines for years fighting to bring services, resources, and development to the area. Neither had backed down in the face of threats from Gates, promises of retaliation from the city's conservative leaders, or quisling-like acquiescence by Bradley. Speaking for her Black, Latino, Asian, and White constituents, Waters stated: "Let me just say that racism is in all of our institutions in America, and it's a problem. People resent it. It is a backlash against it from those that you saw out there in the street."[41]

The damage to South Central and the rest of city was severe and unforgiving. Fifty-eight people were killed (26 Black, 18 Latino, 10 White, 2 Asian, 2 unknown), while another 2,383 were injured seriously enough to seek medical care. There were more than 8,000 structure fires in the city and surrounding county that left more than 5,000 buildings destroyed or badly damaged. It was estimated that property damages would total about $785 million.[42]

In the 1965 Watts rebellion, it was principally the Black community that rebelled against the police and the local White government. Neither L.A.'s small Asian population nor growing Latino residents played a major role in the street battles that occurred then. In 1992, the uprising was a genuine multi-racial and working-class Intifada. As the makeup of those arrested demonstrates, the rebellion crossed all racial groups in the Los Angeles areas. Among those arrested, 45 percent were Latino, 41 percent Black, and 12 percent White. Although Bush and Gates attempted to portray those active in the rebellion as part of America's habitual urban criminal class, in fact, about 60 percent of those who participated in the rebellion and were arrested had no criminal record.[43] Most of those jailed, 60 percent, were arrested for curfew violations.[44]

Smaller uprisings broke out around the nation, most with multi-racial participation. In San Francisco, demonstrations and attempts to stop traffic on some of the bridges surrounding the city led to over 1,500 arrests and forced the mayor to declare a state of emergency. In Atlanta and Las Vegas, Black youths (and others) led demonstrations, and numerous arrests were made. Similar, though less volatile, actions occurred in New York, Washington, D.C., Tampa, and Seattle. In Washington, D.C., students from the area colleges and high schools as well as community activists held meetings and demonstrated in the streets. One effort in D.C. to shut down the 14th Street Bridge, which is a main traffic artery between the city and the Virginia suburbs, prompted an on-site street meeting between the demonstrators and Mayor Sharon Pratt Kelly. Demonstrations, arrests, and looting lasting for several days broke out in Toronto, Canada.[45]

In virtually every instance, the same issues and concerns were raised: how to end police brutality against the Black community, frustration over the lack of discussion by candidates running for office about the problems facing the poor, demands for jobs, lack of faith in government, and questions about the effectiveness of Black leadership. In the main, these confrontations involved young people who felt little connection with black elected officials and older leaders. This did not mean that young people were in disagreement with black leaders over the injustice of the verdict; only in how to respond in both the short- and long term.

Rejection of the verdict was nearly universal. Every major poll taken right after the decision concluded that people of all races opposed the verdict. In the *USA Today* poll, 100 percent of Blacks and 86 percent of Whites viewed the verdict as wrong.[46] A *Newsweek* poll found that 92 percent of Blacks and 73 percent of Whites felt the officers were guilty.[47] Similar polls by *Washington Post*-ABC News (92 percent Blacks and 64 percent Whites) and *Time* (92 percent Blacks and 62 percent Whites) reached the same conclusions.[48]

From coast to coast, the Black community was outraged. For many inner-city young Blacks, who had often and continually had to deal with police brutality, the freeing of the officers was yet another sign that justice was elusive for African Americans. The King beating echoed cases such as Dred Scott, Homer Adolph Plessy, Scottsboro boys, Emmitt Till, Bobby Hutton, Eleanor Bumpers, Sammy Young, and other infamous instances where Blacks were publicly sacrificed by a racist justice system.

While few Blacks condoned the violence or the deaths that occurred in the L.A. uprising, most understood the historical context out of which the rage grew. Most also knew that other outlets of protests had been ineffective or unavailable to those in the streets of Los Angeles.

# King for a Day: Black Leaders Respond

Stunned by the ferocity and depth of the rage expressed by the L.A. community, national Black leaders of every political tendency scrambled to assert themselves into the forefront of the rebellions. On May 6, 1992, in reaction to the Simi Valley verdict and its aftermath, an emergency leadership meeting of Black elected officials; civil rights leaders; fraternal organizations; and religious, labor, peace and justice, education, student, women, and youth activists convened in Washington, D.C. Called and chaired by Jesse Jackson, the meeting was characterized by anxious discussion concerning the verdict, the subsequent rebellions, and the problems confronting urban America. Coretta Scott King, Mary Frances Berry, Al Sharpton, Joseph Lowery, New York Mayor David Dinkins, and D.C. Mayor Sharon Pratt Kelly were all in attendance.

There was general consensus among the group that the underlying cause of the rebellion in Los Angeles—which has produced similar situations in other cities—was fundamentally economic and social in nature. It was also agreed that racism and the lack of political power are playing major roles in elevating the situation in inner-cities to a crisis level.

Among the actions proposed were: a national day of "Protest, Healing, and Voter Registration" to be held on June 19, 1992; massive demonstrations at the Democratic National Convention in New York, July 13–16; and hearings on police brutality to be held in Washington, D.C. and other cities. June 19 is known as "Juneteenth," the date in 1863 when slaves in Texas discovered that they had been legally freed, although the Emancipation Proclamation had gone into effect on January 1, 1863.

In a follow-up meeting in Washington, D.C., attended by a much smaller and less high-powered set of participants, it was agreed that the June 19th activities would be decentralized and that local groups could decide the nature and scope of their efforts. Discussion about demonstrations at the Democratic National Convention evaporated. In the end, as the fires of Los Angeles burned out, so did the "urgency" of the response. Some of the momentum shifted to Congress where Rep. Maxine Waters and a few other Black congresspersons attempted to push through Urban Aid legislation. Beyond that, there was very little effective or challenging response on the part of the Black leadership other than to eloquently (and correctly) denounce the Bush administration.

From the beginning, one problem that arose with the leadership meetings was that very few young people were involved in discussions on how to react to the rebellion. That lack of involvement made it painfully obvious that Black youth generally felt little allegiance to the national Black leadership initiatives. This point was raised at the May 6 meeting by the few young people who attended the gathering, but was basically ignored.

In Los Angeles, Black youth gang members went beyond their elders and developed their own proposal for addressing the issues of the community. The Bloods/Crips $3.7 billion proposal to rebuild and redevelop L.A. came straight from the streets and the experiences of young Blacks in South Central Los Angeles. Some of the demands were surprising, such as calls for more trees, an end to welfare, and teacher merit tests. Other demands concerned education, economic growth, social services, infrastructure repair, and law enforcement.

The proposal was one of the major developments to come out of the truce movement among L.A.'s Black street gangs. Under the theme "Give Us The Hammer And The Nails, We Will Rebuild The City," the simply-named Bloods/Crips Proposal called for $2 billion to reconstruct damaged and long-neglected areas of the city; $1 billion for "human welfare" programs that would bring hospitals and health clinics to South Central; $700 million for an education agenda that would refurbish the schools and build the writing, math and science skills of inner-city youth; and $20 million in low-interest loans for minority businesses. It's most controversial demand was a request for $6 million to fund a new law enforcement program. They proposed the creation of a community-based "police buddy" system that would have former gang members, after completion of a police training course, patrol and help secure the neighborhood side-by-side with L.A.'s finest.

The Bloods/Crips Organization, authors of this historic document, pledged that if their demands were met, they would rid L.A. of drug dealers and would provide matching funds for an AIDS research and awareness center. Few doubted that they could meet those obligations. The proposal was sent directly to Mayor Tom Bradley.

It would be naive, of course, to think that in this transformation process all vestiges of gang mentality disappeared. Some of the macho posturing found its way into the proposal. After a fairly solid and cogent discourse that surely surprised many, the proposal ended with a last word of bravado that demanded a response within seventy-two hours and initial implementation by the city within thirty days, or else!

The proposal buried the lie that all L.A. gang members are unreformable hoodlums whose concern for their community reaches no further than the barrel of an Uzi, and who would be better off in jail than in the 'hood'.

Going beyond the initial objective of achieving peace among themselves, a number of the gang members have shown themselves in the wake of the city's crisis to be articulate spokespersons for their community's grievances and aspirations.

# The Candidates Duck for Cover

The response by President George Bush was predictable. He saw no connection between the response to the verdict and conditions of life faced by Blacks in Los Angles and other inner-city areas. He said, "What we saw last night and the night before in Los Angeles is not about civil rights. It's not about the great cause of equality that all Americans must uphold. It's not a message of protest. It's been the brutality of mob, pure and simple."[49] Bush denounced the people in the streets and called out the troops. Just as he had ordered the military into Panama and the Persian Gulf, he sent massive military personnel to Los Angeles.[50]

All the signals from the Bush White House had, in fact, championed the brutal and terrorist activities of the LAPD. Only two days after the King beating, when thousands of calls from around the country were flooding into the LAPD headquarters protesting the brutality of its police, Bush entertained LAPD Police Chief Daryl Gates at a ceremony at the White House where he singled out Gates as one of his "All-American heroes."[51] The White House initially attempted to place the blame for the uprising on the social programs of past Democratic administrations. White House spokesperson Marlin Fitzwater stated that the "riot was the result of the Great Society programs of the 1960s and 1970s."[52] NAACP Executive Director Benjamin Hooks responded, "Mr. Fitzwater, get your message straight. The Great Society did not cause the riot. It was because of Presidents like Reagan who went around looking for the welfare queens and let the savings and loan crooks get away that we now have a problem in our streets."[53]

In a panic and watching his re-election hopes go up in flames, Bush beckoned twelve Blacks "spokespeople" to confer at the White House. The group was composed essentially of the heads of the traditional—and many would argue out-of-touch—civil rights organizations. One reporter quipped that the list could have come from a "twenty-year-old Rolodex."[54] Among those in attendance were Dorothy Height, John Jacobs, Benjamin Hooks, Coretta Scott King, and Tony Brown. It appears that the only thing to come out of the meeting was an opportunity for Bush to say in his speech to the nation that he had spoken with "leaders of the civil rights community" about the crisis.

Under pressure from the media and looking to enhance his sinking campaign, Bush went to Los Angeles on May 6. Bush explained cynically to reporters why he was going to Los Angeles by stating, "As you know, I planned a trip out there for some time, so it fits in very nicely."[55] Although he had spent more than three years ignoring the problems of the cities, Bush suddenly became an advocate of government aid to urban America. Bush, for all intents and purposes, never spoke of the needs of the cities for the rest of the campaign. It was no surprise that polls taken after the uprising found that less than a quarter of the people in the country felt that Bush would do the best job of the candidates in handling the racial situation in the United States.[56]

Pat Buchanan's response was typically neanderthal. Employing his usual racist and nationalistic rhetoric, he told the media that "foreigners are coming into this country illegally and helping to burn down one of the greatest cities in America."[57] He said greater force was needed to combat "hoodlumism and "thuggery," as he described the people in the streets of Los Angeles. Buchanan said that the looters are "the Brown Shirts of 1992" and denied that poverty was at the root of the trouble or that "budget cuts in the 1980s justify…an orgy of looting, arson, murder and lynching."[58]

Candidate Bill Clinton's remarks were cautious, but more sensitive to the inner-city reality than those of Bush or Perot. He recognized that the injustice of the verdict tapped into feelings of hurt and frustration, especially for the forgotten and left-behind. Referring to the verdict, he stated: "The people in the other America deserve the same law-and-order that the rest of us demand."[59] At a Black church in Washington, D.C., he stated: "We have neglected and denied our problems for so long they have festered. And for this neglect, we have all paid."[60] He even predicted that more rebellions could happen if the situation facing the inner-city poor were allowed to continue to deteriorate. "We literally have to empower and connect these people to the life we want them to live or they will be lost forever, or you'll have more of what you've seen for the last few days," stated Clinton. In a campaign move, he would later harden his words and emphasize a law-and-order aspect that seemed geared for those voters who disagreed with the verdict, but saw the rebellion as a hooligan riot.

H. Ross Perot had the least to say both quantitatively and substantively. He spoke mainly in his usual "let's just do it" terms. Reflecting a simplistic and naive understanding of the rebellions, Perot said that he was disappointed by the acquittal of four police officers, but "We must unite to solve our problems. If we fight with one another, we all lose."[61] In his statements, Perot also linked Bush to other racist incidents when he raised and criticized the Republicans' use of the infamous "Willie Horton" ad. He stated that he found the ad "reprehensible" and that he would never do that sort of thing.[62]

# Conclusion

While it is undeniably true that the Rodney King beating verdict and the revolt that followed it was a watershed moment in American politics, it is also clear that there is little agreement on the character and significance of that moment. In the context of the current state of Black politics and the crisis facing the Black community, the revolt had several implications. First, it forced into the spotlight the issue of race relations in ways neither anticipated nor welcomed by the presidential aspirants, government officials, and many Black leaders. The discomfort visible in Bush, Clinton, Perot, and elected officials in addressing the racial side of police brutality and judicial injustice was, in fact, discomfort at squarely confronting the ongoing racist dynamics of U.S. society. Up until that point, issues that specifically addressed concerns of African Americans and Latinos had not been raised, given the strategies of both parties and Perot to go after White suburban votes. The rebellion opened up an opportunity to not only discuss these concerns, but to develop policy responses.

For some Black leaders, the rebellion exposed the gulf between those who have benefitted from the move from "protest to politics" and those whose conditions deteriorate daily. Few were able to play more than a spectator role as young African Americans decided that street politics were more appropriate, for the moment, than negotiations or compromise.

Secondly, the rebellion in L.A. was as much about class differences as it was about racial ones, if not more. Shattering the myth of the United States as a classless society, the streets of L.A. (and other cities) bore witness to the multi-colored underclass that refuses to go peacefully into the night—to remain hidden behind poverty's walls of shame. If the debates of the 1992 campaigns avoided discussing racial problems, they also did not address issues of the impoverished, unemployed and working poor whose interests were drowned in the campaign rhetoric of "save the middle class." Despite the few Yuppies and Buppies who joined in the looting, the rebellion was centered in the most destitute part of Los Angeles, where residents took to heart and momentarily put into practice the Marxist call for redistribution of the wealth.

The sense of feeling oppressed as a class was articulated in the responses of those who participated in the looting and street actions. In a survey of 245 of those arrested in Los Angeles conducted by *USA Today*, most expressed dissatisfaction with the government and felt it insensitive to the poor and inner-city community. Almost half, 47 percent, said that it was the conditions in which they lived more than the verdict that was the cause of the uprising.[63] About 75 percent said the government does not care about them, while almost 90 percent agreed with the statement that "police mistreat people like me."[64] Finally, the national street demonstration, led mainly by Black youth, exposed the tenuous and tepid quality of today's political leadership, both White and Black. White political figures stood paralyzed while most national Black leaders, with a few distinctions, scrambled aimlessly to catch up with the aggressive cry of justice and respect. However, the incidents following the verdict made it crystal clear that not one national Black figure held the moral or political authority that could direct people's outrage in any particular direction or toward a common strategy.

Issues raised by the L.A. Spring would fade quickly as the weeks and months passed. The rebellion was rarely mentioned during the rest of the presidential campaign or in much of the mass media. Nor were the myriad of concerns of the inner-cities that fueled the rebellion, except in the most general and vague terms. The golden opportunity for leadership to emerge was squandered and avoided and soon the status quo returned.

In the wake of the rebellion, Los Angeles underwent significant changes in leadership. Gates was forced out and replaced by Willie Williams, the former Black chief of police of Philadelphia. After twenty years in office, Bradley also decided to call it quits. The June 1993 mayoral race boiled down to liberal Democratic City Councilperson Michael Woo, who is Japanese, and conservative multi-millionaire Republican Richard Riordan. Despite Woo's endorsement from President Bill Clinton in a city where Democrats outnumber Republicans two-to-one, Riordan won over Woo by 54 percent to 46 percent. The pattern of voting demonstrated that, as one writer noted, the Apartheidization of Los Angeles continues. Although many hoped that the 1992 rebellion would bring the city together, votes in the June runoff split along racial lines. Riordan, a hard-line law-and-order proponent, won 67 percent of the Anglo vote, which accounted for 85 percent of his total vote, 14 percent of the Black, 43 percent of the Latino, and 31 percent of the Asian vote. Woo won 86 percent of the Black vote, 69 percent of the Asian, 57 percent of the Latino, 51 percent of the Jewish, and only 33 percent of the White vote.[65]

All across the city, racial politics pretty much determined how the vote went. In overwhelmingly Black and Brown South Central, Woo won 80 percent of the vote. In the primarily White and upper-middle-class North San Fernando Valley and West Valley areas, Riordan won 75 percent and 71 percent of the vote respectively. What most impacted the election was low voter turnout among Blacks and high turnout among Whites. In South Central, turnout was below 35 percent. In the Valley areas, it was close to 50 percent. Riordan also made substantial in-roads into the Latino and Asian communities. Riordan's Latino vote more than doubled from the 20 percent he received in the primary.

Riordan's victory was part of a tidal change in the color of local mayors' offices in the nation's major cities. In New York, Hartford, CT, Philadelphia, and earlier in Chicago, middle-age, white Republican males would once again occupy the mayor's seat. Central to this turn around was the rising notion that black mayors had failed to revive these cities and had allowed street crime and random violence to flourish. There was little doubt that these new mayors, like the fabled marshals of the old West, were being brought in to clean up the towns that had been taken over by gunslingers and outlaws. There was also little doubt that the chief targets of these administrations were going to be young, black, Hip Hopping, inner-city males— America's latest public enemies.

# Chapter 10

# Public Enemies: Hip Hop's Impact on Black Politics

Do I have to sell me a whole lot of crack
For decent shelter and clothes on my back?
Or should I just wait for President Bush
Or Jesse Jackson and Operation PUSH?

—Ice Cube[1]

The late African leader Amilcar Cabral once wrote, "Whatever may be the conditions of a people's political and social factors...it is generally within the culture that we find the seed of opposition, which leads to the structuring and development of the liberation movement."[2] Cabral's insight seems highly appropriate when looking at the impact of the Hip Hop movement and rap music on the Black community and its political, social, and even economic life.

As one scholar noted, for many, the rappers are "urban griots dispensing social and cultural critiques."[3] While this may be true, the nature of those critiques is duplicitous and simultaneously often painfully naive and incredibly insightful, abjectly dehumanizing and rich in human spirit. It is these dualities that have given rap its power to inspire as well as its ability to infuriate.

For many Black youth in the United States, in the words of the classic song by War, the world is a ghetto. Trapped in and witness to cycles of violence, destitution, and lives of desperation, their aspirations and views find expression in political behavior, social practice, economic activities, and cultural outlets. These themes come together and form a political culture of resistance that has been termed "Hip Hop" and whose most dynamic expression is in the form of rap music.

115

Rap has stepped up to the plate and attempts to challenge the prevailing paradigms and oppressive structures of late capitalism and institutionalized racism. The resulting interaction has led rap to have a fundamental impact on the cultural and political life of the African American community and its patterns of gender relations and identity.

Changes in the last three decades in the political economy of Black urban life have qualitatively shaped the growing unemployment situation of African Americans, particularly its youth. Since 1960, Black youth have suffered the largest decline in employment of all component groups of all races.[4] In 1986, in the middle of the Republican years, Black teenage unemployment was officially as high as 43.7 percent.[5] In October 1992, six years later, the number remained virtually unchanged, with Black youth unemployment officially at 42.5 percent.[6]

It was perfectly logical that Hip Hop culture emerged strongest initially in cities hardest hit by Reaganomics with large minority youth populations— New York, Los Angeles, Houston, and Oakland. For many of these youth, rap became not only an outlet for social and political discourse, but also an economic opportunity that required little investment other than boldness and a competitive edge. In a period when Black labor was in low demand, and if one could not shoot a basketball like Michael Jordan, then the entertainment industry was one of the few legal avenues available for the get-rich conscious-ness that dominated the social ethos of the 1980s.

Rap music is big business. In 1990, according to the *Los Angeles Times*, rap brought in $600 million. In that year, two rap albums alone, Hammer's *Please Hammer Don't Hurt 'Em* and Vanilla Ice's *To The Extreme*, sold fourteen million copies just in the United States, while Public Enemy's *Fear of a Black Planet* and Digital Underground's *Sex Packet*, also sold over a million each.[7] In 1991, sales leaped to about $700 million.[8] 2 Live Crew's *As Nasty as They Wanna Be*, the subject of lawsuits and arrests, sold more than two million copies.[9] In their debut album, *Straight Outta Compton*, Niggahs With Attitude (NWA) sold over a million copies and followed that up in 1992 by breaking all sales records with their *Efil4zaggin* (niggaz 4 life, spelled backwards) album. The album sold an unprecedented 900,000 copies in its first week of release and later went on to sell millions.[10]

Young Black consumers, ages fifteen to twenty-four, spend about $23 billion annually in the United States of which about $100 million is spent on records and tapes.[11] African Americans, however, are not the main purchasers of rap, as increasingly, rap is being bought by non-Blacks. A survey taken in mid-1992 found that 74 percent of rap sold in the first six months of that year was bought by Whites.[12] This is one reason why every major record company and communications conglomerate, from Sony to Atlantic, has made signifi-cant investments in rap music.

The dominant ideological trend of the rappers is Black nationalism. Universally wedded to the notion that Black leadership, for the most part, has sold out, the Black nationalist rhetoric of Hip Hop becomes a challenging and liberating political paradigm in the face of surrender on the part of many political forces in the Black community. While there are leftist rappers, such as the Disposable Heroes of Hiphoprisy and KRS-One, who more embody Jesse Jackson's Rainbow Coalition notion of politics, most range from the soft-core nationalism of Arrested Development to the hard-core nationalist-influenced raps of the political and "gangsta" rappers.

Indeed, much of rap's political pedagogy comes from the so-called gangsta rappers. Dismissed by many as vulgar, profane, misogynist, racist, anti-Semitic, and juvenile—accusations that carry a great deal of validity—gangsta rap, at the same time, expresses what scholar Robin D.G. Kelley calls "the lessons of lived experiences."[13] These "organic intellectuals," such as Ice Cube, NWA, Too Short, the Geto Boys, and others, document the generally hidden conditions and lifestyle choices of many of America's inner-city Black poor.

Gender issues in rap remain controversial. From its earliest days to the present, women and more than a few men have rightfully condemned much of rap music as misogynist and degrading to women. National Council of Negro Women president Dorothy Height states, "This music is damaging because it is degrading to women to have it suggested in our popular music that [women] are to be abused."[14]

Scholar Marilyn Lashley is uncompromising in her denunciation of the portrayal of women in rap music. It is "explicitly and gratuitously sexual, occasionally bestial and frequently violent. These images, in the guise of 'art and music,' exploit, degrade and denigrate African American women as well as the race. They encourage sexual harassment, exploitation and misogyny at their best and sexual abuse at their worst," she states.[15]

Others, mainly men, have defended these projections as part of a continuity in Black culture that is not as harmful as it appears. No less than Harvard scholar and cultural critic Henry Louis Gates walks softly on this turf. He testified on behalf of scandalous rappers 2 Live Crew in their notorious censorship trial in Florida. Gates pooh-poohs the uproar by stating that male rappers are playing out the old Black tradition of "signifying"[16] that is relatively harmless and culturally important.

Rap has become a forum for debating the nature of gender relations among Black youth. The name-calling, descriptions of graphic rapes, and other negative encounters between young Black women and men dominate the music's gender politics. For many of the rap groups, their songs are one extended sex party. This aspect of the music has also drawn fire, though many of the male rappers have argued that they are engaging in meaningless fantasies. However, as one feminist correctly pointed out, it's "not so much the issue of sex as an obsession, but that of sex as a violent weapon against women."[17] She goes on to say that songs like "Treat Her Like a Prostitute," "One Less Bitch," "Pop that Coochie," "Baby Got Back," "Me So Horny," "That Bitch Betta Have My Money," and "She Swallowed It" "not only desensitize their audiences to violence against women, they also help rationalize and reinforce a nihilistic mentality among those who already suffer from the effects of ghetto reality."[18] The escalating incidence of rape and sexual harassment against women in general, and Black women in particular, underscores her concerns.

Positive and competent female rappers, such as Queen Latifah, Monie Love, Queen Mother Rage, Isis, and MC Lyte, will continue to achieve power and fight back against the dehumanizing side of rap. In addition, some male and gender-mixed rap groups, such as the Disposable Heroes of Hiphoprisy and Arrested Development, have shown that a positive perspective on Black female and male relations is possible.

## Souljah Stories: Rap and the 1992 Elections

> George Bush is a terrorist
> He creates terror in the minds
> And neighborhoods of Black people
>
> —Sister Souljah "Killing Me Softly"[19]

In no instance was it clearer that rap has come of political age than in the Sister Souljah–Bill Clinton–Jesse Jackson controversy. In June 1992, Souljah, then a little-known young Black female rapper, became a political vehicle through which Clinton was able to distance himself from Jackson and the progressive wing of the Democratic Party, and at the same time highlight the wide political space that exists between rappers and mainstream politics.

On June 11–13, in Washington, D.C., the National Rainbow Coalition (NRC) held a national leadership summit on the theme "Rebuild America: 1992 and Beyond." Over 200 persons, attended workshops and panels on rebuilding America and the urban crisis, as well as on criminal justice, voter registration, youth, labor, and women's issues. A plan put forth by the NRC, in addition to supporting the American Development Bank, called for new priorities and investments in people—universal health care, education, and children's programs. The Rainbow stressed corporate responsibility and an empowerment agenda supporting equal opportunity and the right of workers to organize. The NRC outlined a visionary proposal for rebuilding the nation. It stated, "We must start with a long-term plan to rebuild America, a surge of political will that manifests itself in a commitment of the resources and energy needed to get the job done. We have a plan for every country in the world except our own."[20]

No one was prepared for what would become the major story to emerge from the conference. One of Jackson's associates had discovered, about forty-five minutes before Clinton was to speak, that Clinton "was going to do something to upset Jackson and the Rainbow Coalition," but had chosen not to inform Jackson because he was engaged in finishing up his introductory remarks.[21] After rising to speak and praising the NRC for its work, Clinton sharply criticized the NRC for inviting rapper Sister Souljah to speak at the event the previous day, given the remarks attributed to her in the *Washington Post*. The catalyst for Clinton's attack was an interview that Sister Souljah had given, in which she was reported to have stated, in response to the Los Angeles insurrection, "I mean, if Black people kill Black people every day, why not have a week and kill White people." Although she contended that the statement had been taken out of context, and subsequent examination of the full text of her remarks seems to support her contention, her remarks set off a firestorm of White protest and Black defensiveness. Clinton went as far as to equate Souljah with racist demagogue David Duke.

Souljah stated that in her remarks she was describing the mentality of gang members who feel little remorse in killing other Blacks and that, in their thinking, killing Whites would be justified. While she herself had made inflammatory remarks, she steadfastly held that she was neither advocating or condoning the murder of Whites (or anyone else).[22] Thomas Oliphant, a *Boston Globe* columnist, agreed with Souljah's claim and wrote, "[I]'ve read the transcript of the May 13 interview ten times, and there is no doubt in my mind that she is reporting on—and reflecting—street-level rage, not advocating murder, which is the impression Clinton's selection of her most inflammatory words was designed to foster."[23]

Clinton's piercing attack on rapper Sister Souljah and the National Rainbow Coalition stunned Jackson and other attendees and, to a great degree, became a pivot on which the prospects of his candidacy turned. Jackson, as the national media captured in photos and film, was livid and found himself forced to sit and virtually be lectured to by Clinton. Immediately after Clinton finished, Jackson and some of his close advisers huddled and contemplated how to respond. Many of those in the audience at the Washington Sheraton were shocked speechless.

There was a political objective to Clinton's remarks that went beyond any moral condemnation he may have felt. As it turns out, Clinton was implementing what his staffers came to term "counterscheduling," i.e., giving

unpopular centrist speeches to left-of-center groups to demonstrate his independence.[24] Clinton's remarks were a calculated tactic on his part to publicly
chastise Jackson, and to show his independence from so-called "special
interests," in general, and Jackson, in particular. Souljah was the vehicle
through which Clinton carried out this political game. He was able to slam
Souljah and, at the same time, allay the anxieties of White voters that he might
be catering to Jackson as had been perceived to be the case with Mondale and
Dukakis.

To add insult to injury, reportedly Jackson was told in a private meeting
immediately after the event by Clinton that he was not being considered for
the vice presidential spot on the Democratic ticket. According to this report,
Jackson had written out a number of reasons why he would be beneficial to
the ticket, but Clinton wasn't interested.[25] Clinton praised Jackson as an
important leader in the party to reporters, but indicated that he was moving
toward someone else even by that early date.

It was doubtful that Clinton had ever seriously listened to rap music,
but, like George Bush and Ronald Reagan, the Clinton camp understood the
racial calculations of political strategy and power in the United States. Rap
represents a culture of resistance and expresses the alienation, frustration,
anger, and rebellious mode of urban Black youth who consciously recognize
their vulnerability and marginality in post-industrial United States. This
social discontent is commodified and marketed by some of the most skilled
advertising agencies and multinational record producers in the world. While
Sister Souljah did not neccessarily represent a constituency that was being
wooed by the Clinton campaign, her celebrity and notoriety made her a
convenient target through which the message of disassociation could be
delivered.

At the time of this incident, Clinton was receiving only about 20 percent
of the White vote[26] and coming in last in most polls behind Perot and Bush.
According to a poll taken by the *Hotline* political newsletter, Perot led in
seventeen states, Bush followed with sixteen states, and Clinton brought up
the rear with only two states—Arkansas and Maryland. In the electoral vote
estimation, Perot had 243, Bush 162, and Clinton only 16.[27]

Clinton received more media attention from his willingness to polarize
himself from Jackson than for his pleas for racial harmony. His rise in the
polls, particularly and almost exclusively among Whites, in June and July of
1992 following this incident was due in no small part to his attacks on Jackson
and Souljah.[28] While it may be an exaggeration to say that Souljah helped
Clinton get elected, the evidence shows that Blacks responded negatively to
the attack three to one and Whites, by three to one, had a favorable response.[29]

In the immediate days after Clinton blind-sided Rev. Jesse Jackson,
Clinton and Jackson became engaged in a war of position that posed new

dilemmas and challenges for them both. Clinton sought to implement a strategy that, in the desperate hope of winning White votes, clearly risked losing massive numbers of Black votes.

Jackson, for his part, found himself facing a Hobbesian quandary of either choosing to support his adversary Clinton; tacking toward the vulpine Perot; or signaling his followers, in either words or deeds, to boycott the election. Jackson's gesture of conciliation had backfired and he had to find new tactics that would allow him the leverage that he sought, but which appeared to be slipping away. His response to Clinton was unbridled anger. He stated that what he called Clinton's "Machiavellian maneuver" had exposed a deep "character flaw."[30] He went on to say that Clinton had deliberately come to the conference to "stage a very well-planned sneak attack, without the courage to confront but with a calculation to embarrass." Arguing that the governor was being divisive, he sneered that "They're celebrating in Clinton's camp. He seems to have an obsession to prove what doesn't need to be proved. They think they've won some kind of victory. But you don't win by splitting your base, and this won't help them to win."[31]

To a great degree, Clinton's gamble paid off. He won support from moderate and liberal White columnists, the *New York Times* editorial page, and a number of Black elected officials including Cleveland Mayor Michael White, Rep. John Lewis and Rep. Mike Espy. White, for instance, dismissed the incident as insignificant. He stated, "The issues we confront are too great to allow this minor flap to divide us."[32] Espy also rose to Clinton's defense. He remarked, "I don't find anything wrong with what Governor Clinton said. She is an influential entertainer and she does have the listening ear of hundreds of thousands of Black youths, and any attempt to encourage actions that would threaten the lives of anyone is something we ought to condemn."[33] Clinton's Black defenders all felt that he would not be politically harmed in the Black community because of his statements. Espy stated, "I can't believe it will [hurt Clinton]."[34] Another Black former Jackson supporter, Joel T. Ferguson of Michigan, said, "Where else are they [African Americans] going to go?"[35]

A number of other Blacks felt, however, that the Democrats could lose many more votes than they gained over the incident. Many of Jackson's supporters, such as Rep. Charles Rangel (D-NY) and Rep. Major Owens (D-NY), responded angrily to Clinton's verbal attack on Souljah and argued that millions of Black voters were being turned off by these kinds of tactics and insults. Howard University Political Science Department Chairman Ron Walters wrote that "this incident will, no doubt, deepen the cynicism in the Black community with respect to the current election and about Clinton's candidacy in particular. The bottom line is that he did not have to comment upon any aspect of the Rainbow convention, so this must have been selective and deliberate."[36]

The debate in Clinton's camp over how to win the White vote sharpened. Jackson and other Black activists believed that this strategy was doomed. They argued that for Clinton, winning the Black vote had gained a new urgency with the possibility of Ross Perot entering the race. It was the belief of many political observers that Clinton had little chance of winning if there was a depressed Black voter turnout, as in the primaries, or a significant split in the Black vote between Clinton, Bush, and Perot. In the last three presidential elections, the Democratic Party has lost about two-thirds of the White vote. Of the three elections won by the Democratic Party since 1960, the Black vote was pivotal in two, in 1960 and 1976. In 1960, Kennedy won 68 percent of the Black vote. In 1976, southerner Jimmy Carter won only 45 percent of the White vote in the South, but won about 85 percent of the Black vote.

It has been argued that if Democratic nominees Walter Mondale in 1984 and Michael Dukakis in 1988 had aggressively registered and turned out traditional Democratic constituencies, particularly in the Black community, they may have won. Dukakis won 86 percent of the Black vote, but only 40 percent of the White vote.

While Clinton struggled over the virtues of different strategies, Jackson had to confront his own contradictory options. If he endorsed Clinton, could he maintain legitimacy with that part of his base that feels increasingly alienated from and insulted by the Democratic Party? If he continued to refuse to back Clinton, would his enemies in the party and outside of it, including those in the media, seize the opportunity to destroy a career that is dependent, to a significant degree, upon party favors? Finally, was he willing to take on those in the Black leadership who had tied their horses to the Clinton cart and planned to remain no matter what noises Jackson made?

# Republican Rapper

> I never heard of them. But I know that rap is the music where it rhymes.
>
> —Bush in response to a question about rappers[37]

The Democrats were not the only ones dealing with rap's political ways and means. While "Republican rapper" may seem to be a contradiction in terms and logic, the political exigencies of 1992 constantly destroyed what appeared to be rational conceptions. The Republican National Convention did indeed feature a young Black rapper known as TRQ. The rapper, whose real name is Steve Gooden, called up the RNC, pledged his allegiance to George Bush, Dan Quayle, and the Republican Party, and wrangled an invitation to attend the convention and perform.

Gooden works as a youth minister for what even he describes as "an evangelical, conservative all-White, church" in the Los Angeles area. He proudly advocates sexual abstinence outside of marriage, he himself being a single virgin, but states that he is looking for a "young, bright, basically conservative professional woman."[38]

Like a lot of rappers, such as the profane 2 Live Crew, TRQ wears a bandanna during his performance. His, however, happens to be an American flag. Hypocritically, Republican flag-wavers and protectors don't accuse TRQ of desecrating their symbol, nor do they call for constitutional amendments whenever he performs. When hard-core rappers 2 Live Crew performed, their flag bandannas were vilified and denounced.

The rap song that he performed at the RNC was called, "We Are Americans." Coming from the mouth of a young Black man, the lyrics are both hysterical and tragic:

> It's our duty to save our America
> From those who would blame America,
> For the ills of their own activity,
> For the riots in Southern California,
> And the murders in the District of Columbia,
> For the hunger and the death in the streets you know,
> And the kids without a dad and a happy home.[39]

TRQ compares the Democrats to old slave masters and, like Bush, blames the social programs of the 1960s for the destruction of the Black family. The song goes on and attacks the pro-choice movement, Ice-T, and Black radicals. He also dedicated a rap to the odious Nancy Reagan titled "Just Say No to Drugs;" one writer commented after hearing it, that it made him "want to go take some—a lot."[40]

TRQ's membership in the Republican Party means that there are at least three Black rappers in the GOP camp. 2 Live Crew's Luther Campbell announced that he would vote for George Bush—hardly a friend of Black free speech—in response to Clinton's choice of the Gore family to be on the Democratic ticket. This was in protest of Tipper Gore's censorship campaign that eventually forced record companies to put warning labels on albums, cassettes, and compact discs.[41] He and TRQ join Easy E (aka Eric Wright) formerly of the notorious rap group NWA. In 1991, due to a $2,500 donation to the Republican Party made in his name by one of his financial advisers, Easy E became a member of an exclusive Republican high-donor set that includes ultra-conservative party supporters Joseph Coors and Arnold Schwarzenegger. He received a letter from Sen. Phil Gramm inviting him to an elite dinner of Republican bigwigs, that stated, "I believe your accomplishments...prove you worthy of membership."[42] He attended the dinner and, reportedly, enjoyed himself.

Black leaders can't simply dismiss the influence of Hip Hop in the Black community, whether it's the nationalist and gangsta rappers or more mainstream rappers. As long as the music reflects, at least in part, the reality of the lives of alienated, angry, and abandoned Black youth, it will find a reception and invade the political space of the nation and the Black community. To win support from Black youth, Black leaders must convince them that the leadership is more committed to changing the conditions that give rise to the music than in changing the music that they find offensive. It is also necessary that Black leaders and activists understand the relationship between cultural consumption and the cultural economies of modern capitalism.

But rappers are not off the hook. The sexist, violent, and dehumanizing raps produced by groups like 2 Live Crew must be condemned. Republican rapper TRQ also underscores the point that even without profanity, the music can be profane. Hip Hoppers themselves must address the contradictory tendencies of rap and its lifestyle even while defining new terrains upon which the music must travel.

In the end, the Black community must be careful not to have African American culture reduced to the commodities and political ambiguities of Hip Hop. Music forms, including jazz and blues and other non-Hip Hop Black cultural expressions deserve criticism, reaffirmation, and validation. Efforts to preserve and pass on these traditions, such as the Smithsonian Institution's program to bring the music of Duke Ellington to junior and senior high schools in Washington, D.C., should be encouraged and reproduced. In the end, Hip Hop is neither the cultural beast that will destroy Black America nor the political panacea that will save it, but is a part of the ongoing African American struggle, often in the realm of cultural assertions, constantly reaching for higher and higher modes of liberation.

# Part III

# Black to the Future

# Chapter 11

# Race, and the Race for the White House

What's wrong is that objectively Blacks, and to a lesser degree Hispanics, are—profoundly are—worse off than the rest of the country, more likely to suffer from economic and social difficulties that are profound and that make the good life much more difficult.

—Bill Clinton[1]

Within the Democratic Party, there were essentially two explanations of why Whites had been leaving the party in droves and as a result explained why the Democrats had not won the presidency since 1976. Liberals and progressives in the party argued that Republicans had consciously and aggressively spread the politics of divisiveness and sought to convince Whites that the causes of their problems were Democrat-sponsored social programs aimed at minorities. Republicans had been successful, it was argued, at not only convincing Whites that these programs were wasteful, but also that Democrats ignored issues like high taxes, crime, and welfare.

Moderates argued differently and began to put their ideas into action, culminating in 1985 with the creation of the Democratic Leadership Council (DLC). The DLC could claim among its members some of the party's leading lights, including Sen. Sam Nunn, Sen. Charles Robb, Rep. Richard Gephardt—all of whom have chaired the DLC—and its most famous alumnus, Bill Clinton. Formed to "revitalize the Democratic Party and lead it back into the political mainstream,"[2] it was fairly clear from the start that the DLC was formed largely in response to the growth of the progressive wing of the Democratic Party sparked by Jesse Jackson's 1984 campaign.

DLC President Al From articulated clearly the agenda of the group. He wrote in the *Washington Post*:

New Democrats believe economic growth generated in the private sector is the prerequisite for opportunity for all; we believe in the values most Americans share—liberty of conscience, individual responsibility, tolerance, work, faith, family and community; we support a new politics of reciprocity in which people who get government help have a responsibility to give something back to the commonwealth; we believe America should lead other nations toward democracy and market economies; and, as advocates of activist government, we want to retool government so it offers more choice in public services and is more responsive to the needs of citizens and more accountable to taxpayers.[3]

The Progressive Policy Institute, a DLC-affiliated, Washington-based think tank, has issued a number of documents arguing the case for abandoning what it calls "liberal fundamentalism." In one document, it states that "the public has come to associate liberalism with tax and spending policies that contradict the interests of average families; with welfare policies that foster dependence rather than self-reliance; with softness toward perpetrators of crime and indifference toward its victims; with ambivalence toward the assertion of American values and interests abroad; and with an adversarial stance toward mainstream moral and cultural values."[4] The document is unambiguous in its condemnation of Jackson. It states, "Jesse Jackson's 1984 and 1988 campaign...were the purest version of liberal fundamentalism."[5]

By the time Clinton had decided to run, the DLC had more than 3,000 members in twenty-seven states.[6] The DLC's few Black members include agriculture secretary and former Rep. Mike Espy, former House majority whip and one-time DLC co-chair Bill Gray, Rep. John Lewis, and Douglas Wilder. In 1991, Espy was chairperson of the Mississippi state chapter of the DLC. The DLC had to contend not only with the Jackson progressive wing of the party, but also with its liberals. Party honchos such as New York Gov. Mario Cuomo had been critical of the DLC's political aims and policy recommendations. Cuomo had referred to the DLC program as "warmed over Republicanism."[7]

## Bill Clinton and the Dilemma of Race

For many in the party and the media, Clinton represented the best of the "New South" White politicians. Baby boomer Clinton grew up in the post-war, civil rights protest era of the 1950s and 1960s. The pressures of the Civil Rights movement eliminated most middle ground from people's consciousness, and political leaders in the period were pushed either to the far Right or to a liberal position on issues of race. Unlike many national White politicians, Clinton grew up around African Americans and the poverty of his youth often found him in the company of poor Blacks. He recalls being repulsed by the segregation of his youth and vowing to fight discrimination and prejudice at every opportunity. The comfort that Clinton demonstrated in Black churches during the campaign was bred by his frequent visits to the many small-town Black churches that dot the Arkansas landscape. In 1987, Clinton testified against the nomination of conservative Robert Bork to the Supreme Court. Bork had been Clinton's constitutional law professor at Yale, but Clinton stated strongly that he was uncompromisingly opposed to the nominee, given Bork's civil rights record, right-wing judicial views, and the potential of his nomination to reopen racial wounds in the South.[8]

The strain between the Democrats and many in the Black community manifested in the relationship between Clinton and Jesse Jackson. That tension exploded when Clinton made a blunder and attacked Jackson personally. Told erroneously by an aide that Jackson had endorsed Sen. Tom Harkin without first informing him, Clinton unleashed a mouthful of venom aimed at Jackson that was recorded on videotape and, ultimately, broadcast to millions. Looking directly into the camera at station KTSP in Phoenix, Clinton shrieked, "It's an outrage. A dirty, double-crossing, back-stabbing thing to do. For him to do this, for me to hear this on a television program is an act of absolute dishonor."[9] Upon realizing his error, Clinton and his supporters quickly brought in the damage control operation, to smooth Jackson's ruffled feathers. Despite the public rapprochement, Jackson reportedly was enraged after seeing the outburst. Jackson told CNN, "I am disappointed with this over-reaction without verification. I am disturbed by the tone of the blast at my integrity, my character. I feel blind-sided by what I finally saw and heard him say."[10]

This was the first of a number of actions on the part of Clinton that Jackson and others would term "insults" or "disrespect" toward the African American community. In March 1992, Clinton's insensitive decision to golf at an Arkansas country club that had no Black members set off a firestorm of criticism and raised anew questions about the depth and sincerity of his commitment to bridging the nation's racial divide. Clinton was exposed as having played golf at least six times in 1991 and more in previous years at the Little Rock Country Club.[11] While Blacks were allowed to play at the club, it had no Black members on its roster. Clinton would later say, "I won't play golf there again until they integrate."[12]

# Blacks and the 1992 Convention

The 1992 Democratic National Convention (DNC), held July 14 to July 17, was a departure from the 1984 and 1988 conventions in a number of ways. The most obvious was the absence of a Black candidate, specifically Jesse Jackson. A second and related distinction had to do with the absence of a clear and coherent Black agenda. Prior to 1984, Black leaders and activists had met before the conventions and developed a set of platform and policy demands that became the bargaining tools with the party as well as a point of unity for Black delegates. In 1976, for example, Black leaders met in Charlotte, North Carolina with the potential candidates to get their position vis-a-vis a Black agenda. A similar gathering happened in 1980 in Richmond, Virginia. In 1984 and 1988, the Black agenda became a part of (some felt subsumed in) Jackson's overall progressive agenda. In 1992, no such gatherings occurred.

In 1992, African Americans were in key positions at the DNC at every level. In addition to DNC Chairperson Ron Brown, key Black participants included Alexis Herman, convention chief executive officer; Mario M. Cooper, convention manager; and Frank Williams, Jr., convention chief financial officer.[13] Other Black DNC officials included Maxine Griffith, director of convention hall planning and management; Hartina Flournoy, general counsel; Michael Pitts, director of transportation; Marilyn Shaw, director of volunteer services; and Lajuan M. Johnson, director of headquarters hotels.[14]

While Black participation in the convention expanded in some areas, it shrank in others. The percentage of Black delegates fell back to about the same level as in 1984. There were 771 Black delegates at the 1992 DNC, representing 17.9 percent of all delegates.[15] This was down from the 962 that were present at the 1988 DNC (23.1 percent) and at about the same level as the 1984 DNC where 697 Black delegates were present (17.7 percent).[16] Most Black delegates, as expected, supported Bill Clinton. Sixty percent of them backed Clinton, 11 percent Jerry Brown, 8 percent Paul Tsongas, 16 percent were unpledged, and 5 percent were uncommitted.[17]

The Democrats' platform, which Clinton referred to as a "new covenant"[18] between the government and the American people, was divided into four parts: "Opportunity," "Responsibility," "Restoring Community," and "Preserving Our National Security."[19] In terms of the Black agenda, the platform pledged to reverse the Bush attacks on civil rights and to ensure that all discrimination is ended. The cities were promised more jobs, a national public works program, an end to red-lining and housing discrimination, and a national network of Community Development banks. To a great degree, the platform differed little from the liberal platforms of the past and may even have been more progressive. However, the platform's rhetoric of "welfare reform" and "shared responsibility" was viewed by many Blacks as racial signals that the Democrats were breaking from supporting programs and policies that could be seen as beneficial to Blacks.

Jackson and Clinton's war of position continued all the way up to the very eve of the DNC. In his belated endorsement statement, only two days before the DNC, Jackson stated, "On November 3, I have decided to vote for Bill Clinton and Al Gore."[20] In his speech at the convention, Jackson said, "The great temptation in these difficult days of racial polarization and economic injustice, is to make political arguments Black and White and miss the moral imperative of wrong and right...Tonight, we face another challenge—ten million Americans unemployed, twenty-five million on food stamps, thirty-five million in poverty, forty million have no health care, the homeless are a source of national shame and disgrace. There is a harshness to America that comes from not seeing and a growing mindless materialism."[21]

Rather than go with the more difficult southern strategy of trying to wrestle White southern votes from the Republicans, the Clinton campaign decided to adopt a strategy that focused on the suburban vote, that carried with it the assumption that the Democrats would win their traditional constituencies, Blacks, labor, Jews, and the urban vote, with minimal effort. This strategy, as outlined by William Schneider in his insightful *Atlantic* article,[22] meant first winning the dozen or so states and Washington, D.C., that have historically voted Democratic: Delaware, Hawaii, Maryland, Massachusetts, Minnesota, Missouri, New York, Pennsylvania, Rhode Island, West Virginia, and Wisconsin. In applying the suburban strategy, the Democrats went after states where they had not done well in the recent past, but had significant suburban populations. These included California, Connecticut, Illinois, Iowa, Michigan, Montana, New Mexico, Oregon, South Dakota, Vermont, and Washington. The campaign counted on winning Arkansas and Tennessee, both of which Dukakis had lost in 1988. With this strategy, the Democrats would end up with a minimum of 287 electoral votes, seventeen more than necessary to win. In this scenario, the Democrats could even afford to lose some states that have a large number of electoral votes such as Texas and Florida, which actually turned out to be the case. In 1988, although the Democrats had won most major cities, those victories were wiped out in state after state by a massive suburban vote for Bush.

Several detailed plans were advanced and implemented by the Clinton campaign, through its African American component, to reach out to the African American community including registration and get-out-the-vote (GOTV) efforts, use of Black surrogates, sponsorship of a tour by the

(GOTV) efforts, use of Black surrogates, sponsorship of a tour by the Congressional Black Caucus, grassroots mobilization, and attendance by Black campaign workers and officials at major Black community gatherings, conferences, and conventions.[23] The campaign had originally planned five major gatherings with groups of African Americans—"Grass Roots Advocates," "National Civil Rights Leaders," an "Urban Strategy Meeting," the "National African American Clergy," and the "Southern Strategy"—but was able to convene only the latter two. Out of the National African American Clergy meeting was formed the National African American Clergy Committee. It developed a GOTV proposal called "Gideon's Army One in a Million GOTV Campaign," aimed at involving the Black clergy nationally in turnout efforts for the final days of the campaign.

Jesse Jackson, to some degree, buried his hatchet with the Democrats and got on board the campaign. From September 12 to November 3, Jackson visited twenty-seven states and led over 200 events on behalf of the campaign. Jackson generated enthusiastic crowds in every small town and city he went to. From Ocala, Florida and Fayette, Iowa to Bangor, Maine; Big Stone Gap, West Virginia; Missoula, Montana; Chillicothe, Missouri; and Ashland, Oregon; the Jackson effort went full-steam ahead.

# George Bush and the Politics of Racial Opportunism

For three decades, the Republican Party's overt appeals to White racial fears have been at the center of U.S. presidential elections. It was not only Reagan's anti-Black policies—cutting social programs, stacking the U.S. Commission on Civil Rights with anti-civil rights commissioners, proposing tax cuts for racist schools like Bob Jones University, vetoing of a South African sanctions bill, appointing hard-core conservatives to the Supreme Court and other federal benches, and other administrative assaults—that angered African Americans. His countless petty insults and racial remarks and gestures made him loathed in virtually every Black community. His refusal to meet with the Congressional Black Caucus, jokes about "welfare queens," forgetting the name of the only Black in his Cabinet, red-baiting attacks on Martin Luther King, Jr., and his visit to a Nazi burial ground in Germany all contributed to the growing racial divisions in the nation. Through all of this, the response from Reagan's vice president, George Bush, was a deafening silence.

George Herbert Walker Bush comes from a long line of traditional Republicans. Born with a silver spoon in his lips, Bush grew up privileged, pampered, and political. In 1980, after losing to Reagan during the Republican primaries, where he jeered Reagan's economic program by calling it "voodoo economics," Bush was tapped to be the Republican vice presidential candidate.

In 1988, Bush was irrevocably the "Willie Horton" candidate. No character in modern times has resounded with as much symbolism of Republican racism as the much-referenced Horton. William Horton, Jr. was a Black prisoner in Massachusetts who had been convicted of the brutal first-degree murder of a seventeen-year-old gas station attendant. Although he was sentenced to life in prison without the possibility of parole, he was allowed to participate in an experimental prisoner furlough program. The program began in 1972, two years before Michael Dukakis was elected governor. On June 6, 1986, while on his tenth furlough, Horton escaped and disappeared for eight months. He resurfaced with a vengeance on April 3, 1987 in Oxon Hill, Maryland, where authorities state that he broke into the home of Clifford Barnes and Angela Miller where he then raped Miller, beat and gagged Barnes, and robbed the place. Horton was arrested while driving Miller's car and was eventually sentenced to two consecutive life terms in a Maryland prison. In interviews in *The Nation* and *Emerge*, Horton states that he stole the car, but did not commit the other crimes.[24] What is more verifiable and interesting is his documented proof that he was visited in prison by Republican officials who wanted him to endorse Dukakis. While these officials will admit to seeing Horton, they deny that they tried to bribe him as he claims.

Although the Bush campaign belatedly claimed that it had not actually run the ads that had Horton in them, it did not object to their use and, in any case, ran similar ads. In one ad that the Bush campaign used extensively in the last months of the campaign—the so-called "Revolving Door" commercial—a line of mostly Black prisoners is shown walking through a revolving door. Before he died from a brain tumor in 1990, Bush strategist Lee Atwater publicly apologized for the Willie Horton ads. Bush never has.

# The Republican Call for American Apartheid

At the Republican National Convention, from Pat Buchanan, Ronald Reagan, and Pat Robertson to Newt Gingrich and George Bush, intolerance was on parade as speaker after speaker used the fig leaf of religious values to hide ugly concessions made to the far Right. Attacks on urbanites, gays, women, and even Hillary Clinton were relentless and denounced even by many Republicans who found the convention repugnant.

Black Republican elected officials, who represent less than 1 percent of all Black elected officials (70 out of 7,480 as of mid-1992),[25] were mostly silent in criticizing the convention's gross expressions of bigotry. One Black delegate, Carol Ward-Allen of Oakland, California, was so disturbed by Buchanan's loathsome speech that she walked out of the convention and questioned whether she even wanted to remain a Republican.[26] In the main, however, Black delegates and the three main Black Republican organizations—the National Black Republican Council, created by then-National Republican Committee Chairperson George Bush in 1972;[27] the Council of 100; and the mostly Black Freedom Republicans—were hushed. Indeed, Black speakers at the RNC, including Health and Human Services Secretary Louis Sullivan, former National Security Agency advisor Condoleezza Rice, and perpetual Maryland candidate for Congress Alan Keyes, echoed the spite and jingoism that came from other speakers.

Many pundits, prodded by the Bush campaign, raised the specter of a late Bush surge that, reminiscent of Democrat Harry Truman's famous 1948 down-to-the-wire victory over Republican Thomas Dewey and Progressive Party candidate Henry Wallace, would overcome the Clinton lead. Yet, an important difference exist between the 1992 and the 1948 races. In the 1948 election, there was genuine contention for the Black vote. Howard University's Ron Walters, writing in the *Black Political Agenda '92* newsletter, refuted the attempt to draw an analogy between the two elections. He noted the critical role that the Black vote played in the 1948 race for Truman, a vote that Bush could not count on. Walters writes:

> Blacks had supported Roosevelt in 1932, in an historic switch of parties. However, by 1948 their vote had become far more strategic to Democrats, becoming concentrated in northern industrial cities. Truman attempted to solidify Black support for Democrats by establishing a Committee on Civil Rights that issued the report, "To Secure These Rights," which called for the elimination of racial discrimination. Then in the election year of 1948, he issued Executive Orders prohibiting racial segregation in the federal services and the Armed Forces.[28]

Hard-core segregationist Strom Thurmond and other southern states' rights advocates left the 1948 Democratic convention immediately and within days had formed the States' Rights Party whose mission was to siphon off White southern votes from Truman. Earlier in the year, the Democratic Party had split to the left when Wallace and his supporters among liberals, labor, and Blacks departed and formed the Progressive Party. Abandoned by the party's Right and Left, Truman had little choice but to frantically seek

Black support. The fleeting southern vote was made up for by a strong Black vote that held "the balance of power in sixteen states with a total of 278 electoral votes, compared to 127 electoral votes controlled by the South."[29]

Fearful that the popular Dewey could possibly win, especially if Wallace were able to pull Black and labor votes, Truman made desperate moves to win Black support. Although he had been silent regarding the rise of racist groups in the post-war years, in 1948 Truman made deals with the NAACP and pledged to support civil rights legislation, promote fair employment procedures, and push for more rapid desegregation with federal contractors.[30] Even with these efforts, Black support for Truman was not universal. The only major Black newspaper to endorse Truman was the *Chicago Defender*.[31] Dewey's and Wallace's effort to court Blacks also paid-off. For example, the *Amsterdam News*, one of the most influential Black newspapers of the time, endorsed Dewey. The paper noted Dewey's appointment of Blacks as one reason for its support.[32] Others Black leaders, such as New York City Councilperson and open communist Benjamin Davis and radical intellectual W.E.B. DuBois, considered Truman a racist and backed Wallace. Activist and artist Paul Robeson was Vice Chairperson of Wallace's Progressive Party and even superstar boxer Joe Louis made a contribution to the campaign.[33] At one rally for Wallace in Harlem, 15,000 Blacks turned out.[34]

There was one aspect of the Truman metaphor that Bush may not have found so desirable. In 1991, it was revealed that Truman held deeply personal racist attitudes before, during, and after his terms in office. Private letters contained some of the most vicious racial slurs ever recorded by any President. In one letter he wrote in 1911 to his future wife Bess, he stated, "I think one man is just as good as another so long as he's honest and decent and not a nigger or a Chinaman. Uncle Will says that the Lord made a White man from dust, a nigger from mud, then He threw up what was left and it came down a Chinaman."[35] In other letters during his presidency, he referred to Blacks who worked in the White House as "an army of coons" and discussed what he called "nigger picnic day."[36]

Despite the fact that he was trailing Clinton, neither Bush nor his campaign staff considered for a moment the tactical option of appealing to the Black vote. Given the Bush record, it is doubtful that such an appeal would have generated more than guffaws from the Black community, but the fact that such a consideration was not possible underscored the live-or-die racial politics of the Republican Party that were faithfully followed in the 1992 race.

# Perotism Percolates

On February 20, 1992, relatively obscure Texas billionaire H. Ross Perot sat down at the microphone with talk show host Larry King and sparked a voter upheaval unseen in decades. He told millions of listeners that if registered in 50 states that he would run as an independent candidate for President.[37] For the major candidates, who had more or less prepared for and survived the Jackson, Cuomo, Duke, and Buchanan threats, the most jarring factor of the entire campaign season was the bizarre candidacy of Perot. For African Americans, Perot's challenge to the two-party system presented new complications, though some Blacks perceived new opportunities.

Perot had put into practice what Ron Walters described as exercising independent leverage upon the political system. Many Jackson supporters felt that what Perot had ignited had always been the potential of the Rainbow Coalition. Even without the structure (or burden) of a third party, Rainbow activists had advocated mobilization outside of the major-party institutions in order to deploy pressure on those institutions vis-a-vis a progressive agenda. The emergence of the Perot movement highlighted that there was a basis for mobilizing independent of the traditional systems, without becoming marginalized, which appeared to be the fear of Jackson and other Black leaders tied to the major parties. In fact, as Perot would demonstrate, one's political hand could possibly be strengthened through the implementation of an independent strategy.

A critical difference exists however between Perot's movement and that of the Rainbow Coalition. Perot is not progressive nor even liberal on most issues. He essentially sees the nation as a business where its board of directors (Congress) is out of control and its workers (the public) have lost their discipline, sense of productivity, and respect for the guidance and brilliance of the company's CEO (the president). Enter Ross the Boss. Like Reagan, Perot understood the value of winning mass support for a political agenda by whipping up anti-authority and anti-big government emotions. His status as an outsider, however, was nothing more than a public relations-concocted illusion. Perot is as insider as they come and, indeed, built his political involvement and financial fortune on that foundation.

He has consistently supported conservative Republicans financially and politically including Richard Nixon, Ronald Reagan, and George Bush. During the 70s, 80s, and early 90s Perot promised Richard Nixon "$10 million to establish a 'pro-Nixon' public policy research institute" although he did not follow through with it.[38] He did, however, spend about $1 million buying advertisements in support of Nixon's war on Vietnam as national opposition to the war escalated.[39] Perot also gave extensive public and monetary support to Ronald Reagan and his cronies while receiving political appointments in return. From 1981 to 1986, for example, Perot was a member of Reagan's President's Foreign Intelligence Advisory Board.[40] He gave $2 million to rogue Col. Oliver North to further his illegal contra activities.[41] Later, North and Perot had a falling out. North claims that Perot told North's lawyer, concerning the Iran-Contra scandal, that North should testify "that the President [Reagan] didn't know" and that if North went to jail he would "take care of his family. And I'll be happy to give him a job when he gets out."[42] Perot, of course, as has countless others, called North a liar.

## Perot's Prejudices and the Black Community

In 1971, *Ramparts* reporter Robert Fitch exposed Perot's racism in an article describing how Perot's Electronic Data System had coldly fired or dismissed Black employees at a computer company that EDS took over. Perot had launched this racial purge at the same time that the company began to take over the processing of California's Medicaid and Medicare claims, many of whom were from Blacks and Hispanics. Perot's takeover of this company put him on the road to becoming a billionaire. Perot did precious little outreach to communities of color in his campaign. His campaign officials and workers, his volunteers, and his targeted constituency were virtually all middle-class and all White. When challenged about this composition, James Squires, a Perot spokesperson, stated, "After we've been up and running for a while...you are going to see we will include everybody."[43] For the entire campaign, however, this situation did not change.

Perot had little to offer in the way of concrete programs to address the concerns of the Black community. Perot, in his speeches and campaign literature, did not address issues such as affirmative action, racist police violence, the crisis of the inner-cities, or foreign policy concerns such as South Africa, Somalia, or Haiti. From what could be gleaned from his public statements, he viewed the role of the federal government in the same way as Reagan and Bush. Meshed with his emphasis on cutting the federal deficit, primarily by cutting spending, he argued that "the problems of poverty and race could best be solved at the local level and not through new government programs."[44]

In his law-and-order drug war campaign in Texas, Perot called for cordoning off Black and Hispanic communities and doing door-to-door house searches, to the enduring ire of local Black leaders. Although Perot now denies making this statement, more than one source claims that he said it. In a 1988 interview with journalist Laura Miller, formerly of the *Dallas*

*Times-Herald*, Perot reportedly stated, "Pick a night and cordon off a section of South Dallas. Send hundreds of police officers—however many it would take—into the area to vacuum it up. Shake down everybody on the street. Search every house and apartment. Confiscate all drugs and weapons."[45] It was Perot who met with Nancy Reagan in the early 1980s and inspired her disastrous, simplistic, and often silly "Just Say No" campaign.[46] In 1988, his intervention led to the weakening of the hard-won Dallas Police Citizens Review Board. The Dallas Police Department's reputation for brutality and mistreatment of Blacks and Hispanics is second only to the Los Angeles Police Department. Although local activists fought hard to establish the board, Perot met secretly with the Dallas police to help them defend themselves against charges of racism that were more than justified.

The Black community, of course, was not immune to the disillusionment, frustration, and anger being felt by many, if not most, of the electorate. By late spring, signs of Black support for Perot were already visible. In California, Perot was attracting support from about 18 percent of Blacks across the state, according to the *Los Angeles Times*. In Los Angeles, 22 percent of the Blacks who voted in the primary voiced support for Perot.[47] Nationwide, however, Perot was not doing as well. In a *Newsweek* poll released in June, Perot was leading Clinton and Bush, but failing woefully to attracted much Black support. According to the poll, only 6 percent of his supporters were non-White.[48] This figure contradicted another poll done between May 27 and 30 by CBS News that had Perot winning 12 percent of the Black vote.[49] Ron Walters argued that these votes meant that Perot could become a "tactical choice for many [Blacks] who want a substantial change."[50] Before he declared in July that he was dropping out of the race, Perot had won the support of a few notable African Americans, including New York's influential Rev. Calvin Butts and former NFL running back O. J. Simpson. Butts would later throw his support behind independent candidate Ron Daniels.

Any opportunity to make further inroads into the Black community was demolished following Perot's political misadventure at the NAACP national convention. Perot turned what could have been a potential political plum into an all-around disaster. At the national convention of the NAACP, Perot repeatedly used the racially irritable terms "you people" and "your people." In one passage of his speech in which he discussed the country's growing economic job loss, he stated, "I don't have to tell you who gets hurt first when this sort of thing happens—you people do. Your people do."[51] He also told patronizing stories of how well his parents had treated their Black workers and Black hoboes who came to beg. NAACP members were angered at Perot's tone and words and some from the audience even heckled him. In his speech, Perot did not address any concerns of the organization or of Blacks nor state how he would work to build racial harmony. Perot, who did not seem to understand what offense he had made, later issued a belated and what many interpreted as a less-than-sincere apology. He said, "Well, okay. I'm sorry. I apologize."[52] His press secretary, Sharon Holman, stated, "It was an unfortunate choice of words."[53]

As the Clinton, Bush, and Perot campaigns unfolded, Black leaders found themselves in a quandary. Most reasoned that Bush had to go, but could Clinton or Perot be trusted? Concerns were raised about what guarantees could be secured from the candidates that would warrant an all-out effort to mobilize the Black vote. Perhaps—most important for many Black leaders who supported Clinton—was whether the"distancing" that many felt was a campaign tactic necessitated by the political climate, was a prelude to a new era in Black-Democratic relations. These unanswered issues nagged Black leadership for most of 1992 and shaped their behavior and stance towards the presidential election.

**Chapter 12**

# Black Leadership and the 1992 Presidential Race

This is a defining moment for African American voters. In a lot of ways it was easier to support Jackson; this time people are really going to have to say why they support a candidate. And people are going to have to decide what issues really are of concern.

—Hulbert James[1]

The 1992 presidential race became a vehicle through which the struggle for political hegemony within the Black community was carried out. In certain respects, nearly all of the political tendencies in the Black community—nationalists, leftists, progressives, conservatives, post-Black liberals, traditional liberals, and new radical reformers—were represented in the presidential race at one level or another. For some of the nationalists, leftists, progressives, and radical reformers, who chose to participate in the election at all, Ohio activist Ron Daniels was their candidate of choice. The controversial Lenora Fulani and her New Alliance Party postured as the quasi-socialist alternative to the two major parties. Black conservatives, if they supported anyone, backed Bush or Perot. The post-Black liberal Democrats could choose either Virginia Gov. L. Douglas Wilder or Arkansas Gov. Bill Clinton. Some traditional liberals and progressives who felt a kinship to labor initially looked to either Sen. Tom Harkin or former California Gov. Jerry Brown.

The majority of the old liberal Black guard and many of the new radical reformers found the choices wanting. For the most part, most of these forces begrudgingly hopped onto the Clinton bandwagon. In the end, they determined that it was more important to get rid of Bush than to punish Clinton for real and perceived racial slights. Even Jesse Jackson, the biggest holdout on endorsing Clinton, became an enthusiastic supporter for the Clinton-Gore ticket in the last months of the campaign.

In the face of what some Blacks felt was a repudiation of the interests of the Black community, the 1992 elections deserve attention, as it crystallized many of the battles that are being fought between different political tendencies within the Black community. The election forces a number of theoretical and political questions onto the agenda of African American political activists, strategists, and thinkers.

What has historically been viewed as the "Black and civil rights agenda," i.e., affirmative action, funding for needed social programs, civil rights legislation, support for struggles in Africa and the Caribbean, and other concerns, was generally downplayed in the campaigns of the major-party presidential candidates in 1992. Except for the voices of a few independents and Black activists outside of the campaigns, these issues were either not raised or, if they were, given a moderate or conservative spin.

Given those political dynamics, how should have the African American community related to the 1992 presidential election? Could a credible threat to withhold the Black vote have forced the candidates to address the "Black agenda?" Should the Black community have supported one of the Black independents who was running for president? Here in the last decade of the 20th century, what exactly does constitute the Black agenda? In the period preceding the campaign season, when these questions should have been widely debated and a possible consensus strategy formed, what occurred among Black leaders was political maneuvering, vacillation, and deal-making, whose consequence was to leave the Black community as a whole without a strategy or plan for the presidential primaries and general campaign.

The nature of the leadership crisis is not the absence of leadership, but rather the lack of vision that has resulted in ineffective strategies and tactics. Theoretician Mack Jones observes that Black leaders have "never articulated a full-blown political philosophy which would have allowed them to understand and explain the connection between the economic and political dimensions of the unequal conditions of Black Americans."[2] This situation exacerbates the gulf that exists between many Black leaders and their purported base. Across the political spectrum, most African American political observers would agree that what is missing is a coherent analysis and prescriptive strategy of the class and social conditions and challenges that face African Americans on the verge of the new century, out of which new leadership will flow.

Some Black intellectuals, such as progressive political writer Manning Marable and conservative talk-show host Tony Brown, have argued that the current crisis in strategy and leadership is due to the slavish relationship that many Black leaders have to the Democratic Party.[3] Conversely, political scientist Adolph Reed Jr. has contended that the Democratic Party plays a critical role, and that "at this moment in American history, it is a vital organizational agency for any broad-scale emancipatory initiative in practical politics, including those that emanate from the Black community."[4] This debate emerged anew in 1992 as Black leaders and activists reflected upon their relationship with the Democratic Party.

In 1992, as noted above, the consequence of this crisis was that the Black community functioned without a common political strategy. Left to spontaneity, the Black community overwhelmingly voted for the Democrats and Bill Clinton as predicted, yet secured few promises in the bargain. While the desire to get rid of Bush and the Republicans fundamentally drove the Black vote in the general election, it declawed the power of that vote, as political scientist Ron Walters contends, to "leverage" concessions that address many of the needs of the Black community.

This confusion contributed significantly to a depressed Black voter turnout during the spring. Like the economy, the Black vote went into serious recession for the Democratic Party in the primaries. In a development that should have created a small panic among party leaders, Black voter turnout in the primaries was significantly down from previous years. For party leaders, who foresaw no major shift of Black voters to the Republican Party, to Perot, or to any of the independents, there was still a clear concern about Black turnout. Although it was a safe bet that Clinton would get an extremely high percentage of the Black vote, it was shaping up to be a much smaller piece of the pie than in recent years.

In southern and border states that would be key to a Democratic victory in the fall—Florida, Georgia, Louisiana, Maryland, Mississippi, Tennessee, and Texas—Black voter turnout during the primaries had dropped off considerably from the 1988 election. The drop was as small as 5 percent in Florida to as much as 68 percent in Tennessee. In 1988, according to the Joint Center for Political and Economic Studies, 132,552 Blacks voted in the Tennessee primary. Jesse Jackson received 113,286 of those votes (85 percent).[5] In 1992, the number of Blacks voting in Tennessee dropped to 42,788. A similar fall-off occurred in Louisiana. In 1988, 256,024 Blacks voted in the primary, 245,784 of them for Jackson (96 percent). In 1992, the number of Black votes fell to 86,146 (see Table 12-1).

Not only did the absolute numbers drop, but the percentage of those registered to vote who actually voted also fell. In the 1988 primaries, 41 percent of Louisiana's Black registered voters came out to vote. In 1992, only 26 percent voted. In Georgia, the percentage dropped from 35 percent to 29 percent.

In the Florida, Georgia, Illinois, Louisiana, Maryland, Mississippi, Tennessee, and Texas primaries, Clinton won less than half of the votes that

**Table 12-1**

**Black Voter Decline in Democratic Primaries**

| State | 1988 Turnout | 1992 Turnout | Percent of Decline |
|-------|-------------|-------------|-------------------|
| AL | 142, 080 | 103,707 | -27.0% |
| CA | 502.197 | 330,243 | -34.2% |
| FL | 178,262 | 169, 465 | -4.0% |
| GA | 217,963 | 131,843 | -39.5% |
| IL | 390,241 | 310, 308 | -20.5% |
| LA | 256,024 | 109,805 | -57.1% |
| MD | 152,642 | 117,160 | -23.2% |
| MS | 165,332 | 82,284 | -50.2% |
| NJ | 183,205 | 103,372 | -43.6% |
| NY | 425,300 | 181,391 | -57.3% |
| OH | 296,517 | 71,503 | -75.9% |
| PA | 256,307 | 139,204 | -45.7% |
| TN | 132,552 | 42,788 | -68.0% |
| TX | 303,272 | 251,950 | -16.9% |

Source: Joint Center for Political and Economic Studies

Rev. Jesse Jackson had received in 1988. In those states, Jackson had won 1,870,132 votes. Clinton's numbers totaled only 852,628. In Georgia, Illinois, Louisiana, Mississippi, Tennessee, and Texas, Jackson had averaged 94 percent of the Black vote in 1988. Clinton averaged about 79 percent in those states in the 1992 primaries. In Maryland, there was a thirty-nine point difference between Jackson's votes in 1988, 134,325 (88 percent) and Clinton's votes in 1992, 54,468 (49 percent).[6]

Jackson's absence from the race, as well as the absence of any other Black on a major-party ticket only explains part of the problem. The strategy of winning back Whites who had voted Republican in the last three elections alienated many Black voters. At the expense of specifically addressing issues of concerns to African Americans, the Democrats were failing to inspire a Black enthusiasm for the ticket which potentially could have meant trouble in the fall election. The drop in turnout was also likely due to a more general alienation with the political system overall. Many Blacks, just like many Whites, were increasingly losing faith that the system would deliver no matter

**Table 12-2**

**White Voter Decline in Democratic Primaries**

| State | 1988 Turnout | 1992 Turnout | Percent of Decline |
|-------|-------------|-------------|-------------------|
| CA | 2,636,537 | 2,340,569 | -11% |
| FL | 1,095,036 | 960,306 | -12% |
| GA | 404,789 | 322,788 | -20% |
| LA | 368,426 | 312,521 | -15% |
| MS | 194,085 | 109,073 | -44% |
| NJ | 471,097 | 276,491 | -41% |
| NY | 1,149,886 | 826,335 | -28% |

Source: Joint Center for Political and Economic Studies

who was in office. Even White turnout was depressed for the Democrats (see Table 12-2).

A number of Black leaders expressed concerns about the drop in Black turnout and placed the blame on the candidates. One of the harshest criticisms came from Jackson. In a newsletter distributed by the National Rainbow Coalition, Jackson wrote that "The plunge in voter turnout reflects the insufficiency of today's presidential debate. The campaign is preoccupied with one-liners, photo-ops, and sound bites. Politics is disconnected from our pains, our problems, and our real needs. The campaigns from both parties are caught up in attacking each other, instead of attacking unmet needs, and putting forth an alternative vision...In the final analysis, change is always initiated by the people who need it. Slave masters will never end slavery—slaves must."[7]

Clinton, of course, proved the doomsayers wrong. In the political circumstances of 1992, the unique coalition forged by Clinton, which included the Black vote, broke through conventional wisdom. A conscious decision was made by Clinton to cultivate alternative and more moderate Black leaders, such as then-Rep. Mike Espy and Cleveland Mayor Michael White, and to project them on the national scene. This tactic, along with the combination of locked-in Democratic Black votes; the nation's economic crisis; the Perot factor, which vacuumed significant chunks of the Republican constituency away from Bush; the revulsion by many moderate Republicans toward the rise of the Buchanan wing of the party; and the peculiarities of the Electoral College all came together to propel Clinton into the White House.

## Jackson and the Democrats' Dilemma

Jesse Louis Jackson remains one of the most fascinating and politically enigmatic figures on the national political stage. The fascination with Jackson is his unique ability to negotiate the murky and dangerous waters of Black community politics, Democratic Party politics, and global politics without going aground. Despite efforts to dismiss him, Jackson continues to be one of the most pivotal actors in the Black community affecting African American-Democratic Party relations. To a significant degree, as demonstrated so dramatically in 1992, what Jackson doesn't do is often more important than what he does do.

Almost from the day the 1988 campaign ended, speculation began over whether Jesse Jackson would run for a third time for the Democratic nomination in 1992. As the summer of 1991 came to a close, Jackson came under increasing pressure from a variety of sources to make a decision. Plans for fundraising and DNC strategy would be influenced by whether Jackson entered the race. There were also political issues, such as Jackson's relation to the DNC and whether or not his entrance in the race would dash the fleeting hopes of beating Bush. Some party activists even felt that Ron Brown, who had been selected to be chair of the DNC after the 1988 race, should tell Jackson not to run.

Following the 1988 campaign, Jackson made efforts to build bridges between the different political wings of the party. Invited to speak before the moderate Democratic Leadership Council's 1990 summer gathering, Jackson delivered a speech entitled, "Delighted to be United." He spoke of the many ways in which he viewed a meeting of the minds between the various wings of the Democratic Party:

> We are united on the need for deep cuts in military spending...We are united on the need for a new progressive challenge on the economy...We are more united on social issues ... We are increasingly united on crime and drugs...We are increasingly united on the need to invest in America.[8]

Jackson put out a call for common ground among all Democrats not just on moral terms, but also for practical purposes. He stated, "If we stand together on this common ground agenda: expand the party, don't divide it; invest in people, change our priorities to address our real security needs; make the rich and the corporations pay their fair share of taxes, we can unite—across race, religion, and region. Common ground can transcend differences on policy, on personality, on prejudice. If we are united, we can keep hope alive. And if hope is alive in this land we can win."[9]

At his rhetorical best, Jackson painted strong verbal imagery to describe the flow of power that would come from Democratic unity. Referring to the different political trends in the Democratic Party, Jackson stated: "When all the streams come together to form a mighty Mississippi River and pour into a common gulf and in that equation of reinforcement, there is mutual respect, sharing where every drop in the new mainstream counts as one, only then will we take the big boat to the big house, the White House, and win and deserve to win."[10]

Despite Jackson's attempt at unity, he was not invited to speak at the Democratic Leadership Council's (DLC) annual meetings in 1991 and 1992. At their 1991 meeting in Ohio, Jackson tried to create a controversy over his not being invited, but it received little press and the DLC did not flinch. Having built their base across the country, the DLC was gearing up to run their candidate, Arkansas Gov. Bill Clinton, who was a founding member and a former chairperson of the organization.

By the summer of 1991, there were plenty of reasons for Jackson (and other leading Democrats) not to run. Bush's relatively successful thrashing of Sadam Hussein during the Persian Gulf War had shot his favorability ratings to over 70 percent.[11] Although Bush had failed in his stated goal of getting rid of Hussein, and his war had cost billions of dollars and, at least, tens of thousands of lives, the White House media machine had carefully crafted the "spin" and won a large amount of public support and sympathy. Revelations about Reagan's and Bush's role in arming Hussein had been ignored by the major press, and only smaller progressive publications were carrying the stories.

All of the top potential Democratic contenders, including Sens. Richard Gephardt, Al Gore, and Bill Bradley, began to declare their intention not to run. New York Governor Mario Cuomo, whom many in the press assumed would be the front-runner, continued to play coy and would not state his intentions one way or the other.

In addition to the above reasons, Jackson confronted a number of political and personal issues. In the summer of 1990, Jackson decided, at virtually the last minute, to seek the local District of Columbia office of Shadow Senator stating upon his announcement, "Statehood for the District of Columbia is the most important civil rights and social justice issue in America today."[12] This position, along with that of an additional Shadow Senator and one Shadow Representative, was created by the 1980 statehood ballot initiative that called for a Statehood Constitutional Convention that was held in 1982. The mission of these offices is to lobby Congress and the general public for statehood for the District. Although the authority to create these offices and hold elections to fill them had been on the books since 1982, it was only when Jackson publicly raised the issue that the District's City Council was embarrassed into putting the offices on the 1990 ballot.

Jackson had initially stated that he was not interested in running for the office, but changed his mind, ran, and won with 46 percent of the vote.[13] Florence Pendleton (26 percent) won the other Shadow Senator seat and Charles Moreland won as Shadow Representative with 72 percent. As written into law, the offices had no clear tasks, nor were they budgeted. The newly elected officials had to secure their own operating funds and could determine whatever course of action they wanted in fighting for the statehood cause. Thus, while winning the seat gave Jackson the elected office mantle that blunted some of the criticism of those who complained that he had never been elected to anything, it did not resolve many other problems.

The position carried no authority with Congress, nor did it make Jackson a member of the Congressional Black Caucus as some early rumors had speculated. Even at the local level, city officials knew that these positions had no legislative power and, indeed, were less influential than the city's myriad of organized community and issue groups. The fact that the positions were not funded also meant that anything that Jackson and the others did in the name of their office had to come from funds that they raised independently. The election then, ironically, put an extra financial burden on Jackson, who now had to generate activities around D.C. statehood while, at the same time, raising money for those efforts and his other operations and activities.

Jackson's biggest organizational problem was the disempowering of the National Rainbow Coalition. His decision to turn the NRC from a fledgling, but potentially powerful mass membership activist organization into, essentially, a national office that works exclusively on the issues and activities that Jackson deems critical, removed a potent organizing force from the national scene. Unlike Clinton's Democratic Leadership Council, Jackson had no activists in place or institutional structures that could be immediately activated into a campaign. The demobilization of the Rainbow forces would be read accurately by Clinton and others as a sign that Jackson lacked the institutional and organizational muscle to respond to a middle-of-the-road presidential campaign or, for that matter, to perceived and real slights and provocations toward Jackson and the Black community. Without an organizational apparatus, Jackson's power lay in his considerable media abilities and networking skills.

Despite these problems, there were still a number of attractive reasons why Jackson should consider a run. First, his name recognition clearly gave him an advantage over other candidates, especially since other potential candidates assumed to have Jackson's stature were dropping out of the race.

In several state polls, Cuomo and Jackson held significant leads over the other candidates and potential candidates. In Florida, Cuomo lead by 20 percent followed by Jackson with 16 percent.[14] In New York, Cuomo's home state, he lead by 48 percent to Jackson's 17 percent, while no one else rose above 6 percent.[15]

Second, the widely perceived right-ward drift of the Democratic Party meant that Jackson would probably have a clear field for the progressive and traditionally liberal vote. If he could win the Mondale and Dukakis Democrats and build upon the seven million votes that he won in 1988, then he would have more than a good chance of winning the nomination. And, it was unlikely that the DNC leadership and party leaders around the country would break with the party if Jackson were the nominee, particularly if he won big in the primaries.

Third, Jackson would also bring a history of experience that few other potential entrants could duplicate. There had been tremendous growth in professionalism and expertise between the 1984 campaign and the one in 1988. Jackson, in all likelihood, would again inspire a level of energy and commitment that the other candidates could not even purchase. Although many of Jackson's supporters expressed frustration over the problems of the Rainbow, a Jackson candidacy would have been hard to resist again, given the moderating mode of the Democratic Party and the war-mongering, increasingly extremist nature of the Republican Party.

Fourth, despite Bush's popularity, there was a growing dissatisfaction with his administration's lack of attention to domestic concerns, particularly the economy. While his approval ratings were high, they were also dropping. By the fall, his approval ratings had dipped into the low 60s and, in one poll, even into the 50s.[16] In one interesting series of polls that received minimal attention, Bush was compared to a generic Democratic nominee to see how he would do against the Democrats in general. In March 1991, Bush out-polled the hypothetical Democrat by 68 percent to 20 percent.[17] By October, however, Bush lead only by 47 percent to 37 percent.[18] Not only had he fallen by 21 points, but the Democrats had risen by 17 points, a trend that spelled trouble for the Republicans.

Jackson held his cards close to his chest and teased reporters and supporters about his intentions. Despite his vacillation, however, he made it clear that he thought that if he entered the race he would have a good chance of winning. He told the media, "The strain of the campaign is substantial." He went on to say, "I got seven million votes and 1,300 delegates in 1988. Ten million votes and 1,800 can win. So, winning is within our grasp. It is a matter for consideration."[19]

In November 1991, a series of closed meetings were held in Washington, D.C. by Jackson to receive input from his closest associates and supporters on his decision whether or not to run. Participants in those meetings included national and local elected officials, labor leaders, community activists, and political operatives of all types. Individuals such as Rep. Maxine Waters, Rep. Charles Rangel, Pennsylvania activist Rick Adams, attorney Kay Pierson, political scientists Ron Walters and Bill Strickland, former and current staffers, and others played key roles in moving the agenda of the meeting and articulating the pros and cons of a third Jackson presidential run.

At one meeting, held at the Washington Sheraton Hotel, there was a presentation by Democratic National Committee Research Director Mark Steitz. He informed the gathering that the Democratic Party was making a strong effort not to repeat the campaign mistakes made in 1988. Among the strategy changes being implemented were an earlier focus on California, more aggressive and better-planned fundraising efforts, more intensive oppositional research on Bush and the Republicans, and plans for a herculean effort at getting a larger turnout in metropolitan areas. The party had concluded that one of its mistakes in 1988 had been not organizing a massive turnout in the cities to offset the large suburban vote that had gone to Bush.

At this same meeting was a somewhat whimsical, but pointed presentation by former Jackson staffer Steve Cobble. He reminded the audience of the achievements of Jackson in the 1984 and 1988 campaigns and that those accomplishments warranted better treatment and more respect than Jackson was getting from the party. He told a parable about a Greek Democratic Party leader—an undisguised reference to Michael Dukakis—who had achieved the same number of votes and had done the same level of registration as Jackson. He elaborated on other contributions of this Greek leader, such as helping other party candidates get elected and healing some of the divisions within the party. This Greek leader after having made all these contributions, in Cobble's parable, was treated royally and widely viewed as the standard bearer of the party. Cobble compared the treatment of this fictitious party leader with that of Jackson. The point was understood without explanation.[20]

At the gathering, Jackson and Waters outlined the pluses and minuses of a Jackson campaign. Waters was unbridled in her feelings that Jackson should enter the race. She stated her extreme displeasure at the conservative direction in which the Democratic Party was headed and warned that Blacks, Latinos, women, and the poor were just about at the end of their rope. She saw Jackson as the one politician on the national scene who could, in effect, save the nation.

Jackson, for his part, stated that his two biggest reservations about running were, first, the still-lingering debts owed from the 1988 race and from the 1990 Shadow Senator race and, second, security for his family. In addition to the campaign debts, Jackson owed money to the Federal Election Commission (FEC), which had initially claimed that the Jackson '88 campaign owed the government $700,000 in federal subsidies that could not be accounted for adequately by the campaign. In 1993, after years of negotiations, that figure was reduced to $122,031.[21]

In a rare open and frank moment, Jackson shared with the crowd the immense and often frightening nature of the many threats that his family had received during his two presidential campaigns. He expressed genuine concern and trepidation about having them (and himself) go through that experience again.

In the discussion from the floor, the overwhelming sentiment from the partisan crowd was that Jackson should run. Some even advocated that he run as an independent, given the conservative political dynamics that were beginning to appear within Democratic Party circles. The session ended with Jackson undecided, but recommending that if people wanted him to seriously consider running, then steps first had to be taken to retire the old debt. Jackson used the metaphor of trying to win an auto race with a car that only has three tires. He said that for him to even contemplate entering the race, he first had to know that his car had four tires, was full of gas, and was ready to drive. The meeting ended with Jackson asking for volunteers who could commit themselves to raising $10,000 each toward retiring the old debts.

## Jackson Bows Out

In the end, on November 2, 1992, citing mainly the financial and personal security concerns, Jackson decided not to run for the nomination. Announcing his decision on the grounds of Potomac Gardens, a Washington, D.C. housing project, Jackson said that he would concentrate his energy on building a "new, independent democratic majority," and "not seek the nomination for the Democratic Party."[22] Jackson elaborated on some of his dissatisfaction with the party:

> There has been too much of an unholy alliance between the two parties—leaving the electorate with two names, but one party, one set of assumptions and no options. Reagan's 1981 tax cut was a wholesale attack on the public sector; it cost thousands of jobs—it was approved by Democrats. Today's Supreme Court represents a radical rightward shift, putting the squeeze on cherished rights—nominated by Republicans, confirmed by Demo-

crats. When the Berlin Wall came down, the Republican and Democratic budgets were 1 percent apart.[23]

Though critical of the Democrats' complicity with the Republicans on a range of issues, Jackson was careful to note that his concerns with the Democratic Party and his call for a new, independent democratic majority were not a break from the party. In a carefully worded passage that reportedly was added at the last minute, Jackson stated:

> Is the new democratic majority a third party? No. It is an overhaul of the process that now serves a narrow elite. I am a strong Democrat, and I have deep pride in what I have been able to contribute to the party and the country...As a Democrat, I hope that the party leadership will expand and reach out with hope and vision. George Bush should be and must be beaten, and he will be beaten by Democrats if they speak authentically for the new democratic majority. Reaching out to everyone, including the locked out, is the way to victory. And so we are not stepping back but building up for a better America.[24]

Citing the physical threats to his family, Jackson said, "My family lives on the edge of considerable risk and danger every day. I am grateful and impressed by their commitment to share the burden of the causes of social justice, economic security, fairness, freedom and peace. They have absorbed more death threats in two campaigns than any candidate's family ever has. And yet they have held their heads high, and remained a close-knit unit, and turned hostility into hope."[25]

The group of reporters who attended the press conference tried to press Jackson on whether he would commit to some other candidate or if he would sit out the race. They also asked him what impact he thought his not being in the race would have on the Black community's role in the coming election. Jackson pointed out that there were still two Black candidates in the race, Virginia Gov. Douglas Wilder and independent Ron Daniels, and that the press should seek them out. He refused to state what he would do in the coming campaign or to offer suggestions to his followers other than what was in his statement.

To some of Jackson's enemies as well as supporters in the Democratic Party, this was welcome news. Despite Bush's drop in the polls, the Democrats still believed that they would have a difficult time defeating the president. Jackson's entrance in the race would have complicated matters. Arguments that he was too liberal and would drive away White voters were raised anew. Those arguments against Jackson's running were echoes of the same views heard in 1984 and 1988. Ron Brown, DNC chairperson at the time, stated that Jackson's decision should "Certainly help us get to a consensus nominee early in the process."[26]

Those Jackson supporters who did not think that Bush could be beaten were relieved for Jackson. A third unsuccessful Jackson candidacy, many believed, would perhaps eliminate Jackson forever from the presidential sweepstakes, something that many did not want to happen. This group felt that if the Democrats lost again in 1992, which would have been the sixth time in the last seven elections, Jackson could come back stronger in 1996. A powerful downside of this strategy was that if the Democrats won, Jackson's ability to run in 1996 (and perhaps in 2000 and 2004, as well) would be severely compromised. Running against a Democratic incumbent had its obvious limits, especially if Jackson were to run as a Democrat, and there was nothing then to indicate that Jackson would ever run as an independent.

For other supporters, however, Jackson's being on the sidelines meant there was a tremendous political vacuum. In 1984 and 1988, Jackson's candidacy pushed the Democrats to address issues of concern to Blacks, Hispanics, labor, and other constituencies whose votes were previously taken for granted. Jackson, who won nearly seven million votes in 1988 and came to the Democratic National Convention with more than 1,200 delegates, was on both occasions able to force the party platform to be more progressive and to inspire millions to go out and vote.

Just what relevance, strategic or symbolic, the absence of Jackson from the presidential race meant for African Americans in terms of 1992 presidential politics was an extremely pivotal question. His refusal to run and unwillingness to elaborate a clear strategy were problematic. Jackson's notion of building an "independent democratic majority" was vague and had little meaning with respect to African American socio-economic and political interests. It was also unclear if this concept was to take on an organizational form similar or different from that of Jackson's National Rainbow Coalition. "Independent democratic majority" also seemed to imply at least a tilt toward building a third party, but Jackson had made it clear that he opposed that option. All of these concerns were left unexplored and, in any case, the term disappeared from Jackson's public statements in a few short weeks. Its main purpose seemed to have been to send a signal of Jackson's dissatisfaction with the political tenor and direction of the Democratic Party. At the press conference held at the housing project site, Jackson's calculated mention of Independent Ron Daniels as an alternative Black candidate, in response to a reporter's question about the absence of an African American in the campaign, also seemed to be part of the signaling that on Jackson's part.

One factor that seemed to be pushing the urgency of Jackson's decision was the growing number of Black elected officials who were beginning to line up behind particular potential candidates as well as the impending candidacy of Doug Wilder. While national Black figures were hesitant to make early endorsements, Clinton and Harkin were winning support from a number of Black local officials and Democratic Party activists.

The Wilder situation was particularly irksome to Jackson, as those in the media began to query if the Virginia governor was Jackson's replacement not only in the coming campaign, but also in national Black political circles.[27] These perceived "defections" and questions perhaps hit home most sharply when two of Jackson's former staffers, Joe Johnson, who had been Executive Director of the National Rainbow Coalition, and Eric Easter, who had been Jackson's press secretary, both went to work on Wilder's campaign. Johnson took the position of campaign manager while Easter fulfilled the role of press secretary.

Without Jackson in the race, many thought it likely that the potential Democratic candidates would once again take African American interests and voters for granted. Jackson's refusal to run meant that a challenge to that trend from progressives would have to take place outside of a Jackson candidacy.

The National Rainbow Coalition, for its part, developed a list of issues, termed the "Ten Commitments." Where a candidate stood in relation to supporting the concerns outlined in the list would determine the level of support, if any, that a candidate would receive from the NRC. These issues were: support for District of Columbia Statehood, support for the National Voter Registration Act known popularly as the "Motor Voter" bill, repeal of Section 14B of the Labor Act; endorsement of civil rights legislation; the creation of a national health-care system, institution of a military conversion plan, support for environmental justice, support for the creation of more affordable housing, backing of an increase in education funding, and endorsement of cutting the military budget by half.

How these programmatic ideas would be fought for was left undetermined. When Jackson dropped out of contention, he did so without a specific plan or strategy for his followers. It was advocated that Rainbow activists go into the campaign of their choosing, but do so as Rainbow representatives. The objective of this tactic, it seems, was that Jackson's forces would infiltrate the various presidential campaigns at the highest level possible as staffers and volunteers with the intention of fighting for the progressive slate of ideas that the Rainbow had articulated over the years. This plan appeared to be one of necessity, given that the momentum to move away from Jackson had already begun by some of his loyal activists and supporters among elected officials.

Jackson himself stated that he had not determined if he would endorse someone during the primary season. This stance, Jackson assumed, would allow him the broadest latitude in working with the individual candidates and, at the same time, exerting pressure on them to treat him respectfully if they were to have any chance of receiving what was thought to be a coveted endorsement. This tactic was contingent on a number of assumptions that would later prove unstable. First, it was assumed that Jackson would have the capacity to turn out the Black vote in large numbers. Jackson's ability to sway Black voters, who would be crucial in winning primaries and probably the general election, had been demonstrated in the past. There was no reason to suspect that he would not have the same power in 1992, despite not being a candidate.

Second, what looked like a relatively weak field of candidates opened the speculation that a brokered convention was possible and thus Jackson could emerge as the kingmaker if he were uncommitted at that time. The belief that none of the candidates could break out of the pack was also tied to the view that the Black vote would probably be fragmented. None of the declared candidates, including Wilder, were very inspiring to the African American community nor were they beginning with much of a base. While Clinton was seen as the front-runner, he was still relatively unknown outside of party circles and had weak ties to Black leaders and activists outside of the South.

Third, it was assumed that Jackson had a legitimate shot at the vice presidential slot, and rumors were already circulating that Jackson was interested in that spot on the ticket. In order to be viable for that spot, Jackson would need not only a strong demand coming from the Black and progressive community, but also good relations with the Democratic candidate. By not endorsing anyone, he theoretically would not have burnt bridges with the eventual nominee. Being noncommittal to any candidate would strengthen his hand on this count.

Lastly, it was also assumed that, for the most part, no other Black leaders had the ability or willingness to challenge Jackson's position as the preeminent Black politician of the day. In 1988, virtually every prominent Black elected official in the nation had jumped on Jackson's bandwagon.

Except for the first assumption—Jackson's ability to motivate Black voters in the general election—all of these beliefs turned out to be false. Clinton emerged fairly early as the front-runner, who never had any intention of seeing Jackson on the ticket, and he got substantial support from a wide range of Black elected officials who were willing, even eager in some cases, to confront Jackson.

# National Rainbow Coalition Presidential Forum

Although he was not a candidate, Jackson was determined not to sit on the sidelines during the election. He understood the need to play, to the extent that he could, a power broker's role in the Democratic Party. At the same time, he also knew that he could not afford to give his supporters too long a leash for fear that they would be reluctant to return to the fold. He decided, therefore, to hold a series of Rainbow meetings where the candidates would come to present their case to Jackson's constituency. These meetings were to be high-profile including national television coverage and endless press conferences and interviews.

On January 25, 1992, the NRC held a presidential forum at Washington, D.C.'s Omni Shoreham Hotel attended by six of the major Democratic aspirants—former California Gov. Jerry Brown, Arkansas Gov. Bill Clinton, Sen. Tom Harkin, former Sen. Eugene McCarthy, Sen. Bob Kerrey, and former Sen. Paul Tsongas.

Desperate for the important Black vote, and wedded to the perception that NRC President Jesse Jackson could deliver a significant chunk of it, the candidates were at their rhetorical best. Determined to be a major player in the race, Jackson's event was as much to position his authority as to force the candidates to address the constituency that he had built over the last seven years.

The structure of the event precluded any serious debate between the candidates themselves, or between the candidates and the questioners. In a sense, the forum became six press opportunities for the candidates. The structure consisted of roughly one hour for each candidate to do a presentation and field questions. Each candidate was allowed to make a fifteen-minute presentation (although no one spoke within that time) and then respond to 45 minutes of pre-written questions from a pre-chosen panel of about ten to twelve people.

The questioners included elected officials, labor activists, student leaders, community activists, civil rights activists, and environmentalists—a significant departure from the media stars who usually pander to the candidates. Among the questioners were Arab American Institute Executive Director Jim Zogby; New York State Assemblywoman Barbara Clark; Alabama State Senator Hank Sanders; Rep. Charles Rangel (D-NY); United Mineworkers of America Vice President Cecil Roberts; North Carolina Farm Alliance President Merle Hansen; New Hampshire AFL-CIO President Mark McKenzie; Ithaca, New York Mayor Ben Nichols; Baltimore Mayor Kurt Schmoke; Operation PUSH Board Vice Chair Willie Barrows; American University Law Professor Jamin Raskin; Howard University Political Scientist Ron Walters; and El Centro de la Raza Director Estela Ortega, among others.

Brown, who spoke first, appeared to be the sentimental favorite among the crowd at the Omni Shoreham and certainly won some converts by calling for a moment of silence for Rickey Ray Rector, the brain-damaged Black man executed the day before in Arkansas under the authority of Gov. Bill Clinton, who was to appear on the podium later. The loudest cheers, however, were for Harkin, who also attacked Clinton's support for the death penalty. Most of the candidates engaged in Bush-bashing. Harkin stated, for example, that Bush is someone who "was born on third base, but believes that he had hit a triple." Brown was the exception in that he blamed both the Democrats and the Republicans for the economic and social crisis that the nation is experiencing.

Clinton arrived late to the forum, on his way back from Arkansas after having overseen the execution of Rector. Stating that he had agonized over the execution, Clinton asked the crowd to "respect his decision" and to "agree to disagree."

McCarthy, who was virtually non-existent in the polls at that time, and subsequently dropped out after an extremely poor showing, mainly entertained the audience with quips and political tales from the past. More than anything, his presence raised the question of the criteria used to determine which candidates had been invited and which had not. Independent candidate Ron Daniels, for example, whose program was much more substantive and progressive than Tsongas', Clinton's, or Kerrey's and closer to the NRC's program, and who was a former executive director of the NRC itself, was not invited to participate. His absence and McCarthy's attendance seem to underscore the idea that the event was as much about Jackson's positioning vis-a-vis the Democratic Party as it was about identifying where the candidates stood on issues important to the Rainbow constituency.

The audience consisted mainly of NRC staff and volunteers, staffers and supporters of the various candidates, questioners and their aides, dozens of members of the media, and a smattering of local and national NRC activists. The crowd tended to ebb and flow with the comings and goings of the various candidates.

In a statement released by the NRC at the forum, Jackson's 1992 strategy was made more explicit. While declaring that Jackson "may or may not personally endorse" one of the candidates before the DNC took place, Rainbow supporters were asked to work aggressively in the campaign of their choice, but as Rainbow cadre.

As Rainbow activists, their tasks inside of the campaigns would be to work on voter registration, voter education on the issues, and delegate selection; to work at the DNC; to participate in the vice presidential selection process; and to work in the general election. The logic of this strategy was that again, in the event of a brokered convention, Rainbow activists could be in a position to influence, if not determine, the selection of the nominee. In addition, following the convention, the Rainbow, through its network of activists in the winning candidate's campaign, would be positioned to impact the strategy and flow of the general election, unlike in 1984 and 1988, when Rainbow activists were ignored or rebuked by Mondale and Dukakis campaign staffs.

By the time of this forum, Clinton had won the endorsement of several members of the Congressional Black Caucus, such as John Lewis, Mike Espy, and Bill Jefferson, as well as that of a growing number of southern Black elected officials and activists who had been identified with the NRC, such as Texan Hazel Obey, a former Jackson delegate and head of the Texas State Rainbow Coalition. Other Rainbow activists, mainly White, were backing Harkin or Brown.

# A Slice of Pecan Pie

Gov. Clinton's attendance, as noted above, was controversial and tense. On January 24, 1992, in a move that had served to distance Clinton further from some in the Black and progressive communities, Clinton authorized and oversaw the execution of a brain-damaged Black man, Ricky Ray Rector. After murdering a White police officer, Rector blew away a three-inch section of his brain during his capture. The injury resulted in a frontal lobotomy which rendered him mentally incapacitated. Because he was unable to grasp even the most fundamental aspects of his situation or even who he was, progressive judicial and civil rights activists agreed across the board that Rector probably should have been designated mentally incompetent and sent away permanently to a pschiatric institution. Instead, Rector went to trial, was found guilty, and sentenced to death.

The brutality of this government-sanctioned and -implemented execution was furthered increased when it took state officials close to fifty minutes to find a suitable vein in which to inject the poison that killed Rector. Unaware that he was about to die, Rector told prison officials that he was going to vote for Clinton in the fall. It had been his habit to save his dessert from his dinners so that he could eat it later. When prison officials returned to his cell after the execution, they found a slice of pecan pie that Rector had left with every expectation that he would return to the cell.[28] He died apparently not even knowing that he was being executed.

Clinton had ignored letters and calls from Black leaders and civil and human rights activists to commute Rector's sentence to life in prison without the possibility of parole, which he had the power to do. In one letter to Clinton, Jesse Jackson wrote, "I join with the National Coalition to Abolish the Death Penalty, the NAACP Legal Defense Fund, and many others across this country in appealing to you to spare the life of Ricky Ray Rector...I appeal to you, in the name of God and conscience, to spare the life of Ricky Ray Rector and to reconsider your position on capital punishment."[29] Jackson also personally called and talked to Clinton in a last-ditch effort to stop the execution. Other Rainbow associates, such as Rep. Charles Rangel (D-NY), Memphis Mayor Willie Henderson, and former New Mexico Gov. Tony Anaya, also pleaded with Clinton to stop the execution.[30]

At the forum, only two of the major Democratic candidates opposed the death penalty: Sen. Tom Harkin and former California Gov. Jerry Brown. Harkin pointed out how Clinton's decision to execute Rector perpetuates a criminal justice system that is unjust and racist. He noted how Milwaukee mass murderer Jeffrey Dahlmer, who had murdered a number of young Black boys as well as others, had not even faced the death penalty, while Rector, "a person with an IQ of 70," was executed.

On the other hand, Clinton, Kerrey, and Tsongas all supported the death penalty. This departure from the traditional Democratic Party position came as a shock to some progressive activists. Embracing the death penalty had been a staple among Republicans as part of their strategy for winning White votes.

This tact by some Democrats, ostensibly in the name of law and order, masked the well-documented fact that the death penalty has historically been applied in a racially discriminatory way. Between 1930 and 1990, 56 percent of those executed were Blacks or other people of color.[31] Of the 453 men executed for rape during the same period, 405 were African American.[32]

Further, the death penalty continues to be reserved primarily for cases in which the victims are White even though African Americans are the victims of more murders in the United States than are Whites. As of March 1992, of the 155 people executed since 1976, when the Supreme Court re-legalized the death penalty, close to 90 percent have been executed for killing Whites.[33] One study concluded that "in Florida, killers of Whites are eight times more likely to receive a death sentence than killers of Blacks."[34] In Illinois and Mississippi, the figure is six times as great. In Georgia, the figure is ten times greater; in addition, the death penalty is sought in 85 percent of the cases in which Whites are the victims, but only in 15 percent of those in which Blacks are.[35] As of mid-1993, only one White in the entire history of the United States had ever been executed for murdering an African American.

As a deterrent to crime, the most popular reason given for its use, the death penalty has had virtually no effect. In states where the death penalty has been abolished, homicide rates average 5.1 murders per 100,000 population. In states where the death penalty is being used, murders average 9.1. In Florida, there were eight executions in 1984, yet the state saw a rise in homicides of 5.1 percent.

There are more than 2,500 poor, uneducated people on death row awaiting execution either by gas, shooting, lethal injection, electrocution, or hanging. Half of the people on death row are from national minority groups, with African Americans comprising the largest proportion, an astounding 41 percent. Most of them were unemployed when they committed their crime. Capital punishment in the United States is still for those without capital.

For White Democrats, calling for the death penalty was made easier by the actions and positions of moderate Black politicians such as Virginia Gov. Douglas Wilder. By the time he announced that he was running for the presidential nomination, Wilder had allowed five executions. It should be noted that the majority of people in Virginia, 59 percent, oppose the death penalty and prefer a sentence of twenty-five years before parole is allowed along with financial restitution to the victim's family.[36] Wilder joins a number of moderate Black officials who support the death penalty. In his ill-fated bid for governor of Georgia, Andy Young jettisoned his few remaining liberal credentials and declared that he supported the death penalty. In Washington, D.C., during her first year in office, Mayor Sharon Pratt Kelly ignited a controversy by intimating that she would support the death penalty under certain circumstances. She backed off of that position after an initial controversy and reversed herself completely in the fall of 1992 when Congress forced the city to include a question on the District of Columbus election ballot concerning the reimposition of the death penalty in the city. Other Black elected officials, such as former Rep. Mike Espy, also supported the death penalty.

It was clear from this meeting that the NRC had its work cut out for it. What some had expected to be a forum for settling which candidate would best carry the Rainbow message had left more confusion than ever. While it was clear that some candidates, such as Brown, Harkin, and McCarthy, were closer to the Rainbow's program and goals than others, it was equally obvious that they were the poorest organized and had the least momentum as they headed into the primaries. Neither did any of these candidates have Black staffers in high-level positions, if they had any at all, or any strong ties to the Black community. For all the problems that Clinton seemed to present, his campaign appeared to be the best organized and well-resourced. In addition, when the forum initially had been planned, many had expected or hoped that

Doug Wilder would attend as a candidate and put some pressure on the presidential race to address issues of concern to the Black community.

## The Race Gets a Little Wilder

On September 13, 1991, acknowledging that he was the "longest of the long shots,"[37] Virginia Gov. Douglas Wilder announced his candidacy for the Democratic nomination. He declared that "as someone who has fought for positive change and the American Dream for all these years, I cannot stand on the sidelines while the country I love stumbles further backwards."[38]

Reflecting the moderate tone that he is known for, Wilder's speech was a combination of hits on the Bush administration, pledges to expand economic opportunities and political rights, and centrist ideas about values aimed at middle America's conservative political expectations. In one passage, he stated, "If elected, I pledge to all of you that I will do everything in my power to heal the growing divisions among us; to restore economic vitality ... so that more people can enter the middle-class...and to secure peace around the world through U.S. economic and military strength."[39]

Although the only African American in the Democratic race, Wilder devoted little of his speech to issues or concerns specifically related to Blacks. He did, at one point, acknowledge the worsening racial relations in the United States, but linked that crisis to the nation's dismal economic situation. He stated, "Washington seems to have lost the passion to fight the deterioration in race relations in this nation...a result—in large measure—of Washington's fiscal mess and the noose it has become around America's future economic prosperity."[40]

On December 2, 1969, Wilder had been elected to the Virginia State Senate, the first Black ever elected to that body. With 48.4 percent of the vote, he beat two White candidates, former Richmond mayor Morrill Crowe (31.5 percent) and outgoing Lt. Gov. Fred Pollard (18.6 percent).[41] Upon his victory, in an effort to distance himself from the issue of race, Wilder stated, "I look forward to the time when all men can run as candidates on their qualifications and not as a 'Negro candidate' or a 'White candidate.'"[42] In 1985, Wilder again made history when he was elected lieutenant governor. In a close vote, he beat State Senator John Chichester, 51.8 percent to 48.2 percent.[43]

Wilder would make history a third time in 1989 when he did what many believed was nearly impossible: win the governorship in Virginia. With the financial backing of the state Democratic Party, to the tune of a $750,000 contribution, Wilder squeaked by with a close victory over J. Marshall

Coleman. He won by 6,854 votes (.37 of 1 percent) out of nearly two million cast.[44] Overall, he had spent over $7 million in the costliest race in Virginia's history. In that election, Wilder won about 39 percent of the White vote.[45]

During the campaign and his subsequent governorship, Wilder sounded a mix of conservative and mildly liberal themes. He defined himself as a fiscal conservative and championed other conservative causes such as the death penalty, Virginia's anti-labor right-to-work laws, and opposition to District of Columbus statehood. He also took pains to distance himself publicly from the Black community. In an analysis of his campaign schedule from June 19, 1989 to September 4, 1989, it was found that of the eighty-five public appearances he made, only ten were to Black organizations.[46]

Wilder was one of the few Black politicians active with the moderate Democratic Leadership Council. In a speech before the DLC's national conference in fall of 1989, following his election as governor of Virginia, he avoided any discussion of race and spoke of his desire for the Democratic Party to become more mainstream and to downscale the role of government in society. He stated, "[We] have worked hard to preserve the Jeffersonian principle of limited government. That means keeping government out of the most personal of personal decisions."[47] Even at that early date, Wilder signaled his interest in the White House and what political views he thought would be necessary in order for the Democrats to win. "In presidential elections, it is time for the Democratic Party to take a plunge into the waters of America's New Mainstream. Mainstream values are the values of the overwhelming majority of the people of this country. It's time our party began focusing on such values at the national level," declared Wilder.[48]

# Wilder Drops Out

Although suspicions arose immediately upon Wilder's entrance into the race about his motives and those of the Democratic Party strategists, it was generally believed that he would at least stay in through the early primaries. After all, his candidacy was unique and would generate media coverage on that alone. Besides, if he stayed in the race through Super Tuesday, when most of the southern states would their cast ballots, he had a good chance of picking up much of Jackson's previous support in the Black community in the South.

Speculation was rampant, however, on why Wilder had chosen to run. Rumors ran the gamut from the belief that he had been coaxed to enter the race to vie with Jesse for the Black vote to the idea that he was really running for the vice presidential slot. For his part, Jackson was lukewarm to the candidacy publicly and, many believed, antagonistic toward it in private.

Many in the media greeted Wilder's candidacy with joy and clearly viewed him as a rational alternative to Jackson. Long before Wilder had even hinted that he was interested in running for president, the media had been portraying him as a replacement for Jackson. As former Jackson staffer Steve Cobble noted, "The pundits had a dream—that Virginia Gov. Douglas Wilder would drive Jesse Jackson from the public stage."[49] One newspaper even reported that Democratic strategists are already calculating that Mr. Wilder's [1989 gubernatorial] victory is bad news for Jesse Jackson.[50] In a similar voice, the *Boston Globe* reported, "We may be seeing the sun beginning to set on the 'Jesse Jackson era.'"[51]

Black reporters who opposed Jackson were even more exuberant about Wilder than their White colleagues. The *Washington Post*'s Juan Williams, who generally gets assignments to do critical pieces on Black leaders, was enthusiastic and inspired about the apparent rise of Wilder. He effusively wrote that the governor is "arguably the most important Black American politician of the 20th Century...It is not just that Wilder is an alternative to the best-known Black spokesman, Jesse Jackson: his success is a rebuke to Jackson's 1980s political vision of Blacks as America's victims."[52]

Wilder's campaign activities left a lot to be desired. He would often show up unprepared and uninformed on key issues. His inexperience in campaigning outside of Virginia was apparent on more than one occasion.

Wilder's campaign was in trouble with many Black politicians and activists from the beginning. His moderate program was a turn-off to a number of the Black elected officials who had backed Jackson in 1984 and 1988. One of Jackson's strongest supporters has been Rep. Charles Rangel. Comparing Wilder to Black conservative Supreme Court Associate Justice Clarence Thomas, Rangel stated, "[If] he can run as a Black candidate, then he will do better getting the Jackson votes. If he wants to run like Clarence Thomas, then hell, he doesn't even have Clarence Thomas's color, but I guess everyone will say he's Black, and some Blacks will say, 'Give the boy a chance.'"[53] Activist Ron Daniels, who was preparing to launch his own independent run for president, stated, "He's a mainstream Democrat, same old Tweedledee-Tweedledum. He is a conservative in brown face."[54]

Wilder, at one point, accused Jesse Jackson of sabotaging his campaign. Wilder told reporters that Jackson had "asked people not to support me."[55] He said that those close to Jackson were spreading the word that Wilder was trying to "reap fruit from trees he hadn't planted."[56] Jackson denied Wilder's charges and stated, "I don't know what prompted this outburst. I don't want to be used as a scapegoat for what's happening in his campaign."[57] One commentator noted, with some degree of accuracy, that the

Wilder-Jackson debate was potentially harmful to both men. He argued that unless they could work something out, then it was likely that both would lose—big.[58]

Despite these weaknesses and obstacles, Wilder did manage to get some Black support. In Clinton's home state of Arkansas, Wilder won the endorsement of state Rep. Bill Walker, who also promised to help him win the support of the other eleven Black members of Arkansas' legislature. Walker chaired the twelve-member legislative Black caucus. Walker stated, "It's not whether we like Bill Clinton, but what has he done for us, and the answer comes up short."[59] Walker accused Clinton of not addressing Black poverty in the state, of failing to secure a state civil rights bill, and of "fighting Blacks on redistricting."[60] For state Rep. Ben McGee, another Black legislator, it boiled down to racial solidarity. He said, "I just could never tell my grandchildren that I didn't support" Wilder, the nation's first elected Black governor.[61]

On January 8, 1992, citing the difficulty of trying to run a national campaign and manage the state of Virginia, Wilder dropped out of the race for the Democratic nomination for president. In a move that stunned even Wilder's highest campaign officials, including his campaign manager, he gave up his quest to become the first Black nominee of a major-party. Although few expected Wilder to reach the level achieved by Jesse Jackson in 1984 and 1988, his departure before the Super Tuesday contests seems inexplicable. In a number of polls taken in the South, Wilder had polled equal to or better than Arkansas Governor Bill Clinton, the tentative front-runner.

"Obviously, I was wrong," stated Wilder in explaining how he had misjudged his ability to juggle two extremely difficult tasks.[62] Wilder spoke of fulfilling his responsibility to the voters of Virginia in its time of financial crisis and said that trying to both run a national campaign and be governor wasn't working. He said, "You can't do both things well."[63] Many believe, however, that he saw inevitable defeat in the early primaries and got out while the getting was good. As one observer noted, Wilder "was trying to make a virtue out of a necessity."[64] Wilder raised the least funds of all the candidates, was the most inexperienced in running a national campaign, had little organization, and was often unprepared in delivering his message. By the time he dropped out, he had only raised $289,026 in presidential campaign funds.[65] Although his campaign could claim that he was "leading in Maryland and South Carolina and otherwise doing well in the South," most polls showed him coming in last or nearly last.[66] In Maryland, where African Americans make up 25–30 percent of the electorate, Wilder led with 20 percent followed by Clinton with 12 percent, Bob Kerrey with 10 percent, Jerry Brown with 6 percent, and Paul Tsongas with 3 percent. In South Carolina, where Blacks often made up 40–50 percent of the Democratic primary vote, Wilder lead by 21 percent, followed by Clinton with 16 percent, and the rest in single digits.[67]

His public squabbles with Jackson and Virginia Sen. Charles Robb, his poor record on trade union rights, his opposition to D.C. statehood, and his pro-death penalty stance were political pitfalls that would have undermined his support from liberals, Blacks, labor, and other constituencies.

By exiting early, he avoided the stigmatizing that he would probably have gotten in states such as Iowa and New Hampshire. At the same time, his four months of campaigning broadened his popular recognition beyond the lonely backwaters of Virginia. Through his aborted candidacy, he positioned himself as a national Black leader, as one of the nation's better-known governors, and, perhaps most important, a force at the Democratic National Convention who could potentially be offered the vice president slot. There was even speculation at that time, mostly unfounded, that Wilder would go to the New York convention as a "favorite son" long-shot candidate.[68]

Although Wilder's appeal to Black voters was more due to racial loyalty than political unity or his policy positions, his absence from the race had a number of important implications. Rather than his departure forcing the other candidates to more aggressively seek the Black vote and address issues of Black concerns—as many commentators had argued would happen—some contended that it actually meant a return to the pre-Jesse Jackson days when the Black vote was taken for granted and few concessions were made by either party. Political analyst Ronald Walters predicted astutely at the time that, "With Wilder out, there could be a disastrously low Black turnout in the primary, which could carry over to the general election."[69] Given the lack of ties that the remaining five candidates had to the African American community, it was questionable whether traditional Black leadership and the masses of Blacks would rally around any particular candidate.

The theme of race-neutrality would emerge as a consistent refrain during the 1992 race. A number of White commentators also echoed these views, one of the better known being Thomas Edsel. In a 1992 edition of his *Chain Reaction: The Impact of Race, Rights, and Taxes on American Politics*, Edsel added an afterword where he heralded candidate Clinton's call for a "new covenant" and for "reciprocal responsibility."[70] He also attacked Jesse Jackson and argued that Democrats were losing votes by the "simple linking of Democratic candidates to Jesse Jackson."[71]

# Chapter 13

# Election Results, Analysis, and Lessons Learned

The worst of Clinton will be a lot better than the best of Bush.

—Rep. Charles B. Rangel[1]

In the end, the American people, like most African Americans, wanted change. The repudiation of the Reagan-Bush era by the electorate—even while embracing many of its assumptions—grew stronger as election day neared. More than anything, the administration's inability to rescue the economy motivated millions of Bush's 1988 supporters to run for cover and desert the hapless president. Bush and the Republicans remained oblivious to the popular demand for new leadership, new ideas, and a responsive approach to the nation's ills throughout the entire campaign and, in the end, paid the ultimate electoral cost.

Indicative of Bush's insensitive and canyon-wide distance from the reality of the country's suffering, and a fitting legacy to his cynical career of racial politics, he vetoed an urban-aid bill the day after the general election, "killing the only urban aid measure to emerge from Congress in the wake of [the spring 1992] riots."[2] Although Bush could have let the bill die from a pocket veto (i.e., by not signing it) because Congress had already adjourned, he made a point of vetoing it as he claimed to be opposed to some minor tax increases included in the bill. In fact, the bill actually would have given tax breaks to the wealthy and repealed luxury taxes on boats, planes, furs, and jewelry.

For African Americans, the election highlighted many of the issues faced by the Black community and Black leadership that go beyond electoral politics. These issues must now be addressed in the new political atmosphere that the change in administration has brought. How African Americans may fare in the new administration and the possibilities of a more efficacious

167

struggle for equality and human rights will be addressed in Chapter 14. This chapter examines the election results and what lessons may be derived from the 1992 campaign.

The election of a Democrat, Bill Clinton, to the White House after twelve years of attacks by Republican administrations was a welcome change to most African Americans. Clinton won 82 percent of the Black vote and came into office pledged to turn the nation around economically and to end a dozen years of racial and social divisiveness. His election and the victories of dozens of Black candidates at the federal, state, county, and local levels signaled for many African Americans and others a new beginning, a new era, a new hope.

Most believed that the Clinton program of reform was the right medicine after twelve years of social and economic castor oil from Washington. For most African Americans, Clinton's promise to build an administration that was racially and sexually diverse was also well received.

Clinton ran an efficient and skillful campaign that remained focused on the need for change. He was good in the debates, though not overwhelming, and took his act on the road where it was well received and stood in sharp contrast to the aristocratic campaign of Bush. Despite the reservations of many Black leaders, Clinton was welcomed in the Black community as he projected the nation's pain and deterioration.

However, jubilation was tempered by caution. Racial incidents during the campaign, many involving Jesse Jackson, stayed in the minds of many African Americans even through the general election. Clinton's behavior during the campaign and his moderate political agenda made some Blacks wary and led to the lowest turnout of Blacks in the primaries in at least a dozen years. African Americans supported Clinton strongly in the general election, but with Ross Perot siphoning off about 7 percent of the Black electorate, Clinton got the lowest percentage of Black vote since 1960.[3]

As the first post-Cold War president, Clinton faces an uncertain and less stable world than any president in this century. The 1992 election thus was important not only to the future of all Americans, but to the global community as well.

At forty-six, Clinton became the third-youngest president, defeating the sixty-eight-year-old Bush, who was the third-oldest president. As the *National Journal* noted, with the election of Clinton and his forty-four-year-old Vice President Al Gore, the "boomers" were taking charge.

# Election Results

The final results of the election for the major-party candidates were Bill Clinton, 43 percent (43,860,888) of the vote, and George Bush, 38 percent (38,220,427). Among the independents, Ross Perot won 19 percent (19,266,862), Lenora Fulani got about 80,595 votes, and Ron Daniels garnered at least 25,833 votes. [4] By all appearances, Perot's candidacy hurt Bush more than Clinton. Perot, in fact, appears to have stolen enough votes from Bush to have quantitatively impacted, perhaps decisively, the election result.

Overall, Clinton more or less kept pace with the 1988 Dukakis vote. In the *New York Times* post-election analysis, Clinton did better than Dukakis had in only twenty-two out of 103 voter categories, and in many categories did worse. He won 39 percent of the White vote, about the same as Dukakis, and 41 percent of the male vote, also the same (see Table 13-1). Clinton got 2 percent less of the overall vote than Dukakis had. [5]

The Democratic strategy of going after the suburban vote seemed to have limited success although Clinton's core votes came from the traditional Democratic constituencies of union households (55 percent), liberals (68 percent), Blacks (82 percent), Latinos (62 percent), and Jews (78 percent). Across the country, Clinton won or held his own in suburbs that Democrats had lost badly in previous elections. In the notoriously Republican Chicago suburbs, for example, he split the vote with Bush. [6] The same occurred in suburbs in the Philadelphia, Atlanta, and Los Angeles areas. Clinton was the first Democrat to be victorious since 1964 in the five heavily suburban states of California, Colorado, Montana, New Hampshire, and Vermont, and the first to carry Illinois, Michigan, and Ohio together in the same election since 1936.

The Democrats also broke the "electoral lock" held by the Republicans in the South and the West. The centrist message was able to win states previously owned by the Republican ticket, including Arkansas, Georgia, Kentucky, Louisiana, and Tennessee. Clinton won 42 percent of the southern White vote, a significant leap over Walter Mondale and Michael Dukakis, both of whom did not reach 30 percent. [7]

As expected, Clinton did better than Bush or Perot with minority voters. Clinton won the majority of the Latino vote, 62 percent, compared to Bush's 25 percent and Perot's 14 percent, and this vote was critical in a number of states. As political writer Manning Marable points out, the Latino vote in New Mexico (38 percent of the state's vote), California (26 percent), and Colorado (13 percent) "gave Clinton crucial support in helping him win these states." [8] Clinton lost Florida, which undoubtedly was due in no small part to losing the Cuban vote which has traditionally been strongly Republican.

Victories of Latino candidates in the U.S. House increased their representation from eleven to eighteen.

Bush won the majority of the Asian vote, 55 percent, compared to Clinton's 29 percent and Perot's 16 percent. Given the smallness of that vote and its tight geographical concentrations, it was of little help to Bush. The number of Asians in Congress, however, did increase from three to four. Bush's Asian support probably reflects who in the Asian community can and does participate in the electoral process, as well as the socio-economic status of those voters, which is higher than that of Black and Latino voters.

Women out-voted men 54 percent to 46 percent, the largest gap ever. This turnout no doubt helped the large number of women who ran for

## Table 13-1

### November Presidential Election Results
### Gender, Race, Age, and Income Comparisons

| % of Total | Classification | Clinton | Bush | Perot |
|---|---|---|---|---|
| 46 | Men | 41 | 38 | 21 |
| 54 | Women | 46 | 37 | 17 |
| 87 | White | 39 | 41 | 20 |
| 8 | Black | 82 | 11 | 7 |
| 3 | Hispanic | 62 | 25 | 14 |
| 1 | Asians | 29 | 55 | 16 |
| 40 | White Men | 37 | 41 | 22 |
| 46 | White Women | 41 | 41 | 18 |
| 3 | Black Men | 77 | 15 | 9 |
| 5 | Black Women | 86 | 9 | 5 |
| 18 | Whites, 18-29 | 38 | 38 | 4 |
| 2 | Blacks, 18-29 | 83 | 9 | 8 |
| 33 | Whites, 30-44 | 37 | 41 | 22 |
| 3 | Blacks, 30-44 | 81 | 11 | 8 |
| 21 | Whites, 45-60 | 37 | 42 | 20 |
| 2 | Blacks, 45-60 | 79 | 15 | 6 |
| 15 | Whites, 60+ | 47 | 40 | 13 |
| 1 | Blacks, 60+ | 89 | 7 | 4 |
| 21 | Whites in East | 45 | 36 | 19 |

Congress. Out of 106 women who ran, forty-seven (44 percent) won in the U.S. House and six won in the U.S. Senate.

Clinton's win does not reflect either a disalignment from the Republicans or a realignment to the Democrats by the American people. In 1988, 37 percent of the voters identified themselves as Democrats, 35 percent as Republicans, and 26 percent as Independents. In 1992, 38 percent of voters identified themselves as Democrats, 34 percent as Republicans, and 27 percent as Independents.[9] Republicans may have voted for Clinton (11

*table 13-1 continued*

| % of Total | Classification | Clinton | Bush | Perot |
|---|---|---|---|---|
| 2 | Blacks in East | 79 | 14 | 8 |
| 25 | Whites in Midwest | 39 | 39 | 22 |
| 2 | Blacks in Midwest | 86 | 9 | 5 |
| 24 | Whites in South | 34 | 48 | 18 |
| 4 | Blacks in South | 82 | 12 | 6 |
| 16 | Whites in West | 39 | 37 | 24 |
| 1 | Blacks in West | 83 | 7 | 11 |
| 22 | 18-29 | 44 | 34 | 22 |
| 38 | 30-44 | 42 | 38 | 20 |
| 24 | 45-59 | 41 | 40 | 19 |
| 16 | 60+ | 50 | 38 | 12 |
| 14 | $15,000/below | 59 | 23 | 18 |
| 24 | $15-29,999 | 45 | 35 | 20 |
| 30 | $30-49,999 | 41 | 38 | 21 |
| 20 | $50-74,999 | 40 | 42 | 18 |
| 13 | $75,000/above | 36 | 48 | 16 |
| 24 | East | 47 | 35 | 18 |
| 27 | Midwest | 42 | 37 | 21 |
| 30 | South | 42 | 43 | 16 |
| 20 | West | 44 | 34 | 22 |
| 35 | Republicans | 10 | 73 | 17 |
| 27 | Independents | 38 | 32 | 30 |
| 38 | Democrats | 77 | 10 | 13 |
| 30 | White Democrats | 74 | 11 | 15 |
| 6 | Black Democrats | 92 | 5 | 4 |

Source: New York Times, November 5, 1992

percent) or Perot (18 percent), but they maintained their party identification as Republicans. In fact, Clinton won less of the Independent vote (39 percent) than Dukakis did in 1988 (42 percent).

## Impact of the Black Vote on the Presidential Race

Although Black turnout to choose a Democratic nominee in the spring primaries had been depressed, a rebound occurred in the general election as the opportunity to oust Bush from office motivated many, if not most, African American voters. It was estimated that Black turnout increased by as much as one million over 1988, a growth of 4 percent.[10]

In 1992, there were twenty-one million eligible Black voters, of which twelve million were registered—57 percent of all those eligible—and 8.1 million actually voted—67.5 percent of those registered. Clinton won 6,634,327 Black votes (15.2 percent of his total); Bush, 889,970 (2.3 percent of his total); and Perot, 566,345 (2.9 percent of his total).[11]

In some states, Black voters came out in dramatically larger numbers than in 1988. Reports filtered in from all over the nation of long lines at many Black precincts as people waited for two hours or more to vote. Black turnout in Illinois increased by 90 percent over 1988, in Texas by 82 percent, in North Carolina by 51 percent, and in New Jersey by 47 percent.[12] In 1988, Black turnout in Illinois was 364,730, in 1992, it increased to 690,226. In 1988, in Texas, 434,193 Blacks came out to vote; in 1992, the number was 791,642. In fifteen states and the District of Columbia, Black voter increase was significant over 1988. These states included Florida (36.8 percent increase), Georgia (34.0 percent), Louisiana (38.6 percent), Michigan (30.8 percent), New Jersey (46.7 percent), North Carolina (51.1 percent), South Carolina (32.5 percent), and Virginia (30.7 percent).[13]

Some analysts have argued that the Black vote was decisive in several key states. The Joint Center for Political and Economic Studies contends that if Black turnout in New Jersey and Georgia had stayed at the 1988 levels, Clinton would have lost those states.[14] Howard University political scientist Lorenzo Morris argues that Blacks made up over 25 percent of the total Democratic vote and, "in all probability, Clinton would not have won California, New York, Pennsylvania, Illinois, Ohio, Michigan, New Jersey, or Georgia if the Black vote had gone to Bush."[15] These states were all critical in Clinton's winning the electoral college quilt. The Black vote was more than 50 percent of Clinton's vote in Louisiana, which he won, and 59 percent in Mississippi, which he lost.[16]

In terms of party loyalty, those who identified themselves as Black Democrats gave Clinton 92 percent of their vote, the highest of any of the categories analyzed in the *New York Times*. In contrast, White Democrats were a lot less loyal to the ticket. They gave Clinton only 74 percent of their vote. There was somewhat of a gender gap between Black men and Black women. Black men tended to be a bit more conservative, giving Clinton 77 percent of their vote, Bush 15 percent, and Perot 9 percent. Black women, on the other hand, voted strongly for Clinton, 86 percent, while giving Bush only 9 percent and Perot just 5 percent of their vote. Black women were Clinton's third-strongest support group among the 103 categories examined.

Although Clinton and Gore are Southerners, their Black support from the South (82 percent) only bested that from the East (79 percent) and fell below both the West (83 percent) and the Midwest (86 percent). Clinton's and Gore's relative youth also did not seem to have much sway with Black voters. The team did better among Black voters over sixty-years-old (89 percent) than among those under sixty-years-old, where they averaged 81 percent.

African Americans voted for Clinton not only to get rid of Bush, but also because of critical program differences between Clinton, Bush, and Perot; differences that were considered important enough to eliminate Bush and Perot as recipients of the Black vote. Clinton had called for $65 billion for public education, increased opportunities for college attendance, and full funding for Headstart. Bush, the "education president," had cut thirty-two education programs, had proposed a discriminatory voucher system that would greatly exacerbate the crisis of public schools, and had never funded workable programs like Women, Infants, and Children (WIC) and Headstart. Although Perot wailed a lot about the crisis of education and had been involved in some education programs in Texas, his views on the issue did not attract African Americans.

Bush's answer to the Reaganist-driven crisis in the cities was a call for more law and order and budget cuts. During the 80s, federal funding to the cities, under Reagan-Bush-Quayle, fell from $37 billion to $13 billion. This massive federal disinvestment meant that for cities with populations over 300,000 the average federal share of local budgets fell from 22 percent in 1980 to 6 percent by 1989.[17] New York City, for example, saw the federal share of its budget go from 19 percent to 9 percent. Federal shares of the budget in Los Angeles went from 18 percent to 2 percent, in Baltimore from 20 percent to 6 percent, and in Philadelphia from 20 percent to 8 percent.[18] On the other hand, during the campaign Clinton proposed a $50 billion urban rescue plan that theoretically would create jobs and begin to attack some of the entrenched economic and social problems of the cities. Critical to Clinton's proposal is the creation of investment banks that would make low-interest loans available to inner-city communities.

Another major difference between Clinton and Bush, particularly in terms of the Black community, concerned health care. In the 1980s, federal spending for health-care services dropped by 49 percent.[19] Clinton promised "universal coverage" while Bush, who had spent three years without addressing the crisis of health care, proposed tax credits that would have absolutely no effect on the nation's health-care crisis.

To finance his program of reform, Clinton called for increasing taxes on the rich, offering economic investments and incentives, and cutting the military budget, steps long sought by Black activists. Bush, on the other hand, called for a tax cut for the wealthy and only superficial cuts in the military budget.

The Black community also understood that when Bush went, so would the Reaganites and Bushites who dominated nearly all the departments and agencies of the federal government. This meant that the opportunity to move the State Department past the Cold War would be possible. It meant that the Labor Department could actually be headed by someone who doesn't fully represent management and is not anti-union. It meant that the Education Department, which the 1980s Reagan-Bush team had vowed to eliminate, could get on with the job of addressing the problems of education.

As in other recent presidential elections, the Democrats lost the White vote to the Republicans. Clinton won 39 percent to Bush's 41 percent. Perot won 20 percent of the White vote. Although Bush won the plurality of Whites, those numbers reflected habit more than satisfaction. In 1988, Bush had won 59 percent of the White vote, eighteen points above his 1992 total. While Clinton averaged 39 percent of the White vote overall, in some states he did much worse. In Mississippi, for example, he won only 22 percent of the White vote.

Bush's Black support ranged from a low of 5 percent (Black Democrats) to a high of 15 percent (Black men and those between forty-five and sixty). Interestingly, although his Bush's numbers dropped in virtually every other category, his average Black vote remained basically the same as in 1988. Perot's Black support ranged from a low of 4 percent (Black Democrats) to a high of 11 percent (Blacks in the West).

# Other Black Election Results

Below the presidential level, African Americans made significant gains in Congress and in the South. Sixteen new Blacks were elected to the U.S.

Congress, including three who replaced defeated or retiring congresspersons, twelve from southern districts newly created out of the 1990 redistricting process, and Carol Moseley Braun, who was elected to the Senate from Illinois. As a result of these additional congresspersons, membership in the Congressional Black Caucus grew to forty.

In a surprising primary battle, Braun squeaked by in a victory over Democratic incumbent Alan Dixon and multimillionaire Chicago lawyer Al Hofeld. The former state representative and Cook County recorder of deeds stated that she was motivated to run for the office in response to the mistreatment of Anita Hill by the all-White and all-male Senate Judiciary Committee during the Clarence Thomas hearings, and by Dixon's vote for Thomas. Braun's chaotic, underfunded, and generally ignored primary campaign was actually the key to her success. Hofeld viewed the race as primarily between him and Dixon and spent wildly to attack Dixon's record across the state. His success was his downfall, because while Dixon's negatives rose, Hofeld failed to convince voters that he was a viable option. As one writer wrote, "assassins are seldom heroes to the disillusioned followers of the assassinated."[20] Enter Braun with her ready made base of Blacks and women. Braun's strong showing in Chicago (51 percent), suburban Cook County (40 percent), and the counties surrounding Chicago (38 percent) allowed her to cross the finish line with 38 percent of the vote to Dixon's 35 percent and Hofeld's 27 percent.[21] While Hofeld spent $4,854,083 on his campaign, and Dixon $3,284,445. Braun coughed up a paltry $488,538. In the end, Hofeld had spent $12.31 per vote, Dixon $6.52, and Braun $0.88.[22]

Braun is the first Black elected to the Senate since Edward Brooke left office in 1978, only the second Black in this century, and the first African American woman. In the general campaign, she won 55 percent of the vote in a tough race. A number of scandals toward the end of her race and soon after her election tarnished her victory somewhat, but her Black support remained strong throughout. Recognizing her historic candidacy, 95 percent of Black voters cast their vote for Braun in the general election. Braun received strong female support, with 58 percent of the women votes, and significant White support, with 48 percent of their vote. She also did well with eighteen to twenty-nine-year-olds and voters with incomes less than $30,000.[23]

Incumbent Black members of Congress won easily, with 62 percent or higher of the vote in the general election. Black congresswomen did better than the Black congressmen. Each of the female incumbents won by 82 percent or higher.[24]

Except for incumbent Gary Franks, every Black Republican who ran for a seat in Congress lost. Franks, who faced a serious challenge from several quarters in his congressional district, was returned on a plurality of only 45 percent.

New Black congresspersons immediately began to assert themselves into leadership roles when they captured five of the eleven seats in elections for the new class of Congress Democratic Representatives. Eva Clayton was elected president of the class for the first term, and Jim Clyburn will serve as president for the second term of the 103rd Congress beginning in 1994. Cynthia McKinney was chosen to be secretary and Cleo Fields, whose election at age 30 also made him the youngest member of Congress, was elected parliamentarian. Former Chicago Black Panther leader Bobby Rush, won one of the three Whip positions that exist for the class.

Gerald Horne's Senate race in California was an important step forward for the Peace & Freedom Party, despite the fact that he lost. Running against the better financed and media-exposed major-party candidates, he came in third with 287,358 votes (3 percent) behind Democratic Dianne Feinstein's 1,457,889 (59 percent) and Republican John Seymour's 824,674 (34 percent).[25]

Blacks also made important political gains in the South in the 1992 elections. The number of Black members of Congress from the South rose from five to seventeen, and African Americans now represent every southern state except for (notably) Arkansas and Kentucky. This means that African Americans now command 13 percent of all southern U.S. House seats.

In southern state legislatures, Black members rose from 174 in State Houses to 204, and from fifty-two in State Senates to sixty-four. In total, Blacks now account for 14 percent of all southern state legislative seats. There were also some gains outside of the legislative offices. In North Carolina, Democrat Ralph Campbell won the state auditor seat and became the first African American elected to statewide office in the state in this century. He won by 53 percent to 47 percent.

## The Elusive Mandate

Beyond all the political twists and tactical turns of the campaign, it appears that it was the (stupid) economy that did in Bush. Almost half of the electorate, 43 percent, said that the state of the economy was the issue that determined their vote. This is in dramatic contrast to the 24 percent in 1988 who said that the economy was their top issue. Of the 43 percent who saw the economy as a priority, 53 percent voted for Clinton, 24 percent for Bush, and 23 percent for Perot.[26] Based on this criterion, Bush's disastrous handling of the economy, and the loss of hundreds of thousands of jobs during the last two years of his reign, the Republicans had little more than a sliver of a chance of winning. As William Schneider points out in the *National Journal*, among the quarter of the electorate who felt that their economic situation was better—disproportionately the wealthy—Bush beat Clinton by 60 percent to 25 percent. However, for the one-third of the voters who felt that their situation had worsened—a decisive block of voters—Clinton whomped Bush by 62 percent to 13 percent.[27]

Unlike the 1980s, the Bush recession of 1990–92 crossed all regions, racial lines, age categories, and class groupings. With foolish denial, the Bush campaign failed to acknowledge that economic suffering, though uneven, was widespread (and growing) across the nation. While Clinton was more or less able to hold on to the number of votes won by Dukakis in 1988, Bush lost voters in every way possible. For instance, his votes among young people and Independents dropped by 18 and 23 percentage points, respectively. Even among his most loyal supporters, Republicans and conservatives, his votes fell 18 and 15 percentage points, respectively. Bush's numbers tumbled among men; women; Whites; the middle-aged; college graduates; White Protestants; Catholics; and Jews; White born-again Christians; and union households by an average 18.5 percentage points.

The so-called wedge issues—issues that have been used to separate liberals from conservatives, and Blacks from Whites—such as abortion, civil rights, crime, and affirmative action—did not emerge as critical or decisive concerns. One issue that did emerge in a number of states around the country was that of gay and lesbian rights. In Oregon, Measure on 9 was defeated by 57 percent to 43 percent. The anti-gay rights bill wanted to define homosexuality as "abnormal, wrong, unnatural and perverse" and proposed that state and local governments could not "promote, encourage or facilitate homosexuality, pedophilia, sadism or masochism."[28] In Colorado, an anti-gay initiative did pass by 53 percent to 47 percent. The law prohibits the state and local governments from enacting gay rights laws. In addition, it repeals gay rights laws that are already on the books in Aspen, Boulder, and Denver.[29]

Bush's inept and arrogant campaign as well as his political blinders, along with the Perot wild card and the Republican Party's frenzied surge to the right, allowed Clinton to put together a winning coalition of change-desiring voters that included the traditional Democratic base, the moderate-to-conservative Democratic Leadership Council, ideologically varied Independents, disaffected liberal Republicans, and anti-Bush moderate Republicans. The instability of this coalition, however, with its conflicting interests and priorities, mitigates against any mandate worthy of the name. While Clinton's (and Perot's) voters wanted change, it was quite clear that everyone did not want change in the same direction. Differences over raising or lowering taxes, increasing or decreasing funding for social programs, and varying approaches to deficit reductions emerged within moments of Clinton's victory.

Electorate tentativeness toward Clinton was demonstrated in the way in which voters shared their congressional district vote with the top of the ticket. Clinton won 257 congressional districts (59 percent) compared to Bush who won 178 (41 percent). However, this did not translate into straight ticket voting. In ninety-nine districts, voters split their ticket between the House candidate and the opposite party. More important for the Democrats, in only five districts did Clinton's vote surpass the winning House candidate.[30] Bush did even worse, winning only four of those splintered contests. Although Perot won no districts, his presence in the race depressed the vote for Clinton and Bush.

In terms of the thirty-eight Black Democratic House members, Clinton's vote was greater than only two, Ronald Dellums and Lucien Blackwell and a tie with William Clay. This suggests that these Black members will not need Clinton's help for reelection and that Clinton won't have as strong a tradeoff promise to campaign for them in their next election. This will probably mean that Clinton has a diminished ability to pressure them on legislative chp concern.

The 1992 race also witnessed the consolidation of the suburban voter majority, which has profound significance in terms of the Black community and the future of urban policy. As radical city planner and historian Mike Davis has argued, the abandonment of the cities in the 1980s through massive federal disinvestment coincided with the suburbanization of congressional representation. The fuse to the current urban crisis was lit during the last two years of the Jimmy Carter administration, but exploded with atomic-bomb fury during the Reagan administration. As the urban collateral damage grew, inner-city federal representation shrank.

Since the days of Carter, the percentage of urban-based Representatives has declined from one-quarter to one-fifth of the U.S. House of Representatives.[31] This transformation has also occurred as the cities have become less and less White. In 1993, people of color constituted majorities in one in six cities in the United States.[32] In 100 of the 555 cities with populations of 50,000 or more—including Pine Bluff, Arkansas; West Covina, California; Mount Vernon, New York; Laredo, Texas; and most major cities—people of color are a majority.[33] Thus, the identification of urban America as Black and Brown *and* as Democratic became popular common sense that exercises itself through public policy. Federal cuts in aid to the cities are the logical result of the syllogism: urban equals non-White equals Democratic Party. As the *National Journal*'s James Barnes notes, Republican Party affiliation is effectively a direct function of distance away from the inner-cities: "The further a suburb was from the central city, the better Bush generally fared," wrote

Barnes.[34] To be anti-urban, a posture powerfully reinforced by the dominant themes of popular culture and campaign strategies of cynicism and deceit, carries little shame while masking the anti-Black and brown sentiment upon which such a position was often constructed.

The degree that the Clinton campaign was perceived to be less than friendly to urban dwellers, whether this was actually the case or not, was the exact measure by which many suburban voters were attracted to the Democrats. By not explicitly promising urban leaders specific benefits or entitlements during the campaign, Clinton protected his suburban flank from the Republicans, rhetorical bombs about Democratic pandering to the cities. The dilemma for big-city mayors was to assess whether Clinton was engaging in a campaign tactic or really meant what he promised. The mayors rolled the dice and bet that, at worse, Clinton could not be as antagonistic toward the cities as had been Reagan and Bush, and, at best, he would rise to the occasion and aggressively address the spiraling crisis of the cities.

Assessments by most Black observers of why Clinton won focused on the objective conditions that he inherited. If it's true that the key to success is the option to pick your predecessor, then Clinton could not have done better than to pick Bush. Jesse Jackson argues that, although Clinton ran a strong and efficient campaign, he won due to five reasons that had little to do with the candidate, but placed Bush in an inescapable quagmire: the objective economic conditions of the country; the end of the Cold War and its domestic political implications; the Anita Hill factor and its impact on women voters; federal reapportionment that had African and Hispanic American candidates running and stimulating interest at the local level, and a growing sleaze factor surrounding the Bush administration.[35]

The worst economic situation since World War II became Clinton's other running mate. According to Jackson, Clinton was protected from the usual Republican tactic of race-baiting because "diversion through racist appeals to fear by Republicans—i.e., Willie Horton, quotas, etc.—only work when Whites feel relatively economically secure, something they were not feeling on November 3, 1992."[36] Neither did Bush have the Cold War bogeyman with which to scare voters. Reagan and Bush's dubious declaration that they had brought the curtain down on the former Soviet Union had a measurable downside. Though Bush meekly tried to red-bait Clinton during one of the debates, this tactic fell flat.

As Jackson saw it, the Clarence Thomas-Anita Hill hearings galvanized women to come out to the polls. Their 54 percent voting balance as well as a historic number of women who ran for office in 1992 underscored the anger and energy that flowed out of those polarizing hearings and the all-male Judiciary Committee's treatment of Hill. Just as women candidates motivated an increase in women's turnout—disproportionately Democratic—so did the 1990 reapportionment process that created new southern congressional districts with Black majorities. Where Black candidates running for Congress with a chance to make history sparked a greater Black turnout. There was also increased Black voter turnout in districts to ensure that an African American won, which was obviously beneficial to Clinton.

Finally, the growing exposure of Bush's role in the scandals of the Reagan years, in particular the S&L fiasco and the Iran-Contra shenanigans, undermined his claim to moral leadership. Evidence that Bush actually lied about his knowledge of the Iran-Contra deal knocked out the last pillar of respect that many soft Republicans and Independents had for him.

## Lessons of 1992

For the Black community, there were a number of lessons to be drawn from the 1992 election experience. The uniqueness of the 1992 presidential race produced new political phenomena that must now be factored into future strategies and plans concerning Black intervention into the presidential campaign process. Among the issues that arose in 1992 that must now be examined were the problems inherent in having no consensus Black agenda, the impact and significance of the Perot phenomenon, understanding the new dilemmas of race that remain central to U.S. politics, and acknowledging that the contemporary crisis of strategy and Black leadership has deepened.

These are critical differences between 1988 and 1992. In 1988, with Jackson as a candidate, a unity of necessity existed between Black moderates and Black progressives in terms of what platform priorities were needed, how to relate to the nominee, and the manner in which the Black community moved as a block. Although differences, often sharp, did occur, and after the Democratic National Convention Jackson had to struggle to keep his radical supporters in tow, a sense of purpose and mission rallied Black voters and a feeling of growing empowerment inside of the Democratic Party dominated the discourse.

None of these factors existed in the 1992 campaigns. A public and rancorous split happened between Black moderates and Black progressives, with the former backing the Democratic nominee and the latter, as a distinct group, backing no one. Among Black progressives, differences also surfaced over whether to support the Democrats, Clinton, Perot, or one of the Independents.

## *No Consensus Black Agenda*

In the 1992 campaign, for the first time in many years, the Black community failed to gather and develop a "Black agenda" of issues and demands related specifically to the concerns of the Black community. Since the glory days of Fannie Lou Hamer, Black activists inside the Democratic Party have worked closely, if not always cozily, with activists outside to develop and present an agenda of interests, demands, and principles. Although the programs of the Jackson Rainbow campaigns of 1984 and 1988 did not express themselves as solely Black initiatives, his progressive agenda flowed through the prism of the Black experience, and the Black community's concerns were highlighted.

Even though often the agreed upon Black agenda put forth by Black leadership would be compromised in the wheeling and dealing that went on with the various candidates and parties, it served as a guideline by which to measure gains or setbacks vis-a-vis the election. Since no agenda was established in 1992, it was virtually impossible to adequately challenge the political direction and proclivities of the major-party candidates, particularly the Democrats, either in the primaries, debates, convention platforms, or general election. Equally important, it became impossible to mobilize the Black community beyond voter registration and turnout activities, the most benign forms of political participation and activism.

The Democratic Leadership Council developed an extensive agenda and implemented a coherent strategy to realize it, even to the point of appropriating the label "progressive" as flagrant foul against liberals and political radicals. Through their institutions and careful use of the media, Democratic moderates were able to accent their agenda at the expense of a wider discourse that included liberal and progressive ideas on policy. Bludgeoned into muteness by the media reaction to the "liberalism is bankrupt" dogma of Bush and others, and hopeful that a strategy of silence would win the day, Black liberals and progressives failed to effectively challenge the discourse of repudiation as it unfolded during the campaign season.

Jackson's National Rainbow Coalition developed a number of points with which it sought to challenge the aspiring candidates. The NRC and other progressives, however, lacked the capacity to make those concerns and others a concentrated movement among Black, progressive, and working people. Thus, those demands were either acknowledged by the friendlier candidates and then ignored, or just ignored in the first place.

## The Perot Phenomenon

For a number of years, some African American activists have called for an "inside-outside" strategy toward the major parties. These activists have argued that while it is important that African Americans play a critical role within the party structures and attempt to influence the direction and policies of the parties from within, pressure from outside of the authority of those structures is also key in achieving the policy outcomes desired. For the most part, those external pressure vehicles have not existed within the Black community in recent years in any significant way. One of the reasons that Black leaders have hesitated to associate with any motion to act outside of the parties, specifically the Democratic Party, has been the fear of being marginalized and ostracized by White Democratic officials.

The lesson of the Perot movement is that if any constituent effectively and strongly exercises external pressure, not only will that constituency not be isolated, but its inside game will be strengthened. Perot's nineteen million votes clearly have given him the kind of influence and sway that is far from outside of the system. The balance between playing an inside or an outside game is a delicate one, and an error on either side of the equation can be disastrous, yet any minority or dispossessed group that seeks policy reward must also exercise traditional modes of protest, grassroots organizing, and demonstrations. These methods of being heard are as legitimate as running candidates, lobbying, and policy negotiating.

## The Continuing Dilemma of Race

Efforts to "deracialize" U.S. politics, though often from sincere and honest feelings, continue to fail for the simple reason that racial equality remains elusive. The multi-racial Los Angeles festival of resistance, in the middle of the campaign, though not strictly a race riot, underscored the perils of ignoring the festering boil of economic disparity that disproportionately impacts poor communities of color.

What may appear to be a strategic maneuver to win an election, as well as a noble attempt to avoid the seamy side of racial politics, exacerbates the racial and class tensions lying on the surface of United States today. More important is for candidates to engage in an honest dialogue about the reasons behind racial tensions and how communities and the political system can work to erase those tensions. Too many politicians fear, with some justification, that old wounds are best left alone as though they are dealing with some kind of political pregnancy that will somehow self-abort. This view reflects a loss of faith in the masses of American people's ability to overcome these differences, with all the pain and sacrifice (and benefits) that the process would entail.

Racism, discrimination, prejudice, and bigotry will continue at the individual level, for some people, for many, many years to come. However, society can deconstruct the institutional and systemic racism that profoundly shapes the life and life's chances of millions of people of color in the United States and globally. This process would mean encouraging not only a cultural pluralism that is an actual strength of the nation, but also an economic and political pluralism that will arrest the social deterioration that is currently destroying countless communities—of all colors—and further eroding the system's legitimacy.

The changing racial demography of the nation requires different solutions to the various ways in which institutional racism affects distinct groups of people of color. For example, language barriers discriminate disproportionally against people of Hispanic and Asian origins, while housing discrimination overwhelmingly is a racial bias affecting African Americans. Civil rights and racial justice concerns in the future must acknowledge these distinctions. More important, leaders from the different communities of color must bridge the different issues. While the manifestation of racial prejudices and racism may be different, more than likely, they emanate from similar sources—unresponsive politicians, bureaucratic conservatism, corporate profiteering, and consumer-driven culture practices.

## *The Deepening Crisis of Black Leadership*

As scholar Robert Smith has shown, the complaint by the Black community that its leadership is in crisis has a long history and has appeared in every era. At times, that critique has reflected a mistaken sense of the balance of power between African Americans and the dominant social and political institutions, i.e., a failure to appreciate the objective limits on Black leadership. At other times, the criticism has represented a genuine understanding that the times called for a fresh vision, political (and personal) risk-taking, and a more passionate urgency about the conditions of Black life. This is such a time.

By all indices, life for one-third to nearly one-half of all Blacks is in shambles. Many other African Americans live close to that edge. Collectively, half of all Black children are born into destinies of desperation that they escape only by luck, extraordinary individual effort, or crisis intervention. The most optimistic projections are that things will worsen.

While Black leaders have not created these conditions and, indeed, are themselves imprisoned by their implications, they must rise to this heroic

challenge if they are to move history. New visions, new strategies, new
leadership, while always desirable, have become a necessity.

# Chapter 14

# Black Agenda 2000: A Vision, A Plan, A Strategy

Give us a plan of action...a 10 Black Commandments; simple, strong, that we can carry in our hearts, and in our memories no matter where we are and reach out and touch and feel the reassurance that there is behind everything we do a simple, moral, intelligent plan that must be fulfilled in the course of time even if all of our leaders, one-by-one fall in battle.

—Ossie Davis[1]

## The Struggle for a Black Agenda

Which way forward? As Black America stands at the crossroads of its future, this question gnaws at the intestines of the Black community and its leadership. The current state of debilitating circumstances confronting large and growing sectors of the Black community demands a new, imaginative vision, a new agency by Black leadership, and a new sense of historic purpose on the part of African Americans. The construction of a new Black agenda of struggle requires a grasp of past efforts to achieve group solidarity, a sober and critical awareness of the obstacles to group solidarity in the present period, and an exploration of the possible remedies to these obstacles with a turn toward the next century.

The African American effort to collectively forge a "Black agenda" dates back to at least 1830, when fifteen representatives from five states gathered in Philadelphia. These ministers, ex-slaves, business leaders, and newspaper editors, as noted by political historian Hanes Walton, "adopted programs aimed at improving the status and security of the Free Negro population."[2] This process started the National Negro Convention Movement

(NNCM) which would meet six more times between 1831 and 1836. The movement would eventually split over the issue of whether the most efficacious strategy for African Americans was to remain in the United States and struggle for reform, or go to Canada and set up a colony of Black American emigrants.

In 1853, the NNCM again gathered and created a Black agenda of issues and concerns. Among the items demanded by the group was the "complete and unrestricted right of suffrage, opening of admission to all colleges and universities, equal justice for all under the law, and repeal of America's racist laws."[3] They also sought the abolition of slavery.

In the post-slavery era and in the first half of the 20th century, similar agendas and manifestos were developed by Black and civil rights organizations of the period. These included the Niagara Movement, NAACP, Marcus Garvey's United Negro Improvement Association movement, the Nation of Islam, and the National Negro Congress, among others.[4] In addition to serving as fulcrums for ideological debate within the Black community, these programs shaped the ways and manners in which African Americans related to the broader political status quo. In the period prior to Fannie Lou Hamer and the Mississippi Freedom Democratic Party's turbo assault on the Democratic Party, the major-parties ignored these agendas with a snickering impunity.

Since the 1964 Democratic National Convention, Black agendas inside and outside of the body politic have flourished and multiplied. From the insurrectionary platform of the Black Panther Party to the revolutionary writings of Black theorist James Boggs, programs that called for the overthrow of the system challenged the normative paradigms of reform that generally defined Black political participation.[5] The Panthers 10-point program, "What We Want; What We Believe," demanded for African Americans full employment, decent housing, exemption from military service, and the release of all Blacks held in jails and prisons in the United States. It echoed the program of the Nation of Islam, from which it was derived.

While most of these programs made demands on the state, one important document focused on the "White Christian churches and Jewish synagogues" as the source of racial power in the United States. In 1969, led by activist James Foreman, the National Black Economic Development Conference meeting in Detroit issued a Black Manifesto that called for $500,000,000 in reparations to Black America. These funds would be used to establish a southern land bank for Black farmers, publishing and printing facilities, four television networks, a research center, a labor strike fund, a Black university, and to organize welfare recipients. In his speech to the conference, Foreman called for armed revolution and guerrilla warfare in the cities in order to "bring this government down."[6] He called for massive sit-ins and disruptions at White churches and synagogues. It should be noted that the conference was sponsored by the Interreligious Foundation for Community Organizations which received its funding from Christian and Jewish organizations.

Other agendas that specifically sought a response from the political system and the major political parties also developed in the post-1965 era. As Robert Smith notes, these include:

> the platform of the 1972 National Black Convention in Gary, Indiana, the CBC's sixty Recommendations to President Nixon and its watered-down version of the Gary platform called "The Black Declaration of Independence and Bill of Rights," a series of "True State of the Union" messages inserted in the Congressional Record in response to the annual addresses by Presidents Nixon and Ford, a series of recommendations developed by ad hoc meetings of Black Democrats in 1976 and 1980 for presentation to the party conventions and nominees, a series of "mandates" issued by the National Institute of Black Public Officials, meetings of several thousand people convened several times since 1973 by the Joint Center for Political Studies, and, most recently, the alternative CBC budgets developed in response to administration budget proposals since 1981 and the platforms developed by Jesse Jackson as part of his campaigns for president.[7]

One of the most full-blown and ambitious plans to develop which outlined a particular role for every sector of the Black community, from the churches to those incarcerated, was the Black Leadership Family Plan (BLFP) put together in February 1982 by Black organizations and individuals affiliated with the Black Leadership Forum, the Black Leadership Round Table, and the Congressional Black Caucus.[8] Activist Ben Chavis, now NAACP Executive Director, wrote that the plan "comes closest to being a plan that can not only effectuate a progressive change in the condition and state of Black America, but also, I believe that the Plan is a plan for African American self-determination."[9] Among the responsibilities with which it charged the Black community were to "support the Black church, protect the elderly and the youth, excel in education, oppose crime, contribute to the Black Development Fund, buy and bank Black, register and vote, hold your elected officials accountable, support Black family and community life, challenge and boycott negative media and support positive media, secure and defend the Black community, and support mother Africa and the Caribbean."[10]

One of the goals of the plan was the creation of a Black Development Fund that would be built by contributions from the African American community. Based on estimates of how much would be received if the community promised monthly to follow through on its donations, the Fund would grow to about $1.5 billion annually, or roughly 10 percent of the estimated national Black income (circa 1982).

The plan also called for the development of an Action Alert Communications Network, which would respond to crisis situations, and for building coalitions with "Whites, Hispanics and other minorities whose interests coincide with ours."[11] The plan, dependent upon the voluntary participation of the Black community, had little success. Unfortunately, it also made little demand on the institutions and systems of power that exerted decisive control over the lives of African Americans.

In hindsight, the central defect of the BLFP, as well as other agendas cited above was—that despite their necessary and timely response to the perilous state of Black America—they failed to meet the challenge of outlining a wide reaching visionary projection of the future of the nation, the global community as a whole, and the role of African Americans in it. It is within that broad scope that concrete proposals—from inner-city Marshall Plans to grassroots political campaigns—are best articulated and struggled for. Without that vision, no useful or galvanizing strategy (or viable leadership) is possible. A Black agenda for the next century, determined by what is done now, must have clear goals and demands, and concrete objectives, but also much more. It must have an engrossing vision of the new century, rooted in a solid theoretical grasp of the economic, social, political, and cultural dynamics that move society's engine forward, and a commitment to principles of democracy, inclusiveness, and equality. A Black agenda for the next century must promote and constantly recreate a new leadership prepared to tackle the issues and political demands of the coming decades.

Any liberating vision must embrace principles and values that have too rarely existed in Black leadership praxis. These principles include, but are not limited to:

- the goal of democracy and democratic practices both within the movement for social change and equality, and in society as a whole;
- ideological pluralism that allows for a broad array of viewpoints and ideas about the organization of society, including those that are critical of capitalism;
- the leadership of women at all levels of political, cultural, and economic life;
- the inclusive incorporation and recognition of the particular contributions that each generation brings to the struggle;

- the necessity of ongoing coalition with other people of color and Whites that may sometimes mean following the leadership of non-Blacks;
- strict accountability on the part of those who claim to represent Black leadership;
- collective leadership that does not inhibit or repress individual contributions and talents, but also does not elevate individual interests over the collective need.

These principles distinguish an approach to Black leadership that has begun to emerge from the electoral and non-electoral struggles of the last decade. History teaches that strong, charismatic individual leaders will arise regardless of desires to the contrary. The significance and role of those individual leaders must be seen, however, in the proper context. Cuban leader Fidel Castro, in an enlightening interview with former Congressman Mervyn Dymally, provides some instructive insight on this point. He says:

> History is full of leaders. Wherever a human community has existed, a leader has emerged. The times determine what is required of them...It's a mistake, a serious mistake, to think that these qualities are rare or infrequent. I'm convinced of this. For a leader to emerge, the only thing needed is the need for a leader...I believe that human beings, all human beings, have a great capacity for political leadership. What must have happened on countless occasions is that the possibilities for developing those abilities did not arise, because the person lived in a different era, under different circumstances.[12]

The contributions of individual leaders will be significant and, in many instances, decisive. The Black community, however, must not succumb to the dangerous tendency to believe that individual leaders, with their immense strengths and weaknesses, should be allowed to determine the political agenda, strategy, and program of the entire Black community. The appropriate balance between the will of strong, charismatic leaders and the necessity of collective decision making will be a difficult one to maintain, but one that must be struggled for if the movement is to advance.

Where will and where should the Black community be in the 21st century? This is the pivotal question that must be addressed jointly and collectively by the Black community and its leaders at all levels. In a report issued by the Congressional Task Force on the Future of African-Americans, five possible futures—ranging from worst-case scenario to best-case scenario dependent upon changes in the social and economic conditions of the nation—are identified. The five paths are responses to either major economic and social collapse, moderate economic and social collapse, business as usual, moderate economic and social expansion, or major economic and social expansion. In all instances but the last, Black life declines. This means that even if there is moderate economic and social expansion, poverty will continue to rise among African Americans; Black health will most likely deteriorate relative to Whites; communities may become somewhat more stable, but violence is likely to escalate; access to higher education will remain stable or decline; and racism will persist. Racism in this sense is seen as institutional and systemic rather than just as individual practice.

In other words, by even the most optimistic congressional estimate, unless there is major economic and social transformation, "there will be increasing calamity for African Americans."[13] Most Black leaders and, indeed, the African American community as a whole, have expressed similar dismal projections. If the Black community is to be rescued from a calamitous future, it is clear that Black leadership in the days and years ahead must be bolder, more strategically efficacious, and more politically astute than it has ever been in the past. The struggle for and over the future of Black America gets to the very essence of the historic crossroads that African Americans confront.

## Agenda-Setting: The Role of Black Political Leaders

If there is any lesson to learn from struggles and agendas of the past, both successful and not, it is that a progressive vision must be broadly institutionalized and organized and not just left to spontaneity. The need for organization has never been greater. In the words of Martin Luther King Jr., "If we realize how indispensable is responsible militant organization to our struggle, we will create it as we managed to create underground railroads, protest groups, self-help societies and the church that have always been our refuge, our source of hope and our source of action."[14] In this context, progressive Black political leaders and Black intellectuals have distinct roles to play in the restructuring of society toward equality, expanded democracy, and development.

A "Black agenda" for the future must make as a priority a number of concerns both external and internal to the African American community. The crisis of the cities—specifically the material poverty and spiritual despair—must be addressed without delay and with mammoth urgency. More than twenty years ago, writer William K. Tabb wrote prophetically in his classic *The Political Economy of the Black Ghetto* that if there was no change in policies towards the inner-city ghettos, those policies would lead "to racial warfare and urban apartheid."[15] Unfortunately, much of that prediction has come true.

A Marshall Plan of historic proportions must be put forth. An idea that has most aggressively been articulated by the National Urban League, and supported by a wide array of Black political activists and Black, liberal, and civil rights organizations, the Urban League plan calls for a $500 billion investment in the cities over a ten-year period that would "address both long-term economic productivity goals and short-term improvements in social well-being."[16] Seen as both halting the U.S. economic decline and advancing the educational and skill levels of African Americans, the plan advocates comprehensive, long-term financial investments, major reform in education, and the rebuilding of the nation's physical infrastructure. Due to the concentration of African Americans in urban centers and their expanding role in the workforce, "the nation's interests are intimately tied to the conditions of African Americans," writes the National Urban League's Billy Tidwell.[17] Critical of the federal government's lack of investment in youth and infrastructure maintenance and development, and cuts in funding for employment training, the Urban League argues that these trends disproportionately impact African Americans and, unless reversed, will see the nation ill-prepared for economic growth in the coming century.

The focus on improving the skills of the U.S. workforce through education and investment echoes the views of many of the liberals in the Clinton administration. Labor Secretary Robert Reich, for example, argues that in order for the United States to address the increasing "globalization of economic competition" and the "accelerating pace of technological change," it must "reform primary and secondary education...[develop] a system of voluntary skill standards to let citizens improve the payoff to training investments...[create] a school-to-work apprenticeship...[and increase] direct college loans."[18]

As noted earlier, Jesse Jackson's "Rebuild America" plan demands a similar, though larger, outlay of funds. He supports the ten-year, $500 billion proposal of New York financier Felix Rohatyn and would focus spending on jobs for the inner-cities, universal health care, educational equality, and the creation of an American Development Bank that could seed a national network of urban development banks. Reductions in military spending, fair and progressive taxation, sensible borrowing, and judicious investment of workers' pension funds would be the chief means of raising the necessary capital.[19]

In 1992, the Congressional Black Caucus, in response to the Los Angeles uprising called for a $30.90 billion package of emergency aid to the cities.[20] This included $5 billion for job training, $3.45 billion for housing,

$10.09 billion for education, $4.12 billion for economic investment, $7.6 billion for community development, and $640 million for crime and violence prevention programs. The CBC insisted that funding could be obtained by lowering the spending cap on the defense budget while elevating caps on domestic spending. Unfortunately, this proposal (and other legislative maneuvers) required the agreement of President Bush which was not forthcoming. In the end, as mentioned earlier, a scaled-down version of urban aid was finally passed by Congress—and later vetoed by Bush.

Other liberal and progressive groups have also called for large investments in the cities. The Eisenhower Foundation recommends in a wide-reaching 1992 report that the federal government invest $300 billion over ten years to save the cities—"$150 billion in investment for children and youth and another $150 billion for housing, infrastructure, and investment in technology to rebuild cities."[21] Much of this aid would go toward "training for high-technology jobs, affordable housing, and community development banks that can finance inner-city projects," according to Foundation director Lynn Curtis.[22] This program of saving the cities would be financed by "reductions in the military budget, reductions in the budget of the Agency for International Development, taxes on the very rich...higher taxes on tobacco and alcohol—and a gasoline tax as long as lower income groups receive tax credits, so they do not end up paying."[23] The Foundation also calls for the creation of a non-profit Corporation for Youth Investment that would replicate successful youth programs being run by community organizations.

Although the Eisenhower Foundation wants a substantial increase in federal dollars, it is much more hesitant about government involvement in the running of social programs. It states that it has "grave doubts about whether the gridlocked American federal political process would ever or could ever enact informed solutions to the problems of the inner cities and the persons who live in them."[24]

The African American reparations struggle shifted into high gear in 1988 when Congress gave $20,000 each and an apology to Japanese Americans who had been interned in U.S. concentration camps during World War II. In 1971, in another reparation precedent, Congress paid Alaskan natives as a whole $1 billion and gave them forty-four million acres of land.[26] Reparations activists argue that the payments could take many forms such as African-centered education and training institutes, 200 years of tax-exempt status, the provision of land or several separate states, the funding of a return to and settlement in Africa or the creation of viable and profitable manufacturing and production businesses.

In another call for economic salvation and parity, there has been an increased demand for reparations. From the grassroots activities of many nationalists, longtime community activists, and civil right leaders to legislation being proposed by Congressman John Conyers, a demand has been made for financial compensation for 400 years of Black oppression by the United States. Led by the National Coalition of Blacks for Reparation in America (NCOBRA), the movement has held national and local conferences and produced educational materials about reparations. In 1993, NCOBRA hosted the fourth annual Holocaust Memorial and Reparations Conference in Baton Rouge, Louisiana. Seven commissions were established to advance the work of the reparation movement including the commissions on Youth; Legal Strategies; Internationalization; Human Resources; Information Systems and Education; Economic Development and Plebiscites; and Organizational Development.[25]

Conyers' bill, H.R. 40, titled "The Commission to Study the Impact of Slavery and Discrimination Act." was first introduced to Congress in 1993. H.R. 40—the number is symbolic of the post-slavery government promise of "forty acres and a mule"—calls for the establishment of a two-year federal commission that would study the impact of slavery and racism. According to the bill, its purpose is "to acknowledge the fundamental injustice, cruelty, brutality, and inhumanity of slavery in the United States and the thirteen American colonies between 1619 and 1865 and to establish a commission to examine the institution of slavery, subsequent de jure and de facto racial and economic discrimination against African Americans, and the impact of these forces on living African Americans, to make recommendations to the Congress on appropriate remedies, and for other purposes."[27]

Jackson State University economist David Swinton, in testimony before Congress, has also called for a program of reparations as the only means of reversing the economic slide that the Black community is on. He stated, "The only possibility for achieving economic parity in the near future would be large-scale infusions of resources from outside the Black community."[28] Swinton argues that the social and economic forces of the past that contributed to Black economic growth—industrialization, Black migration patterns, liberal public and economic policy, and desegregation—have been historically exhausted and that laissez-faire capitalist market forces or self-help efforts, no matter how sincere and vigorous, will be insufficient to address the absence of resources in the Black community. Why are African Americans missing the necessary power and tools for economic development? As Swinton argues, "The current lack of ownership and limited educational attainment are direct consequences of the racial economic history of America. These historical deficits mean that the resources do not exist in the Black community to overcome the disadvantages that are preventing the attainment of equality."[29] He calls for a reparations program for the Black community of $50 billion annually for twenty years that would "establish a business ownership development fund, a community development fund, and a human capital development fund."[30]

In sum, one of the most persistent demands of the Black liberation movement has been for the systemic redistribution of wealth based on the consensus assumption in the African American community that much of the nation's wealth was accumulated through Black enslavement and continual economic exploitation. From nationalists to liberals to civil rights leaders to leftists and radicals to Black elected officials, a Black Marshall Plan as an economic solution is seen as necessary to even begin to ameliorate the hardships faced by significant segments of the Black community. This demand stands in sharp contrast with the view held by most Whites, even those who support equality and the elimination of racism in U.S. social life, that any such transfer of funds contradicts fundamental principles of the Protestant Ethic and U.S. creed of "earned" wealth. Underscoring the resistance to Black reparations or massive emergency aid to the inner-cities are the current tortured contours of U.S. capitalism in the face of international changes and challenges that have reverberated in domestic economic suffering that has crossed all racial lines and geographical boundaries.

This period of transformation through which U.S. capital is working its way provides a somber context in which to view the reformist and radical economic proposals being sought by Black leaders and activists. Reforms, though necessary, have in the past insufficiently addressed what amounts to the recurring structural crisis of capitalism, i.e., the inability of a system based on profit to rationally eliminate unemployment, poverty, and perpetual crisis. The historic challenge confronting Black leaders (and others) is to fashion a program of economic reform that, given the global economic crisis, must assume a long period of instability and transition that at the same time progressively meets the needs of the nation's poor and disadvantaged. While it is clear that the socialist models of the Soviet Union, Eastern Europe, and elsewhere did not have the answer to either questions of economic development, mass democracy, or political pluralism, it is equally clear that Western-style capitalism, as noted even by Black leaders of the past such as W.E.B. DuBois and Martin Luther King, Jr., has reached its historic limits. Not only has economic restructuring become necessary, but the political will and movement to create the kind of economic democracy that begs for deliverance must be mobilized, organized, and institutionalized. The next century will witness the abandonment of both leftist and rightist models of political institutions that, in effect, undermine democratic participation and act out assumptions that can't serve to move humanity forward.

Much of the debate within the Black political community over whether African Americans should remain in the Democratic Party, migrate to the Republican Party, or participate in third party efforts misses the point. The further democratization of the nation, essential to the advancement of the Black community and other ill-served sectors of the society, will not be achieved through traditional political party activities, be they right, left, or center. A genuine democratic flowering will witness numerous political models—some in the form of parties, others not—that will correspond with the real needs, interests, and political culture of those most in need of those vehicles of empowerment. This is not a call to or sanctioning of anarchy or social chaos; it is a recognition that traditional political party structures and cultures are non-democratic in nature and depreciate the contributions of those who are unable to negotiate the political and ideological norms that inevitably develop.

Participation in party politics should not be abandoned, however. Indeed, a more intensified and strategic involvement in major- and minor-party politics is necessary. As long as the major parties determine policies and institutions that affect the lives and destinies of tens of millions of people, it is suicidally foolish to surrender opportunities to shape, influence, or control those decisions. Third-party efforts have also been important to African Americans. As vehicles of radical anti-racist proposals, third parties have the potential to construct the type of coalition politics that can collectively pressure policy makers to institute necessary reforms and broaden the level of participation of those dispossessed in the governance of society. These activities do not prevent the creation of other political forms that more appropriately address and meet the interests of local, state, and national groups. Specifically, these emergent forms, already in existence from coast to coast, can more effectively attack the problems of the current system in ways that are more progressively democratic, egalitarian, and concrete.

The Alabama New South Coalition (ANSC) is an important example of a progressive effort to build a statewide organization that is capable of engaging in electoral and non-electoral struggles. Born out of the 1984 Jesse Jackson for President campaign, the ANSC organized to challenge the conservative Whites and Blacks within the state's Democratic party who had historically blocked progressive Black participation and empowerment. Comprised of farmers, civil rights activists, elected officials, and others, the mostly multi-racial organization began to win electoral victories at the local and county levels as well as to launch and become involved in economic projects that focused on the immediate and long-term needs of the state's poor and working population. Their work helped Jackson win big in Alabama in 1984—when he faced harsh opposition from the local Black Democratic power-wielders—and in 1988.[31]

The need to build coalitions will grow in the years ahead. There are compelling political and practical reasons why African Americans dare not attempt any "go-it-alone" strategies. African Americans and Whites will continue to be a shrinking proportion of the population as Latino and Asian population groups grow. In 1990, African Americans represented 12.5 percent of the population, non-Latino Whites 74.2 percent, Latinos 9.5 percent, and Asians 3.8 percent. The Census Bureau estimates that by 2050, the non-Latino White population will have shrunk to 53 percent while the African American population will have increased slightly to 15 percent. The big gains, however, will be in the Latino community, which will grow to 21 percent, and among Asians, who will increase to about 10 percent. The Native American population will remain about 1 percent.[32]

These new racial configurations will either create new tensions between racial and national groups, or become an opportunity for a truly pluralist, non-racist foundation upon which to build U.S. society. It should be noted that differences between African Americans and other groups may become secondary to differences within national ethnic groups, as Latinos break down into various Central American groups who will probably occupy a lower socio-economic status than the older Mexican or Cuban communities. In a similar way, older Asian immigrants, such as the Chinese, Korean, and Japanese American communities will probably separate from the newer Southeast Asian groups of Vietnamese, Cambodians, and others. Black leaders will need to grapple with the complexities of these new relationships even while confronting classical forms of racism and discrimination.

In the short run, political reform within the present system is desperately needed. This includes everything from campaign finance reform—not normally seen as a "Black" issue—to ballot access. In terms of electoral politics, easing access to voter registration and voting at every level still is an unfulfilled goal. The Motor Voter bill, signed into law by President Clinton, is a significant step in the right direction. The new law allows for registration when drivers' licenses are renewed, at military recruitment centers, and at social service centers, thereby reaching millions of unregistered voters. Supporters of the bill also wanted unemployment centers included as sites, and sought to have codified into law provisions that would allow same-day registration for federal elections. These recommendations were gutted in the congressional bargaining that surrounded the bill. Although organizers could claim victory in getting the bill passed, they were quick to point out that it does not address the more numerous instances of democratic violations which occur at the local and state levels. In too many jurisdictions around the nation, it is still a burden to register and vote. Inconvenient locations, insensitive registration hours, and lack of registrars dilute the voting potential and democratic involvement of millions of voters.

Also, ballot access provisions that prevent or make it difficult for non-major-party or individuals to get on the ballot must be overturned. Currently, the leading advocates of this reform have been activists affiliated or tied to the New Alliance Party, with which many Black activists have difficulty working. In 1992, non-major-party Black federal candidates Ron Daniels, Gerald Horne, and Gwen Patton all struggled to get on the ballot against unfair state ballot access laws. An expansion of democracy clearly means equalizing the playing field so that candidates not tied to the either Democratic, Republican, or traditional state parties can get on the ballot without extraordinary and biased effort.

Outside of the electoral arena, other political goals and strategies must also be applied. Historically, protest has been a critical part of the arsenal of weapons used by African Americans to advance their agenda. On civil rights issues, such as statehood for the District of Columbia, it is clear that nothing short of massive and ongoing protests that disrupt and create an atmosphere of political disequilibrium will shock the national consciousness into addressing the concerns being raised.

Howard University political scientist Ron Walters often points out the difference between *symbolic* protest and *disruptive* protest. In the former, there is a preemptive agreement with the forces of the state or target of the action about the limits and parameters of the protest. Pre-arranged arrests or bargains ensure that neither side is made uncomfortable for any extended length of time. More important, there is a tacit, though often explicit, understanding that there will be no fundamental change in the behavior of those being protested against. In disruptive protests, however, the goal is to stop business as usual over a prolonged period or as long as necessary. Protesters are willing to disobey the rules of the game and go beyond what is acceptable to the state or the opposition. The civil rights sit-ins are an example of disruptive protests that confronted a hostile populace and an even more hostile police apparatus. Although marches, rallies, and symbolic protests have been and remain important weapons in the arsenal of resistance, protest leaders must also be prepared to advance peaceful tactics that disrupt systems of discrimination and inequality. A march on Washington, whether with 100,000 or one million people, does little to challenge the system except in symbolic or rhetorical forms. On the other hand, a poor peoples' march on the nation's capital with the commitment to pitch tents and stay until legislation is passed that addresses the concerns of those constituents quite dramatically challenges policy makers and political leaders to respond.

# The Struggle Within

Black and White conservatives have consistently declared that neither Black nor civil rights leaders have addressed the issue of Black behavior, and they demand internal changes. In fact, in no period in history have Black leaders avoided the need for internal and external change. In the 1980s, neoconservatives were able to set the parameters of the political debate about the value and utility of the Black and civil rights agendas. At the same time, cuts in social programs, from housing to education, removed any semblance of a social safety net and contributed fundamentally to the very real deterioration in material conditions in Black life, inaugurating an era of internal violence and self-destruction virtually unparalleled in Black history. Yet, as argued below, these changes must also be seen as a form of (negative) response and resistance to racism and Reaganism.

It is within this context that the current wave of apocalyptic behavior has matured and must be understood. While Black political leaders must be careful not to fall into the ideological trap of Reaganism, and like some Black conservatives consistently blame the victim, it is critical that the crisis of spirit and escalating self-destructive behavior that has come to grip too many Black communities be addressed. In particular, the savage Black-on-Black violence, dramatized brazenly in Hollywood films and rap music, poses a new challenge for Black leaders and political activists, who must propose concrete resolutions to a situation that has left Black, Latino, and poor communities terrified and open to draconian, final solutions.

Professor Amos Wilson in his *Black-on-Black Violence* reminds us that Black violence, criminal behavior, or self-destructive proclivities do not happen in a vacuum. He provides some valuable insight in his argument that racism has fueled false notions of a Black criminal class, fostered the criminalization of Black male youth, and led to the deadly and pathological consequences being played out on the streets of the cities. He contends that "Black-on-Black criminality and violence represents quests for power and outraged protests against a sense of powerlessness and insignificance."[33] He argues that this behavior operates as a response to racism and in the interest of racism. This perspective echoes the views of other Black political psychologists such as Frantz Fanon, William Grier, and Price Cobbs.[34] Wilson recommends as a preventive measure the "appropriate socialization of children, equitable and fair organization and distribution of national and community resources, the provision of Afrocentric educational training and of equitable occupational opportunities."[35] While Wilson's perspectives are important in framing the context in which Black violence and self-destruction occur, they do not address the means by which communities and Black leadership can reverse these trends in a timely manner.

Writer Cornel West has been another voice attempting to sort through what he terms the destructive "nihilism" that has created widespread despair, frustration, and fear among many African Americans. He states in frustration that "the major enemy of Black survival in America...is neither oppression nor exploitation, but rather the nihilistic threat—that is, loss of hope and the absence of meaning."[36] He and others point out that African Americans went from having the lowest suicide rate in the nation before the 1970s to having the highest suicide rate in the nation in the 1990s. West believes that there is a direct link between the self-destructive and outer-destructive behavior of young Blacks, capitalist market relations, and the crisis of Black leadership. An omnipresent corporate and consumer culture has promoted a market morality that places little value on human life, caring, or service. He concludes that "new models of collective Black leadership" must emerge that promote an "affirmation of Black humanity" that rescues Blacks from the despair and hopelessness that prevents movement forward. This collective leadership, West argues, "must exemplify moral integrity, character, and democratic statesmanship within itself and within its organizations."[37] Only in this manner can Black leadership intervene effectively and positively in halting the murderous cycles of Black violence permeating the community.

Dr. Deborah Prothrow-Stith has developed one of the most useful and comprehensive approaches to addressing the problem of violence in the Black community. She makes the case that escalating violence in U.S. society, not exclusive to but including Black-on-Black violence, should be viewed primarily as a health emergency. In that sense, the problem should be approached in the same way that successful efforts at reversing negative social trends, such as drunk driving, smoking, and teenage pregnancy, have been targeted. She states forcefully that "No single form of intervention, no single institution can bring about the kind of change needed to restore a sense of safety and order to everyday life. Comprehensive, multi-institutional, community-wide solutions that address the violent behavior of the young, while redressing the social conditions in which violence flourishes are needed."[38] In her writings, she cites numerous examples of programs that have been initiated that are working to reduce violence and turn communities, many of them poor, around.

There are specific tasks and challenges confronting Black intellectuals in this period also. Black progressive intellectuals, similar to the Democratic Leadership Council, Perot, and conservative Republicans, need to create institutions of power and influence that vie for a place on the nation's political landscape. These efforts face considerable difficulties, not the least of which are financial, political, and organizational. As discussed below, numerous efforts have been made to establish some of the institutions suggested, but have failed for various internal or external reasons. It is critical that Black progressives learn from those failures and commit to putting in place the building blocks of a social movement that can create, sustain, and develop the kind of institutions that are sorely needed in the new world that African Americans face.

## Progressive African American Think Tank

A number of efforts have been tried in the past few decades to create a progressive African American think tank. One important attempt was the experience of the Atlanta-based Institute of the Black World. Begun in 1969, the IBW was home to many of the nation's most stellar Black radical intellectuals. Among its associates and leaders were historian Vincent Harding, political scientist Bill Strickland, activist Howard Dodson, and radical theoretician James Boggs. Black radical scholars from other nations also participated in the IBW's work, including the brilliant Marxist historian Walter Rodney and author, activist, scholar, and the "father" of Black radicalism, C.L.R. James.

The IBW's mission was to "develop politically conscious print and audio materials for the arena of Black education [and] impart the philosophy, values, knowledge, and skills needed to understand ourselves and the world in which we live and to change both."[39] Along these lines the IBW produced papers; distributed a newsletter, *Black-World-View*; and held conferences on critical domestic and international issues facing the Black community. The IBW was also important as a forum for debate and the airing of political differences in an atmosphere of solidarity. It ultimately succumbed to a lack of resources and closed down.

Today, the major national Black think tank is the Joint Center for Political and Economic Studies. Begun in 1970 with a $820,000 Ford Foundation grant, the Center grew out of two conferences of Black elected officials in the late 1960s.[40] These officials recognized that as their leadership role and their ranks expanded, there would be an increasing need for technical assistance and research. Thus, in the early years of the Center, its principle task was to provide those services, but its responsibilities soon grew much larger. One task has been to track the growth and development of Black elected officials, resulting in the annual publication of its *National Roster of Black Elected Officials* and the sponsoring of conferences on a wide range of political and policy issues. It also produces a monthly newsletter, *Focus*, and policy papers from its own in-house scholars as well as from outside academics. Politically, the Center has attempted to remain nonpartisan. Members of its staff and board have been Republicans, Democrats, and Independents.

There are some smaller efforts, such as the William Monroe Trotter Institute located at the University of Massachusetts-Boston. The institute is headed by scholar and activist James Jennings and has focused much of its work on identifying and documenting efforts at the grassroots community level by Black and Latino activists. Jennings strongly advocates that people of color and progressives participate in third-party politics. In a paper he delivered at Harvard University's Kennedy School of Government, he charged that the major parties have ignored all findings and studies that demonstrate that racism remains a serious problem in the United States and that "it is essential that an organizationally significant third party or independent national force emerge in this country's political landscape."[41]

Despite these valuable and useful efforts, there remains a need for a nationally focused, appropriately funded, politically broad, independent, and explicitly progressive African American think tank. This new think tank would be distinct from current efforts in a number of ways. Its first task, through the use of a wide cross-section of scholars, would take up the challenge of vision and theory necessary to guide the Black community in the years and decades ahead. The liberal paradigm is no longer adequate to addressing the complexities of race, class, gender, and nation that confront African Americans in the waning years of the 20th century. A bold and wide debate on these and many other theoretical and ideological questions should be generated as soon as possible.

This new think tank would also be more organically linked with the day-to-day struggles being waged in the Black community and in other sectors of the nation and the world. This means not only being in touch with the circles of leadership and movements occurring within those spheres, but also bringing forth a challenging, yet cooperative intellectual spirit that echoes the tradition established by scholar-activists such as W.E.B. DuBois, Johnnetta Cole, and Walter Rodney, as well as grassroots intellectuals such as James Boggs and Fannie Lou Hamer.

Public policy concerns will also play a key role in the work of this new think tank. Black progressive intellectuals must demonstrate an ability not only to develop the "big picture," but also solid proposals and detailed plans for meeting the needs of the Black community and other communities in trouble in the United States and beyond. What should distinguish these efforts from others is the content of the materials produced and the means by which political and theoretical products develop. A progressive think tank must also discover methodologies for building organic links between itself and communities of color that foster democratic participation between intellectuals, activists, and others. This does not mean, of course, surrendering the discipline and scholarly standards necessary to produce quality documents. However, the separation of intellectuals, and activists from the community should be bridged as much as possible.

Finally, though unabashedly progressive, this new entity must also build ties with other progressive and liberal think tanks. Rather than see these other institutions as rivals, it is more useful and productive to search for means by which the exchange of ideas, scholars, and resources can happen. Additionally, it is unnecessary to reproduce or duplicate the expertise that a number of these institutes have demonstrated on questions and issues of the nation. The Eisenhower Foundation, for example, has produced excellent reports and studies on urban issues. The Institute for Research on Poverty, based at the University of Wisconsin-Madison, does perhaps the best research on poverty in the nation.

In 1992, a number of Black scholars and activists met in an effort to put such an institution in place. In a gathering in Washington, D.C., sponsored by the Center for a New Democracy, a broad array of Black scholars and activists spent two days discussing the state of African American politics and means of addressing the problems facing the Black community. Among those involved were professor Manning Marable, who chaired most of the meeting; voting rights activist Greg Moore; anti-apartheid leader Sylvia Hill; National Rainbow Coalition International Affairs Director Jack O'Dell; human rights activist Keith Jennings; political scientists Linda Williams, Ron Walters, and Bill Strickland; political consultant James Steele; women of color rights advocate Linda Burnham; and southern organizers Gwen Patton and Leah Wise.

Although there was strong agreement on the idea of a progressive African American research center, the meeting and several follow-up meetings were inconclusive in pushing the plan forward. Financial considerations and the difficulty of bringing together the major participants, who were spread out across the country, were the major factors in slowing down the effort to launch the institution. In 1993, Marable became director of the Institute for Research in African-American Studies at Columbia University in New York City. The position, as he envisioned it, will allow him to implement many of the proposals discussed in the center meetings of the year before, including organizing public forums, conducting annual conferences, organizing programs in Washington, D.C. and in Congress, and identifying grassroots leaders to become involved in the institute's activities.[42] Most of the activists and scholars who had met with Marable committed to working with him in his new position.

## Domestic Public Policy Lobby

Former Gary, Indiana Mayor Richard Hatcher has correctly suggested that an African American domestic public policy lobby be established. A number of Black and civil rights organizations already do lobbying work in Washington, D.C. The NAACP, for example, has a national office in Washington that focuses solely on tracking and lobbying congressional legislation. Headed by Wade Henderson, a politically astute and strategic thinker, the NAACP national office has been instrumental in leading the fight against

Reaganism, the Clarence Thomas nomination, and other campaigns in the interest of people of color and working people.

Another powerful people-oriented lobby has emerged in the Children's Defense Fund (CDF). Initiated and headed by Marian Wright Edelman, the CDF has produced numerous studies and documents on the impact of poverty on the nation's children. Edelman's strategy is to advance a civil rights agenda through the vehicle of children's rights, where there is little organized opposition. The CDF's star rose considerably with the election of Clinton. Hillary Clinton is a former CDF staffer and chair of its board as well as a friend of Edelman's. Although Edelman was not offered nor did she seek a position in the new administration, with the Clintons in the White House, it is likely that the CDF agenda will at least get a strong hearing.

In 1993, the CDF initiated the Black Student Leadership Network. The network seeks to involve young African Americans in the resolution of the social and economic crises effecting the Black community, particularly its young. Leaders of the BSLN stated in their newsletter, *WeSpeak!*, "Only by building a cross-class, multi-generational social movement within the Black community can we achieve the transformation in government policy and private initiative necessary to save Black children, their families, and communities."[43]

In establishing such a lobby, it is instructive to examine the development and achievements of TransAfrica, which was begun in 1977 by Randall Robinson, a former staffer to ex-Congressman Charles Diggs, who was then Chairman of the House Subcommittee on Africa. TransAfrica was launched to lobby Congress on issues concerning Blacks in the diaspora. Although already widely respected by policymakers and anti-apartheid activists, TransAfrica received its greatest accolades in 1984 when it started a wave of protests against the South African apartheid government on Thanksgiving eve. Robinson, Civil Rights Commissioner Mary Frances Berry, and then-D.C. Delegate Walter Fauntroy were arrested in the South African embassy in Washington, D.C. That action started a prairie fire of similar protests aimed at pro-apartheid targets around the nation, leading to thousands of arrests over the next year or so.

As a consequence of that movement, the anti-apartheid movement won its most important victory to date with the passage of the Anti-Apartheid Act of 1990, which imposed sanctions against the South African apartheid government. This bill would later be rescinded by President Bush, although anti-apartheid activists complained that the release of ANC leader Nelson Mandela and the unbanning of South Africa's anti-apartheid militant organizations did not constitute sufficient change to end U.S. sanctions. What was important, however, was the clear relationship between protest and policy-making on an issue that originally had a low priority on the legislative agenda.

## Political Training Institute

In the 1970s and 1980s, the Center for Third World Organizing functioned as a training center to prepare activists of color to help communities organize themselves to address issues. Led by Hulbert James on the East Coast, and Gary Delgado on the West Coast, CTWO followed in the tradition of other organizing institutes such as the Highlander Center in Tennessee—attended by activists such as Martin Luther King, Jr. and Rosa Parks. CTWO was different, however, in that it also provided its trainees with a historical and political framework through which to understand the struggles that they sought to engage themselves in.

Today, more than ever, there is a need for a training institute that prepares the next generation of organizers and leaders. The campaign and electoral experience garnered in the last thirty years needs to be codified, criticized, and translated into lessons of struggles for the young generation and those to come.

Preparation for electoral and non-electoral campaigns has to become a priority if implementation of public policy goals of concern to the African American and other dispossessed communities is to be efficacious. The political power to win public policy victories will, to a great degree, be conditioned by the application of the science of organizing. Among the skills that need to be transmitted are: building coalitions, ballot access skills, organizing mass mobilizations, lobbying strategies and tactics, voter registration and turnout techniques, campaign management, fundraising, and media skills.

## New Publications

There are a number of publications that are needed in the new political environment of this decade and those to come. While some of these may come from the think tanks described above, that is not necessarily so. First, it is critical that progressive publications be established and promoted that are independent of narrow ideological and political concerns. That independence will guarantee a wider receptivity, distribution, and dissemination of ideas and perspectives.

In addition, even if think tanks and other institutions are producing newsletters and other publications such as journals, fact sheets, and policy studies. The expansion of avenues of open debate is badly needed in the current atmosphere, where intellectual isolation prevails and few ideas are contested and critically examined.

What are some of the types of publications needed? First, a newsletter or journal that tracks the legislative and political activities of Black elected officials and Blacks in the administration would be welcome. The newsletter *Black Congressional Monitor* serves this purpose to some degree. However, it is difficult for those outside of Washington to obtain, and mainly reports the legislative activities of Black members of Congress without comment or analysis. Black publications, like *Emerge* or the Joint Center's *Trendletter*, strive to be more analytical, in-depth, and prescriptive.

Given the large body of Black elected officials, at all levels, and the number of African Americans who are in decisionmaking power within the administration and federal bureaucracy, it is way past time for systematic study and examination of these political activities to happen. Among the issues to look at include policy and legislative initiatives, ideological and political trends, staffing, and relations with other political groups. The publication would also be an opportunity for intellectuals, activists, Black elected officials and others to elaborate a theory of governing and politics that heretofore has had little public forum in the Black community.

There is also a need for a public policy journal. Ideas by Black intellectuals, interest groups, and policymakers about everything from housing to health care to foreign aid have been dispersed and difficult to identify, if they exist at all. This journal would allow for the ongoing debate over what policy initiatives benefit or harm the Black community. To some degree, *The Black Scholar* engages in those types of discussions, but its concern with a broader array of political issues makes it unable to solely concentrate on public policy issues.

The producers of the aforementioned journals could and should also produce special reports on specific public policy issues from an African American perspective. These reports could be developed as needed.

What is needed, more than ever, are more political and theoretical journals similar to *The Black Scholar* and the former *Black World*. Written forums of debate, which those journals would allow, would provide the type of public exchange among Black intellectuals that has all but disappeared.

## Clinton's Pledges, Congressional Actions, and Black Interests

What can Black America expect from Congress and the Clinton administration in the years ahead? How will the growth of the Congressional Black Caucus to forty members and the appointment of a number of African Americans to high-level Cabinet positions affect the Black community?

What are the strengths of the CBC, its weaknesses, and its contradictions? What posture should the Black community take toward the Supreme Court given the possibility that it is unlikely that another Black will be appointed in the near future? The answers to these questions must inform, though not determine, Black political activity and strategy over the rest of the decade, if not beyond.

Despite popular notions to the contrary, candidate Bill Clinton made a number of policy pledges that, if implemented, would have a dramatic impact on the Black community. Some of his initiatives would begin the necessary process to reverse the damaging effects of the Reagan and Bush years, while others have caused many Black activists and scholars to raise questions about their usefulness and political purpose. How Clinton will execute these promises—and, as writer James Steele notes, the term "execute" has a double meaning—will be a function of the balance of forces and pressures from Clinton's left and from his right. On the left will be the Black community, labor, women's groups, and other liberals and progressives calling for social reform and government intervention to ameliorate poverty and inequality. On Clinton's other side will be Democratic moderates and conservatives, the minions of Ross Perot, and the wounded, but breathing Republican Party.

In terms of civil rights and voting concerns, Clinton pledged to oppose racial quotas, raise caps on damages in workplace discrimination cases, support D.C. statehood, sign the Motor Voter bill that would ease access to voter registration, and appoint more minorities and women to top-level administration positions.[44] On economic issues, Clinton stated that he would raise taxes on the wealthy, offer middle-class families tax cuts, end tax incentives that encourage and allow companies to export their plants and jobs, and raise the minimum wage—all initiatives generally supported by the Black community. Given the escalating crisis in Black health care, as noted in Chapter 1, Clinton's pledge to create a fair, affordable and quality universal health care system was well-received in the Black community. True to his word, Clinton gave universal health care a high priority in the early days of his administration and guaranteed that it would remain so by placing Hillary Clinton in charge of developing the administration's health care proposal. Beyond just being the President's wife, Hillary Clinton is an accomplished and respected lawyer. Her position as former chair of the board of the Children's Defense Fund demonstrates a strong commitment to social advocacy and reform. She convened meetings about the nation's health care crisis in Washington, D.C., and around the nation—many involving people of color—and helped to create an atmosphere where even formerly reluctant conservatives agreed that universal health care was necessary although major disagreements exist on how to bring that about and whose interests will be served.

One early incident in the new administration that shocked many Blacks who had supported Clinton involved his withdrawal of Lani Guinier for the nomination of assistant attorney general for civil rights. A longtime friend of both Bill and Hillary Clinton, Guinier came under attack from conservatives—Republican and Democratic—some Jewish organizations, and some members of the Senate Judiciary Committee, almost immediately after being nominated by Clinton. Their purported criticism had to do with her views on how to make voting rights more effective for African Americans.

Guinier was a veteran of legislative battles over voting rights. From 1977 to 1981, she served in the Carter administration as special assistant to Assistant Attorney General for Civil Rights Drew Days. She also worked for the NAACP's Legal Defense and Education Fund for seven years as the director of its Voting Rights Project. As a professor of law at the University of Pennsylvania, she had written numerous articles on the complicated judicial concepts for correcting voting rights violations. In particular, she advocated "cumulative voting" and "legislative super majority requirements" as possible remedies in some situations where the Voting Rights Act had been repeatedly and brazenly violated. She stated, in her defense, that "the Voting Rights Act has not yet completely succeeded in giving all Americans an equally effective voice in their government."[45]

Guinier advocates cumulative voting as a means to give voters more power to select leaders of their choice. In cumulative voting, all voters are given the name number of votes to cast and can choose to give any one candidate one vote, more than one vote, or all of the votes that they have available. For example, if three seats are available for a school board election, each voter will be given three votes and can give them to one candidate or split the votes among three candidates. The value of this voting method is that it gives each voter the same amount of power and allows for fairer selection of representation. Black voters in rural Alabama were able to elect black candidates in areas where blacks had never been able to win—even though blacks were a substantial part of the local population—when winner-take-all elections ruled. This voting method has been used in Illinois, Alabama, and other states and been approved by federal courts and even the Reagan and Bush Justice Departments.

Guinier describes the Alabama case: "Cumulative voting makes it impossible for any one bloc of voters to capture an unfairly high number of seats. Under the old system, 51 percent of Chilton County's voters could capture all the seats all the time, completely shutting out the other 49 percent of the voters. Under the cumulative system, however, many more voters can elect the candidates they want. A majority of the voters still elects a majority of commission, but smaller groups get some representation too. This is not minority rule; it's democratic fair play." Guinier's advocacy of supermajority minority rule; it's democratic fair play." Guinier's advocacy of supermajority voting under certain circumstances was the basis of her being accused of being undemocratic by some conservatives. Supermajority voting means that more than 51 percent is required for victory. She points out, however, that supermajority voting is used broadly throughout the United States including in the U.S. Senate where accusations against her were most shrill. In order to close debate on the Senate floor, for example, three-fifths of the Senate must vote yes.

The purpose of supermajority, Guinier argues, is to encourage broad-based consensus and to "oblige the majority to consult with and take into account the viewpoint of a substantial minority." She contends that while she has "never suggested that supermajority requirements be imposed wholesale on localities against their will," she has suggested that voluntary supermajority rules should be considered in efforts to resolve voting rights violations. She cites the example of Mobile, Alabama where the legislature agreed that decisions of the new seven-member city council would require a five-to-two majority—more than 51 percent—thereby creating greater consensus on issues coming before the council.

Guinier had also played a key role in several well-known civil rights cases including the case of the Wilmington 10 (described in Chapter Four) and the trial of Alabama civil rights activists who were unjustly accused of voting infractions. Despite the fact that the Clintons are her friends, she also filed a suit against Clinton's Arkansas for imposing racially discriminatory laws that disenfranchised Blacks in one poor, delta county.[46]

As pressure built from the right to scuttle her nomination, Black leaders belatedly rallied to her defense, many seeing it as a line in the sand for Clinton in terms of defense of Black interests. Both NAACP leader and Guinier friend Ben Chavis and Jesse Jackson went to the White House, though neither was able to meet with Clinton. The Congressional Black Caucus, led by its chair Kweisis Mfume, also warned the president not to pull the nomination. All of these leaders and others held several press conferences in a last-ditch effort to save Guinier.

In the end, however, the Clinton administration decided that it was better to face the wrath of Black leaders than to promote a nomination that it felt would be divisive, probably defeated, and, more important, damage the prospects of passage of other key legislation. Clinton stated, to the disbelief of many, that he had not actually read Guinier's writings until the very day that he pulled her name and that once he did, he could no longer support her nomination because her views "clearly lend themselves to interpretations that do not represent the views that I expressed on civil rights during my campaign, and views that I hold very dear."[47] He argued that her remedies were "inappropriate" and "anti-democratic."[48] This characterization was refuted by no less than the usually politically pragmatic *Washington Post*, which stated that, contrary to her critics, "she is most definitely not the 'anti-democratic' ogre of their portrayal [and] she deserves the hearing she was denied."[49]

The incident created a great deal of turmoil among Black leaders who felt betrayed and embarrassed. Many stated that Clinton's actions echoed the Sister Souljah controversy and that Guinier had become another Black woman sacrificed on the alter of White male expediency. Others felt that the affair raised questions about the administration's commitment to civil rights and that after this fiasco Clinton would indeed have a difficult time finding someone to replace Guinier acceptable to both conservatives and the civil rights community. Some prominent Blacks also took a great deal of heat. Sen. Carol Moseley Braun, who sits on the Senate Judiciary Committee, was criticized by Black and women's groups for not taking a strong public stand in defense of Guinier or demanding that she have a hearing. Jackson called her silence a "betrayal."[50] Black Cabinet officials also came under bitter criticism as they remained silent throughout the entire episode. In contrast, Attorney General Janet Reno received praise for her support of Guinier, and allowed her the use of a room in the Justice Department to have a press conference following Clinton's withdrawal of her name.

The thrust of the attack on Guinier was two-fold: first, to continue the conservative assault on civil rights and civil rights advocates, and, second, to send a message to Clinton not to veer left. It would have been naive to believe that just because Bush lost the election, the conservatives still in positions of influence would just wither away. However, although Clinton had kept his distance from the civil rights leaders during the campaign, most Blacks believed that his administration would attempt to recapture some of the civil rights momentum lost under Reagan and Bush.

Stunned by Clinton's reversal, particularly after having been given reassurances that the nomination would go forward, Black leaders called for a reevaluation of the relationship between the White House and the Black community. Members of the CBC felt that part of the problem had to do with the lack of a Black liaison in the White House. Tensions between the administration and elected and civil rights leaders would eventually ease as Clinton signaled his support for legislation favored by Blacks.

It is likely that under Clinton there will be a revival of the Civil Rights Commission (CRC) which fell into dispute during the Reagan and Bush years. In the fall of 1993, Clinton appointed civil rights activist Mary Frances Berry to lead the CRC. Clinton has an opportunity during his first term to replace the conservative, anti-civil rights commissioners appointed by Bush with people who actually support civil rights. He is also likely to request and receive more funding from Congress for the Commission. Given Clinton's receive more funding from Congress for the Commission. Given Clinton's statements during the campaign, he is not going to support new initiatives for affirmative action.

Clinton's Equal Employment Opportunity Commission will move back to more class-action suits rather than focus on individuals as in the past three administrations. Finally, it is expected that the Justice Department will attack red-lining and apply stronger enforcement of the 1988 Fair Housing Act.

One other civil rights issue that will confront Clinton is that of statehood for the District of Columbia. While Clinton is on record as a supporter of statehood and would sign a statehood bill if presented with one, it's doubtful that he will campaign heavily for it unless there is a wholesale increase in public pressure. Although the Democrats would welcome and could certainly use two additional Democratic Senators—who would without question be elected in any senatorial election in D.C.—the opposition to statehood is strong and crosses party lines. Some members of Congress and conservatives oppose D.C. statehood on the grounds that the U.S. Constitution designates that the area making up the District must be under the control of the federal government. Other opponents reject statehood for far less lofty reasons. Some state that the city is too poor and could not sustain itself financially as a state while others point to mismanagement and high levels of crime and violence as concerns that should disqualify giving the District more autonomy.

Statehood supporters have responded to all these concerns. They argue that statehood legislation meets the constitutional requirements of ensuring that a federal enclave continues to exist even while establishing a state around that area. Supporters also claim that if the city becomes a state, it will have the ability to raise funds and receive a fairer tax compensation from the federal government than it does now that would create greater financial solvency. Finally, they argue that arguments that focus D.C.'s problems are spurious given that nearly every major city in the nation is experiencing similar dilemmas, yet no one would seriously consider denying the citizens of Oakland or New York full representation in Congress or political control of their community. Beyond responding to their critics, the arguments for statehood are strong on their own merits: D.C. is larger than three other states that have full representation; it pays more federal taxes than all but two other states; it sends its youth to war to defend the nation; and it is unfairly subject to the kinds of congressional interference in its local affairs that no member of Congress would tolerate against their constituents for one second. Many District and non-District residents feel that race and anti-urban politics plays a large role in opposing statehood.

Clinton has promised other initiatives that would positively affect the Black community, such as his pledges to implement a national health-care system, to make available loans for college attendance that can be repaid with community service, to enact tougher penalties for assaults against women and children, to crack down on hate crimes, to fully fund the Head Start program, to transfer 10 percent of the federal housing budget to churches and other non-profit agencies for the homeless, and to expand local authority to make more low-income rental units available. All of these promises face considerable conservative opposition, and few will be implemented or sustained without organized pressure from the Left.

In terms of foreign policy, except for a few notable exceptions, Clinton's campaign positions did not differ significantly from Bush's. While some in the Black community felt, and many more hoped, that the new administration's policies toward Africa would be more egalitarian in terms of aid and less tolerant of human rights violations, the paucity of discussion of this issue during the campaign left most to speculate. One pledge that Clinton did make but completely retreated from was his promise to give temporary asylum to Haitian refugees. Angering Black activists and leaders from coast to coast, Clinton stated only a few days after his inauguration that he would maintain the Bush policy of returning Haitians who attempted to "illegally" enter the United States and keep the blockade that was supposed to stop oil shipments from reaching the island. He stated that he would bring more human rights monitors to Haiti so that people on the island would feel safer about applying for asylum, and also bring more U.S. officials who would screen applicants in Port-au-Prince as well as in the countryside. At the end of 1993, deposed President Jean-Bertrand Aristide remained out of power. Clinton was initially praised for brokering an agreement in August 1993 between Aristide and the Haitian military leaders that overthrew him in September 1991. That agreement stated that Aristide would return to power on October 30, 1993 and the military would step down. The military betrayed their end of the deal and steadfastly refused to give up power and virtually dared the United States to invade. Economic sanctions, that had been lifted after the agreement, were again put in place. As the generals continued to murder and intimidate Aristide supporters, Haiti remained the largest frustration in terms of foreign policy for Clinton and many in the black community.

Many activists pointed out that there appeared to be a racial double standard on the issue of refugees. While those from Eastern Europe and Cuba, all overwhelmingly White, were welcomed with open arms as political refugees, Haitians were labeled economic refugees and turned back.

While the State Department appeared ready to purge many of the most jingoistic characters that ran foreign policy under Reagan and Bush, it was

clear that progressives must keep the pressure on. The opportunity to implement a foreign policy guided by respect for human rights, sovereignty,
economic justice, and political pluralism exists only to the degree it is fought
for. That requires the kind of organization and determination that thus far has
primarily come from the right wing.

In terms of Clinton's cabinet, a number of important changes occurred.
Clinton promised to make appointments that would make his administration
"look like America," and to a great degree, he was true to his word. He
appointed five African Americans to his Cabinet—Jesse Brown, Secretary
of Veteran Affairs; Ron Brown, Secretary of Commerce; Lee Brown, Director of the Office of National Drug Control Policy; Mike Espy, Secretary of
Agriculture; and Hazel O'Leary, Secretary of Energy. There has also been
an increase in the appointment of other people of color and women. While
appreciative of this greater diversity, some have complained that most of the
top positions of government are still held by White males. Some have also
noted that diversity in appearance is not the same as diversity in ideas and
that few progressives are identifiable in the top levels of government. Each
of the Black members of Clinton's cabinet, for example, are generally
considered to be political moderates. Liberal and progressive fears of a
political retreat were raised when Clinton appointed former Republican
David Gergen as White House counselor to the president, a position in which
he was essentially put in charge of managing the political life and future of
the Clinton administration.

Clinton's appointment of former Florida prosecutor Janet Reno as
attorney general is generally considered a grand slam on his part. Reno brings
a tough but fair perspective and, in the early months of the administration,
stood out as a committed public servant who was willing to go to the source
of problems and take on tough issues. She argued for reform of mandatory
minimum sentencing laws that have disproportionately affected the Black
community. Her relationship with African Americans has generally been
positive and is consistent with the good ties that she built with Florida's Black
community. Reno's popularity in the Miami Black community, partially due
to her persistent efforts to prosecute fathers who did not pay child support,
was so high that she inspired a rap song. Miami rapper Anquette's "Janet
Reno" rapped:

Janet Reno comes to town, collecting all the money
You stayed one day then ran away and started acting funny
She caught you down on 15th Avenue, trying to hide your trail

She fined your ass and locked you up. Now who can't post no bail?[51]

Ultimately, what the Black community obtains from the new administration and Congress will be determined by the level of organization and clarity of purpose developed by Black leadership outside of those bodies and with the community as a whole. The most dangerous posture is to simply wait for deliverance. The spontaneous and circumstantial events that unseated George Bush will not suffice to bring the type of policy, political, and economic transformations that the times are calling for. Only the most audacious and sober approach to the new administration and Congress in alliance with other needy groups in the United States will truly see a reversal of the Republican decade.

# Black Resistance and the Call of History

A number of futures face the Black community. It is critical that Black leaders not dwell on what is certain to be the bleak and desperate future if current trends remain constant, but instead focus on a positive alternative future that can be a result of disciplined and committed struggle. New leaders must bring to the Black community another vision of development and of the future. In the Black America that can be in the next century, there will be startling differences in the political, social, and cultural life of African Americans. Black women will play a much more visible and central political leadership role than in the present. The new (and perhaps some of the old) civil rights organizations will be woman-led and more profoundly democratic. More African American women will be elected at the local, state, and national level. More African American women will guide community organizations and cultural enterprises. From local community politics to national and international concerns, leadership in the Black community will be more diverse and gender-balanced.

In the next century that can be, a revitalization of positive and developmental values will also have been reborn within the Black community. Black leaders will exhibit and demand a morality and value system that is nurturing, caring, sacrificing, and humanistic. These values will translate into attitudes and perspectives on social and economic policies. A commitment to educational excellence, for example, will be the norm. Anything less will be unacceptable to students, parents, teachers, administrators, school board members, and political leaders.

A new spirit of community and willingness to serve will also exist. The sense of contributing to community and society, discouraged in this age of materialism and individualism, will dominate and be a major component of child-rearing and educating. The impact of this new spirit will be broad and revolutionary in its impact on how people in the community relate to each other and to those outside of the community. Homicides, as well as substance abuse, will drop considerably as communities also wrestle changes in the criminal justice system that no longer criminalizes whole generations and as alternatives to trafficking are implemented. Community security will be rooted in the organic community.

A visionary perspective on Black life in the next century does not necessarily or romantically see an end to racist views, personal discrimination, and racial intolerance, but it does see a path to the elimination of systemic and institutional racism. How we think about race and what actually constitutes "racial relations" will continue to expand beyond the paradigm of Black and White. A cultural flowering will witness more cross-cultural, multi-ethnic patterns of living and relating while, at the same time, preservation and promotion of the rich, uplifting, and valuable cultural heritage of African Americans, Latinos, Asians, Arabs, Native Americans, and other peoples.

It will be important for the Black community to acknowledge both similarities of conditions as well as important differences that give rise to critical policy questions that for the most part have not affected the Black community. These would include issues such as language and legal status.

Battles will be fought on a much higher plane to redefine popular culture and to purge the racist, sexist, and nationalistic images that contribute to the climate of discrimination and hate that currently permeates much of U.S culture. As part of the world community, images of internationalism will also become more common and necessary.

The central task of Black leadership in the period ahead is to restore hope and a sense of purpose to the community. It is unlikely that the politics of accommodation will be able to meet this challenge. At this point, however, neither is it clear that those who have been critical of the move from protest to politics will be able to rise to the occasion. The difficult days of which Martin Luther King, Jr. spoke in his last hours are upon us.

Perhaps the most important step that Black leaders can take at this point is to recognize the means and manners by which African Americans resist oppression on a daily basis. In this time when frustration with leadership is high, the Black political movement is in retreat and on the defensive, and conditions rapidly abrade, it is critical to identify and grasp the significance of individual resistance. As the brilliant young historian Robin D.G. Kelley observes, the gulf between the "everyday" and what is thought of as political struggles must be bridged. In his writings on the struggles of working-class African Americans during the civil rights era, Kelley examines the means by which the Black community forged a collectivist view of itself that had important relevance to the political struggles of that era. His insights on the period, I believe, are of immense value in the present as when he writes, "In the end, whether or not African Americans choose to join working-class organizations, their daily experiences, articulated mainly in unmonitored social spaces, constitute the ideological and cultural foundations for constructing a collective identity."[52] A Black collective identity, fettered and molded by class and gender experiences, still exists and must be creatively melded into the effort for progressive social transformation.

Breaking through the Black rage that has engulfed so many and channeling that passion into a movement for collective social change is the challenge before Black leadership across the political and ideological board. Encouraging signs abound as lessons from the distant and recent past are being absorbed and analyzed. If changes on the Black political landscape that have occurred in the last decade have clarified the mission and responsibilities of Black leadership, particularly of the new radicals, then a future of hope is not only possible, but well within our grasp.

# Notes

## Notes to Chapter 1

1. Martin Luther King, Jr., "Where Do We Go From Here: Chaos or Community?," in James M. Washington, ed., *A Testament of Hope: The Essential Writings and Speeches of Martin Luther King, Jr.* (New York: Harper Collins, 1986), pp. 562–563.

2. *It's Time to Reinvest in America* (Washington, D.C.: The Campaign for New Priorities, 1992), p. 4.

3. Ibid., p. 8.

4. Donald L. Barlett and James B. Steele, *America: What Went Wrong* (Kansas City: Andrews and McMeel, 1992), p. 8.

5. Ibid., p. 4.

6. Ibid., p. 1.

7. Ibid., p. xi.

8. "The Bush Bust on Job Growth," *Special Report*, Democratic Study Group, No. 102–11, October 1, 1991, p. 1.

9. See Isaac Shapiro, *White Poverty in America*, a report from the Center on Budget and Policy Priorities, Washington, D.C., 1992.

10. Ibid., p. 10.

11. Manning Marable, "The Crisis of the Black Working Class: An Economic and Historical Analysis," *Science & Society*, Summer 1982, p. 156.

12. Rochelle Stanfield, "Black Frustration," *National Journal*, May 16, 1992, p. 1163.

13. Gerald David Jaynes and Robin M. Williams, Jr., eds., *A Common Destiny: Blacks and American Society* (Washington, D.C.: National Academy Press, 1989), p. 275.

14. Ibid.

15. Ibid., Stanfield, p. 1165.

16. National Urban League, *State of Black America 1993* (New York: National Urban League, 1993), p. 168; Ibid., Shapiro, p. 4.

17. Barbara Vobejda, "Children's Poverty Rose in '80s; Suburbs, Rural Areas Also Show Increase," *Washington Post*, August 12, 1992.

18. Christopher Farrell, Michael Mandel, Michael Schroeder, Joseph Weber, Michele Galen, and Gary McWilliams, "The Economic Crisis of Urban America," *Business Week*, May 18, 1992, p. 38.

19. "Slow Economic Growth Lowers Median Household Income and Increases Poverty Rate in 1991, Census Bureau Says," Press Release, U.S. Department of Commerce, Bureau of Census, September 3, 1992.

20. William Fletcher and Eugene "Gus" Newport, "Race and Economic Development: The Need for a Black Agenda," in James Jennings, ed., *Race, Politics, and Economic Development: Community Perspectives* (New York: Verso, 1992), p. 117.

21. Mack Jones, "The Black Underclass as Systemic Phenomenon," in Jennings, ed., p. 53.

22. "Plight of Black America," *USA Today*, January 22, 1992.

23. William Dunn, "Study: 30% of USA's Blacks Segregated," *USA Today*, April 10, 1991.

24. Isabel Wilkerson and Angela Mitchell, "Staying Alive!: The Challenge of Improving Black America's Health," *Emerge*, September 1991, p. 25.

25. Leslie Miller, "Curing Health Care Inequities for Blacks," *USA Today*, August 3, 1992.

26. Mary Jordan, "Local Child Abuse and Neglect Cases Reach a Record Number," *Washington Post*, December 18, 1992.

27. Chris Booker, "Racism: Challenges and Changes for the 1990s," unpublished report, 1992, p. 8.

28. Ibid., p. 8.

29. Ibid., pp. 7–8.

30. Ibid., Wilkerson and Mitchell, p. 28.

31. Manning Marable, "In Critical Condition: Black Health Care and the 1992 Election," *Black Political Agenda '92*, September 1992, p. 7.

32. Mike Snider, "Blacks' Medical Care Often Lacking," *USA Today*, July 20, 1993.

33. Ibid., Booker, p. 7.

34. Ibid., Stanfield, p. 1166.

35. Marc Mauer, *Young Black Men and the Criminal Justice System: A Growing National Problem* (Washington, D.C: The Sentencing Project, 1990).

36. Gary Fields," D.C. Spends Less to Educate than to Jail," *Washington Times*, June 26, 1991.

37. Claudette E. Bennett, *The Black Population in the United States: March 1991*, U.S. Department of Commerce, Bureau of the Census, Current Population Reports, p. 5.

38. Mary Sawyer, "Harassment of Black Elected Officials: Ten Years Later," *The Journal of Intergroup Relations*, Fall 1991, p. 6.

39. "Mission Statement of the Center for the Study of Harassment of African Americans," *The Journal of Intergroup Relations*, Fall 1991, p. 67.

40. Andrea Stone, "Bomb Attacks Put NAACP on Nationwide Security Alert," *USA Today*, July 29, 1993.

41. "Race Top Cause of Hate Crimes," *USA Today*, July 29, 1993.

42. Jesse Katz and Andrea Ford, "Ex–Gang Members Look To Mideast For A Peace Plan; Truce: Group Uses 1949 Cease–Fire Agreement Between Egypt And Israel As The Basis For An Agreement Among L.A.'s Bloods And Crips," *Los Angeles Times*, June 17, 1992.

43. Ibid.

44. Ibid.

45. Sylvester Monroe, "Trading Colors for a Future," *Emerge*, July/August 1993, p. 47.

46. "National Summit for Peace and Justice Report," National Council of the Churches of Christ in the USA, May 25, 1993.

47. "Lowery and Black Leaders Meet With Clinton," *SCLC National Magazine*, January/February 1993, p. 43.

# Notes to Chapter 2

1. Cornel West, *Race Matters* (Boston: Beacon Press, 1993), p. 37.

2. Robert C. Smith, *Black Leadership: A Survey of Theory and Research* (Washington, D.C.: Mental Research and Development Center, Institute for Urban Affairs and Research, Howard University), pp. 3–4. Also see Donald R.Matthews, and James Warren Protho, *Negroes and the New Southern Politics* (New York: Harcourt, Brace and World, 1968); James Q.Wilson, *Negro Politics: The Search for Leadership* (New York: The Free Press, 1960); Donald Thompson, *The Negro Leadership Class* (Englewood Cliffs, N.J.: Prentice–Hall, 1963); Margaret Elaine Burgess, *Negro Leadership in a Southern City* (Chapel Hill, N.C.: University of North Carolina Press, 1962).

3. Ibid.

4. Lewis M. Killian, "Community Structure and the Role of the Negro Leader–Agent," *Sociological Inquiry*, Vol. 35, No. 1, Winter 1965, p. 70.

5. Ibid.

6. Ronald Walters, "Imperatives of Black Leadership: Policy Mobilization and Community Development," *The Urban Review*, Vol. 9, No. 1, Summer 1985, p. 33.

7. Franklin E. Frazier, "Desegregation as an Object of Sociological Study," in Arnold M. Rose, ed., *Human Behavior and Social Process* (Boston: Houghton Mifflin, 1962), p. 609.

8. Harold Cruise, *The Crisis of the Negro Intellectual: From its Origins to the Present* (New York: Quill, 1967), p. 564.

9. Gunnar Myrdal, *An American Dilemma* (New York: Pantheon Books, 1944), pp. 720–735.

10. See Manning Marable, "Black Politicians and Bourgeois Democracy," in his *Black American Politics: From the Washington Marches to Jesse Jackson* (London: Verso, 1985).

11. Ibid., Smith, p. 6.

12. Robert Smith, "Leadership in Negro and Black: Retrospect and Prospect," *The Urban League Review*, Vol. 9, No. 1, Summer 1985, p. 9.

13. Lerone Bennett, *The Negro Mood and Other Essays* (New York: Ballantine, 1965), p. 36.

14. Linda Williams, "Black Politics in the Late 1980s: Where Do We Stand and Where Do We Go From Here?" unpublished paper, May 24, 1987, p. 1.

15. Marcus D. Pohlmann, *Black Politics in Conservative America* (New York: Longman, 1990), p. 141.

16. Ibid.; Smith, "Leadership in Negro and Black" p. 9.

17. Morgan J. Kousser, "The Undermining of the First Reconstruction: Lessons for the Second," in Davidson, Chandler, ed., *Minority Vote Dilution* (Washington, D.C.: Howard University Press, 1989), p. 31.

18. Ibid., Pohlmann, p. 134.

19. Ibid., Smith, *Black Leadership* pp. 35–36.

20. Harold Baron, *The Demand for Black Labor: Historic Notes on the Political Economy of Racism* (Somerville, MA: New England Free Press, 1971), p. 20.

# Notes to Chapter 3

1. William L. Clay, *Just Permanent Interests: Black Americans in Congress, 1870–1991* (New York: Amistad, 1992), p. 165.

2. Marguerite Ross Barnett, "The Congressional Black Caucus: Illusions and Realities of Power," in Michael B. Preston, Lenneal J. Henderson, and Paul L. Puryear, eds., *The New Black Politics* (New York: Longman, 1987), p. 33.

3. Sheila Collins, *The Rainbow Challenge: The Jackson Campaign and the Future of U.S. Politics* (New York: Monthly Review Press, 1986), p. 90.

4. See "Who Speaks for Black America," *Detroit Free Press and Detroit News*, February 23, 1992 and the *Detroit News*, February 24, 1992 and February 25, 1992.

5. Ibid.

6. Ibid.

7. Ibid.

8. Rochelle Stanfield, "Black Frustration," *National Journal*, May 6, 1992, p. 1163.

9. Chester Higgins, Sr., "NAACP Convention Roundup," *Washington New Observer*, August 1, 1992, p. 5.

10. See Salim Muwakkil, "Hooks Leaves NAACP with Many Decisions to Make," *In These Times*, March 11–17, 1992, p. 7.

11. James Harney, "Dissension Clouds NAACP Recruitment," *USA Today*, February 24, 1992.

12. Ibid.

13. Jesse Jackson's letter to NAACP National Board Chairman William Gibson, April 7, 1993, p. 4.

14. Lynne Duke, "Civil Rights Activist Chavis Selected to Head NAACP; Cleveland Minister Wins Vote Over 2 Others," *Washington Post*, April 10, 1993.

15. Robert C. Smith, *Black Leadership: A Survey of Theory and Research* (Washington, D.C.: Mental Research and Development Center, Institute for Urban Affairs and Research, Howard University), p. 65.

16. Ronald Walters, "Imperatives of Black Leadership: Policy Mobilization and Community Development," *The Urban Review*, Vol. 9, No. 1, Summer 1985, p. 29.

17. Ibid.; Barnett, p. 52.

18. "The Friday Buzz," *Congress Daily*, September 24, 1993, p. 4.

19. Editorial, "The Black Caucus Gets Mugged," *New York Times*, September 25, 1993.

20. Dorothy Gilliam, "Peace Pact Toward True Black Power," *Washington Post*, September 18, 1993.

21. William Raspberry, "One that Fell Out of the Sky," *Washington Post*, September 20, 1993.

22. The Congressional Black Caucus, News Release, September 29, 1993.

23. Ralph Bunche, in Grantham, Dewey, *The Political Status of the Negro in the Age of FDR* (Chicago: University of Chicago Press, 1973), p. 88.

24. Manning Marable, *Black American Politics: From the Washington Marches to Jesse Jackson* (London: Verso, 1985), p. 177.

25. Frances Fox Piven and Richard Cloward, *Poor Peoples Movements: Why They Succeed, How They Fail* (New York: Vintage–Random House, 1977), p. 36.

# Notes to Chapter 4

1. Todd "Ty" Williams, "The Last Poets and Gil Scott–Heron are Pioneers of Rhythm and the Spoken Word," *The Source*, May 1992, p. 43.

2. Martin Luther King, Jr., *Stride Toward Freedom* (San Francisco: Harper & Row, 1958), p. 224.

3. Manning Marable, "A New Black Politics," *The Progressive*, August, 1990, pp. 20–21.

4. Andrew Hacker, *Two Nations: Black and White, Separate, Hostile, Unequal* (New York: Scribners, 1992), p. 209.

5. See Georgia A. Persons, ed., *Dilemmas of Black Politics: Issues of Leadership and Strategy* (New York: Harper Collins, 1993), for an extended discussion and examination of a number of case studies on the concept of deracialization.

6. See Clayborne Carson, "Civil Rights and the Black Freedom Struggle," in David Lewis, *The Civil Rights Movement in America* (Jackson, MS: University Press of Mississippi, 1986), pp. 19–37. Other relevant works include Aldon D. Morris, *The Origins of the Civil Rights Movement: Black Communities Organizing for Change* (New York: The Free Press, 1984) and Doug McAdam, *Political Process and the Development of Black Insurgency, 1930–1970* (Chicago: University of Chicago Press, 1982).

7. James Jennings, *The Politics of Black Empowerment: The Transformation of Black Activism in Urban America* (Detroit: Wayne State University Press, 1992).

# Notes to Chapter 5

1. Linda Williams, "Black Political Progress in the 1980s: The Electoral Arena," in Michael B. Preston, Lenneal J. Henderson, Jr., and Paul L. Puryear, *The New Black Politics: The Search for Political Power* (New York: Longman, 1987), p. 111.

2. Ron Daniels announcement speech, Oct. 14, 1991, Washington, D.C.

3. Manning Marable, *Race, Reform and Rebellion: The Second Reconstruction in Black America, 1945–1982* (Jackson, MS: University Press of Mississippi, 1984), p. 137.

4. Ibid.; Daniels, pp. 5–6.

5. Ronald Walters, *Black Presidential Politics: A Strategic Approach* (Albany: State University of New York Press, 1988), p. 142.

6. Ibid.; Daniels, p. 7.

7. Paulette Pierce, "The Roots of the Rainbow Coalition," *The Black Scholar*, March/April 1988, p. 9.

8. Ibid.; pp. 6–7.

9. Ibid.; p. 8.

10. Ibid.; Marable, pp. 220–221.

11. Ibid.; Walters, p. 149.

12. Kathryn Flewellen, "The National Black Independent Political Party: Will History Repeat?," *Freedomways*, No. 2, 1981, p. 100.

13. James Vann, "Ron Daniels: Reaching Toward a New Political Party," *NCIPA Discussion Bulletin*, Winter 1992, p. 12.

14. Lee Kiburi, "President Daniels?," *Pittsburgh Post–Gazette*, August 17, 1991.

15. Matthew Rothschild, "Beyond the Lesser of Evils: The Case Against Clinton," *The Progressive*, October 1992, p. 22.

16. Letter to author from Dr. Gwen Patton, undated.

17. Tom Hughes, "Shelby Opponent Files Suit Over Ballot Access Laws," *Montgomery Advertiser*, July 24, 1992.

18. "Independent Sort," *Montgomery Advertiser*, July 24, 1992.

19. "Making Political History in Alabama," *NCIPA Discussion Bulletin*, Winter 1992–93, p. 23.

20. Ibid.

21. "Decision '92: Special Voters' Guide to State and Local Election; The Third Parties," *Los Angeles Times*, October 25, 1992.

22. Tracey Wilkinson, "California Elections: U.S. Senate; Third Party Candidates Fight Obscurity," *Los Angeles Times*, October 30, 1992.

23. "A National Call to a People's Progressive Convention," document, 1993, p. 1.

24. Ibid.; pp. 2–3.

25. James Vann, "Ypsilanti: Filling the Rainbow Void," *NCIPA Discussion Bulletin*, Winter 1992–93, p. 10.

26. Ibid.; "A National Call to a People's Progressive Convention," p. 3.

27. Phil Hutchings, "Progressives Meet in Michigan," *Black Political Agenda '92*, August 1992, p. 7.

28. See "Where We Stand: A Declaration of Principles of the Committees of Correspondence," June 1, 1992, p. 1.

29. "NCC, At First Meet, Maps Activity," *Corresponder*, October 1992, p. 1.

30. Dallas L. Denby, Jr., *Statistics of the Presidential and Congressional Elections* (Washington, D.C.: U.S. Government Printing Office, 1989), p. 57.

31. Bruce Shapiro, "Dr. Fulani's Snake–Oil Show," *The Nation*, May 4, 1992, p. 586.

32. Ibid.

33. Ibid., p. 587.

34. "Advisory," *Rainbow Organizer*, NRC newsletter, Spring 1988, p. 7.

35. Ibid., Shapiro, p. 591.

36. Larry A. Still, "Dr. Fulani Leads Presidential Race," *National Chronicle*, December 20, 1991, p. 14.

37. Ibid.

38. Ibid., Shapiro, p. 589.

39. Ibid., p. 588.

40. Ibid., p. 589.

41. "The Democracy in Presidential Debates Act: Strengthening Political Pluralism," *Rainbow Lobby Membership Alert Newsletter*, Fall/Winter 1991, pp. 1–2.

42. "The Democracy in Presidential Debates Act: Strengthening Political Pluralism," Rainbow Lobby *Special Report*, Washington, D.C., 1991, pp. 2–3.

43. Ibid., Shapiro, p. 590.

44. Ibid., Still, p. 14.

45. Michael Meyers, "Final Election Returns," *Los Angeles Times*, June 4, 1992.

46. Taylor Branch, *Parting the Waters: America in the King Years, 1954–63* (New York: Simon and Schuster, 1988), p. 735.

47. Bill Carpenter, "Quayle, Gore and Stockdale, But Bevel?," *New Observer*, October 31, 1992, p. 10.

48. For a fuller discussion of the religious Right's efforts to recruit blacks, see Clarence Lusane, "The Far Right Goes After Black Support," *Covert Action Information Bulletin*, Spring 1987, pp. 50–52.

49. Omar Tyree, "Civil Rights Leader Jailed in Protest Against KKK Memorial," *News Dimension*, April 23, 1993.

# Notes to Chapter 6

1. Ronald Walters, *Black Presidential Politics: A Strategic Approach* (Albany:State University of New York Press, 1988), p. 179.

2. "Marion Barry Makes Political Comeback in D.C. Council Win," *Jet*, October 5, 1993, p. 7.

3. Rene Sanchez, "Barry Wins by Landslide in Ward 8; Crawford Loses Seat, Jarvis Squeaks by in D.C. Primaries," *Washington Post*, September 16, 1992.

4. Ibid.

5. "Vital Signs: 1992 Election Returns Statewide Initiatives and Referenda," *Campaign*, March 1993, p. 29.

6. Ibid.

7. Catherine S. Manegold, "The Reformation of a Street Preacher," *New York Times Magazine*, January 24, 1993, p. 21.

8. Ibid., p. 22.

9. Ibid., p. 20.

10. *The Voting Rights Act: Ten Years After* (Washington, D.C.: The United States Commission on Civil Rights, January 1975), p. 330.

11. Chandler Davidson, "Minority Voter Dilution: An Overview," in Chandler Davidson, ed., *Minority Voter Dilution* (Washington, D.C.: Howard University Press, 1984), p. 3.

12. See Walters, *Black Presidential Politics*; Ralph Gomes and Linda Williams, *From Exclusion to Inclusion; The Long Struggle for African American Political Power* (New York: Greenwood Press, 1992); Adolph Reed, Jr., *The Jesse Jackson Phenomenon: The Crisis of Purpose in Afro–American Politics* (New Haven, CT: Yale University Press, 1986), Katherine Tate, *From Protest to Politics: The New Black Voters in American Elections* (Cambridge: Harvard University Press, 1993); Lucius Barker and Ronald Walters, *Jesse Jackson's 1984 Presidential Campaign: Challenge and Change in American Politics* (Urbana, IL: University of Illinois Press, 1989); Lucius Barker, "Ronald Reagan, Jesse Jackson, and the 1984 Presidential Election: The Continuing American Dilemma of Race," in Michael B. Preston, Lenneal J. Henderson, and Paul L. Puryear, eds., *The New Black Politics* (New York: Longman, 1987); Hanes Walton, *Invisible Politics: Black Political Behavior* (Albany: SUNY Press, 1985); Lorenzo Morris, Charles Jarmon, and Arnold Taylor, eds., *The Social and Political Implications of the Jesse Jackson Presidential Campaign* (New York: Praeger, 1990); and ibid., Walters.

13. Ibid., Walton, *Invisible Politics* (Albany: SUNY Press, 1985), p. 93.

14. Ibid., Walters, p. 27.

15. Ibid., p. 112.

16. "Who Speaks for Black America?" *Detroit News*, February 24, 1992.

17. One recent comprehensive study on the impact of television on African Americans concluded that not only do blacks "watch more television than whites, even when social class is controlled...they also rely more on television for news and information." See Aletha C. Huston, et al; *Big World, Small Screen: The Role of Television in American Society* (Lincoln: University of Nebraska Press, 1992), p. 15.

18. Ronald Walters, "Fording the New Mainstream: The Death of Black Politics?," paper delivered at the annual meeting of the National Conference of Black Political Scientists, Atlanta, GA, March 15–17, 1990, p. 3.

19. J. P. McCormick, II, "Black Tuesday and the Politics of Deracialization," paper delivered at the symposium, "Blacks in the November '89 Elections: What is Changing?," sponsored by the Joint Center for Political Studies, Washington, D.C., December 5, 1989.

20. Joseph P. McCormick, II and Charles E. Jones, "The Conceptualization of Deracialization: Thinking Through the Dilemma," in Persons, p. 70.

21. William Julius Wilson, "Race–Neutral Programs and the Democratic Coalition," *The American Prospect*, Spring 1990, p. 81.

22. William Julius Wilson, *The Truly Disadvantaged: The Inner City, the Underclass, and Public Policy* (Chicago: University of Chicago Press, 1987), p. 120.

23. In Kenneth S. Tollett, "Racism and Race–Conscious Remedies," *The American Prospect*, Spring 1991, p. 94.

24. Thomas D. Boston, *Race, Class & Conservatism* (Boston: Unwin Hyman), 1988, p. 1.

# Notes to Chapter 7

1. Clarence Thomas, Opening Statement before the Senate Judiciary Committee, *Federal News Services*, Federal Information Systems Corporation, September 10, 1991, p. 2.

2. *Plessey v. Ferguson* began as a simple act of individual resistance against the violation of one's dignity. Homer Plessey, who was one–eighth black, refused to sit in the black section of a Louisiana railroad car. He was arrested and convicted of violating the state's segregation law, which he eventually appealed to the Supreme Court. The infamous eight–to–one ruling of the Court was issued in 1896 and stated that legal segregation, enshrined in the doctrine of "separate, but equal," could be practiced.

3. National Association for the Advancement of Colored People, *A Report on the Nomination of Judge Clarence Thomas as Associate Justice of the United States Supreme Court*, August 1, 1991, p. 20.

4. Tom Squitier, "Poll: Blacks Split on Thomas," *USA Today*, July 5, 1991. The poll had an margin error of plus or minus five points.

5. Ronald Taylor, "Hold off on Thomas, Leader to Advise SCLC," *Washington Times*, August 13, 1991. Thomas' approval rating among blacks rose to 57 percent in a poll taken one month after his nomination.

6. Ibid., Squitier.

7. Ibid., Taylor.

8. Calvin Rolark, "The CBC and Thomas," *The Washington Informer*, July 18–24, 1991, p. 12.

9. Ibid.

10. Ibid.

11. Margaret Bush Wilson, "The NAACP is Wrong on Thomas," *Washington Post*, August 6, 1991.

12. Ibid.

13. Ibid.

14. Fox Morning News interview with Rep. John Conyers (D–MI) and Robert Woodson, President of the National Center for Neighborhood Enterprises, September 18, 1991.

15. *In Opposition to Clarence Thomas: Where We Must Stand and Why*, Congressional Black Caucus Foundation, Washington, D.C., September 1991, p. 16.

16. Ibid., p. 4.

17. Ibid., p. 16.

18. Ibid., p. 1.

19. Sonya Ross, "Urban League President Calls Thomas An 'Affirmative Action,'" AP Wire Service, July 19, 1991.

20. Ibid.

21. Louis Stokes, *Remarks of the Honorable Rep. Louis Stokes (D–OH) Before the United States Senate Committee on the Judiciary Confirmation Hearings on Judge Clarence Thomas*, September 19, 1991, pp. 3, 6.

22. Ibid., p. 4.

23. John Lewis, *Testimony of Congressman John Lewis Before the Senate Judiciary Committee*, September 19, 1991, p. 4.

24. Adjoa Aiyetoro, *Testimony Concerning the Nomination of Judge Clarence Thomas, United States Court of Appeals, District of Columbia, to the Supreme Court of the United States Before the Senate Committee on the Judiciary*, National Conference of Black Lawyers, pp. 1–2.

25. Archie Waters, "More About Black Judges Who Far Surpass Thomas," *El Paso Times*, August 18, 1991.

26. William Lucy, *Testimony of William Lucy, President, Coalition of Black Trade Unionists*, September 19, 1991, p. 1.

27. Julian Bond, "NAACP Judged Thomas by His Character, Not by His Skin Color," *The Washington Star*, September 5, 1991, p. 1.

28. Ronald Walters, "Thomas: Estranged from His 'Blackness,'" *Washington Post*, July 16, 1991.

29. Clarence Thomas, "Why Black Americans Should Look to Conservative Policies," Heritage Foundation speech, June 18, 1987, p. 2.

30. Ibid., Wilson.

31. Thomas Sowell, "Desperation in the Opposition Camp," *Washington Times*, August 31, 1991.

32. Ibid.; Thomas, "Why Black Americans Should Look to Conservative Policies," p. 4.

33. "Talking Points on the Nomination of Judge Clarence Thomas for the United States Supreme Court," NAACP, August 13, 1991, p. 2.

34. Ibid., p. 65.

35. Ruth Marcus, "The Thomas Hearings Witness List: Notable for Its Absences," *Washington Post*, September 27, 1991.

36. Ibid., Aiyetoro, p. 20.

37. J. Lee Anderson, *Inside the League* (New York: Dodd, Meade, 1986), p. 153. For more information on Thomas' connection to the apartheid government, see Russ Bellant, "The Thomas Connection Has White South African Angle," *National Catholic Reporter*, August 2, 1991; and Herb Boyd, "Clarence Thomas and His Right–wing Bedfellows," *Amsterdam News*, August 31, 1991.

38. Joan Biskupic, "ABA Weighs In," *Congressional Quarterly*, August 31, 1991, p. 2360.

39. Dawn Ceol, "Bar Association Rates Thomas as 'Qualified,'" *Washington Times*, August 28, 1991.

40. Ibid., Biskupic.

41. Ibid., Congressional Black Caucus Foundation, Washington, D.C., p. 2.

42. Ibid., NAACP, p. 33.

43. Cornel West, *Race Matters* (Boston: Beacon Press, 1993), p. 29.

44. Timothy M. Phelps and Helen Winternitz, *Capitol Games: The Inside Story of Clarence Thomas, Anita Hill, and a Supreme Court Nomination* (New York: HarperPerennial, 1992), p. 74.

# Notes to Chapter 8

1. "Rights Hero for Duke," *Newsday*, December 3, 1991.

2. James Ridgeway, *Blood in the Face* (New York: Thunder's Mouth Press, 1990), pp. 146–148.

3. For a review of the growth of White supremacist and hate groups during the 1980s, see *Intelligence Report*, December 1989, distributed by Klanwatch, Southern Poverty Law Center, Montgomery, Alabama.

4. "The Republicans: Plusses From Thomas, Problems From Duke," *The American Political Report*, October 25, 1991, p. 3.

5. Ibid.; Ridgeway, p. 153.

6. Arnold R. Hirsch, "David Duke in the U.S. Senate?," *Washington Post*, September 23, 1990.

7. Ibid.; Ridgeway, p. 154.

8. Bill Nichols, "Past Follows Ex–Klansman on Campaign," *USA Today*, October 23, 1991.

9. Ibid.; Hirsch.

10. Ibid.

11. Ibid.

12. John Maginnis, "The Hazards of Duke," *The New Republic*, November 25, 1991, p. 29.

13. "Gubernatorial Primary Results," *USA Today*, October 21, 1991.

14. David Maraniss, "Again, Duke Shows He's a Force in Louisiana," *Washington Post*, October 20, 1991.

15. "Louisiana: Duke Still the Favorite," *Southern Political Report*, November 12, 1991, p. 3.

16. Bill Nichols, "Past Follows Ex–Klansman on Campaign," *USA Today*, October 23, 1991.

17. Bill Nichols, "Duke Says He'll Win Louisiana Race, GOP Recognition," *USA Today*, October 22, 1991.

18. David Maraniss, "With Week Left, Duke's Chances Remain Unclear," *Washington Post*, November 11, 1991.

19. "Mason–Dixon Poll," *Washington Times*, November 17, 1991.

20. George Archibald, "Edwards Routs Duke," *Washington Times*, November 17, 1991.

21. Jason Berry, "Louisiana Hateride," *The Nation*, December 9, 1991, p. 728.

22. Thomas Edsall, "Duke Announces Bid for the Presidency; Former Klansman Plans to Challenge Bush," *Washington Post*, December 5, 1991.

23. Maralee Schwartz, "Duke Ballot Bar Upheld," *Washington Post*, January 24, 1992.

24. "Duke's Battle of the Ballot," *USA Today*, February 5, 1992.

25. Thomas B. Edsall, "S. Carolina Picks Bush, Clinton," *Washington Post*, March 8, 1992.

# Notes to Chapter 9

1. Langston Hughes, *The Panther and the Lash: Poems of Our Times* (New York: Alfred A. Knopf, 1967).

2. James Jennings, *The Politics of Black Empowerment: The Transformation of Black Activism in Urban America* (Detroit: Wayne State University Press, 1992), p. 84.

3. John O. Calmore, "Metropolitan America and Racism," *Poverty & Race*, July/August 1993, p. 9.

4. Cynthia Hamilton, *Apartheid in an American City* (Los Angeles: Labor/Community Strategy Center, 1991), p. 5.

5. "L.A, Neighborhoods," *USA Today*, May 11, 1992.

6. Ibid.

7. Thomas Pettigrew and Denise Alston, *Tom Bradley's Campaigns for Governor* (Washington, D.C.: The Joint Center for Political Studies, 1988), pp. 1,3, 27.

8. Mike Davis, *City of Quartz* (New York: Vintage Books, 1992), p. 306.

9. Ibid., p. 305

10. Ibid., p. 306

11. James H. Johnson, Jr. and Walter C. Farrell, Jr., "The Fire This Time: The Genesis of the Los Angeles Rebellion of 1992," *North Carolina Law Review*, June 1993, p. 906; and Earl Ofari Hutchinson, "The Continuing Myth of Black Capitalism," *The Black Scholar*, Vol. 23, No. 1, p. 17.

12. Johnson and Farrell, p. 909.

13. Stephen S. Cohen, "Where the Jobs Were: Unemployment Isn't Equal—It's in L.A.," *Washington Post*, March 14, 1993.

14. Ibid.; Johnson and Farrell, p. 912.

15. Ibid., Davis, p. 308.

16. Raphael J. Sonenshein, *Politics in Black and White: Race and Power in Los Angeles* (Princeton, NJ: Princeton University Press, 1993), p. 160.

17. Ibid., Johnson and Farrell, p. 913

18. Ibid., pp. 913–914.

19. Melvin L. Oliver, James H. Johnson, Jr., and Walter C. Farrell, Jr., "Anatomy of a Rebellion: A Political–Economic Analysis," in Robert Gooding–Williams, ed., *Reading Rodney King, Reading Urban Uprising* (New York: Routledge, 1993), p. 127.

20. Murray Campbell, "Blacks Angry as Korean Gets a Probation for Killing," *Washington Times*, November 19, 1991.

21. Ibid.

22. Mike Davis, *L.A. Was Just the Beginning: Urban Revolt in the United States* (Westfield, NJ: Open Magazine, 1992), p. 5.

23. Mike Davis, "Burning All Illusions in L.A.," in *Inside the L.A. Riots* (New York: Institute for Alternative Journalism, 1992), p. 99.

24. "'At Last They See We're Not Lying to Them,'" *Los Angeles Times*, May 11, 1992.

25. *Police Brutality in Los Angeles, California* (London: Amnesty International, 1992), p. 5.

26. Ibid.

27. Ibid., p. 25.

28. Ibid., p. 27.

29. Ibid.

30. Ibid., pp. 29–33.

31. Marc Cooper, "L.A.'s State of Siege: City of Angels, Cops from Hell," in *Inside the L.A. Riots* (New York: Institute for Alternative Journalism, 1992), p. 14.

32. Ibid., Davis, *City of Quartz*, p. 272.

33. Sonia L. Nazario and David J. Jefferson, "LA Law," *Wall Street Journal*, March 12, 1991.

34. Frederic Dannen, "Gates's Hell," *Vanity Fair*, August 1991, p. 104.

35. Ibid., p. 104.

36. Ibid., Sonenshein, p. 213.

37. Ibid.

38. The twelve jurors were Dorothy M. Bailey, Alice Debord, Thomas Gorton, Henry B. King, Jr., Retta E. Kossow, Virginia Bravo Loya, Gerald R. Miller, Christopher C. Morgan, Amelia M. Pigeon, Charles A. Sheehan, Kevin Paul Siminski, and Anna Charmaine Whiting. See Nina Bernstein, "Bitter Division In Jury Room; How 12 Ordinary Citizens Met For 7 Days To Produce Verdict That Shook L.A.," *Newsday*, May 14, 1992. Nina Bernstein's article is an intriguing description of the fierce battles that occurred among the jurors with Whiting leading the fight for at least partial conviction while most were steadfast in defending the officers from beginning to end.

39. Thomas L. Dumm, "The New Enclosures: Racism in the Normalize Community," in Robert Gooding–Williams, ed., *Reading Rodney King, Reading Urban Uprising* (New York: Routledge, 1993), p. 178.

40. Marc Cooper and Greg Goldin, "Some People Don't Count," *Village Voice*, May 12, 1992, p. 39.

41. Carleton R. Bryant, "Leaders Can't Agree on Solutions," *Washington Times*, May 4, 1992.

42. "Path of Destruction," *Los Angeles Times*, May 11, 1992.

43. Ibid.; Davis, *L.A. Was Just the Beginning* p. 1.

44. Shawn McIntosh and Robert Davis, "L.A. Arrest Survey Finds Deep Scars," *USA Today*, May 11, 1992.

45. Ibid.

46. Richard Morin, "Polls Uncover Much Common Ground on L.A. Verdict," *Washington Post*, May 11, 1992.

47. Ibid.

48. Ibid.

49. "The President's Message; Excerpts From Bush's Speech on Los Angeles Riots: 'Need to Restore Order,'" *New York Times*, May 2, 1992.

50. Ibid.

51. Ronald J. Ostrow, "Bush Cites Gulf Victory In Call To Battle Crime; Law Enforcement: President Says A Soldier May Have Been Safer At Kuwaiti Front Than In His Own Hometown," *Los Angeles Times*, March 6, 1991.

52. Linda Greenhouse, "NAACP Chief Assails Bush as Graduates Cheer," *New York Times*, May 10, 1992.

53. Ibid.

54. Steven Waldman, "Filling the Political Void," *Newsweek*, May 18, 1992, p. 31.

55. "Overheard," *Newsweek*, May 18, 1992, p. 23.

56. "Opinion Outlook," *National Journal*, May 16, 1992, p. 1204.

57. Ronald Brownstein," Buchanan Links Border Problem to Riots that Gripped Los Angeles," *Los Angeles Times*, May 14, 1992.

58. "Riots In Los Angeles; Candidates' Reactions Vary Widely," *New York Times*, May 2, 1992.

59. E.J. Dionne Jr. and Maralee Schwartz, "Clinton Issues Plea for Racial Harmony; Candidate Plans to Visit Los Angeles Today," *Washington Post*, May 3, 1992.

60. Ronald Taylor, "Clinton Call Riots Product of Neglect," *Washington Times*, May 4, 1992.

61. "Riots In Los Angeles; Candidates' Reactions Vary Widely."

62. Ibid.

63. Shawn McIntosh and Robert Davis, "L.A. Arrest Survey Finds Deep Scars," *USA Today*, May 11, 1992.

64. Ibid.

65. All exit poll numbers are from Richard Simon, "The Times Poll; Anglo Vote Carried Riordan to Victory; Survey: Exit Poll Shows Racial Divisions of Primary Also Were a Factor in Runoff. Results Indicate that the New Mayor May Have a Tough Task Ahead," *Los Angeles Times*, June 10, 1993.

# Notes to Chapter 10

1. Ice Cube, "A Bird in the Hand," *Death Certificate*, Priority Records, 1991.

2. Amilcar Cabral, "National Liberation and Culture," in *Return to the Source* (New York: Africa Information Service, 1973), p. 43.

3. Michael Eric Dyson, "Performance, Protest, and Prophecy in the Culture of Hip Hop," *Black Sacred Music*, Summer 1991, p. 22.

4. National Urban League, *The State of Black America 1986* (New York: National Urban League, 1986), p. 214.

5. Keith Jennings, "Understanding the Persisting Crisis of Black Youth Unemployment," in James Jennings, ed., *Race, Politics, and Economic Development* (New York: Verso, 1992), p. 155.

6. National Urban League, *The State of Black America 1993* (New York: National Urban League, 1993), p. 181.

7. Paul Grein "It was Feast or Famine in '90 Certs; Platinum Ranks Thin, But Smashes Soar," *Billboard*, January 12, 1991, p. 9.

8. Ibid.

9. John Leland, "Rap and Race," *Newsweek*, June 29, 1992, p. 4 9.

10. James T. Jones, IV, "NWA's Career Gets a Jolt From Lyric's Shock Value," *USA Today*, June 21, 1991.

11. Bruce Horovitz, "Quincy Jones, Time Warner Launch Rap Lovers Magazine," *Los Angeles Times*, September 15, 1992.

12. Chuck Philips, "The Uncivil War: The Battle Between the Establishment and the Supporters of Rap Opens Old Wounds of Race and Class," *Los Angeles Times*, July 19, 1992..

13. Robin D.G. Kelley, "Straight From Underground," *The Nation*, p. 796.

14. "Other Rappers Accused of 'Nasty' Influence," *Washington Times*, June 16, 1992.

15. Marilyn Lashley, "Bad Rap," *Washington Post*, September 25, 1992.

16. Ibid., "Other Rappers Accused of 'Nasty' Influence."

17. Sonja Peterson–Lewis, "A Feminist Analysis of the Defenses of Obscene Rap Lyrics," *Black Sacred Music*, Summer 1991, p. 78.

18. Ibid., p. 79.

19. Sister Souljah, "Killing Me Softly," *360 Degrees of Power*, Epic, 1992.

20. "Rebuild America: 1992 & Beyond," National Rainbow Coalition, program, p. 3.

21. Jack Anderson and Michael Binstein, "Sourness in the Jackson Camp," *Washington Post*, July 12, 1992.

22. See transcript of Sister Souljah's interview with the David Mills in "In Her Own Disputed Words," *Washington Post*, June 16, 1992.

23. Thomas Oliphant, "The Right Way—and the Wrong Way," *Boston Globe*, June 17, 1992.

24. Mark Miller, "'Manhattan Project,' 1992," *Newsweek*, November/December 1992, p. 55.

25. Ibid., p. 56.

26. Richard Benedetto, "Perot Attracts Support from Swing Voters," *USA Today*, June 17, 1992.

27. "Perot's Progress," *Los Angeles Times*, June 18, 1992.

28. For more of an extended discussion on the politics of rap see Clarence Lusane, "Rap, Race and Politics," *Race and Class*, No. 35, July–September, 1993, pp. 41–56, and Robin D.G. Kelley, "Kickin' Reality, Kickin' Ballistics: The Cultural Politics of Gangsta Rap in Postindustrial Los Angeles," unpublished manuscript, 1992.

29. Thomas B. Edsall, "Black Leaders View Clinton Strategy With Mix of Pragmatism, Optimism," *Washington Post*, October 28, 1992.

30. R.W. Apple, Jr., "Jackson Sees a 'Character Flaw' in Clinton's Remarks on Racism," *New York Times*, June 19, 1992.

31. Ibid.

32. David S. Broder and Thomas B. Edsall, "Clinton Finds Biracial Support for Criticism of Rap Singer," *Washington Post*, June 16, 1992.

33. Ibid.

34. Ibid.

35. Ibid.

36. Ronald Walters, "...Clinton's Gall," *Washington Post*, June 16, 1992.

37. "Overheard," *Newsweek*, May 18, 1992, p. 23.

38. Lloyd Grove, "Rapping to a GOP Beat," *Washington Post*, August 5, 1992.

39. Ibid.

40. Ibid.; Dan Couture, "The Republican's Right–wing Rapper," *Houston Chronicle*, August 19,1992.

41. Edna Gundersen, "Tipper Gore Faces the Music," *USA Today*, July 22, 1991.

42. Mike Smith, "Celebrity Buzz; Rap Singer Joins Republican Club," *Atlanta Journal and Constitution*, March 19, 1991.

## Notes to Chapter 11

1. The Editors, "A Visit With Bill Clinton," *The Atlantic*, October 1992, p. 23.

2. "About the DLC," *The Mainstream Democrat,* March, 1991, p. 25.

3. Al From, "Hey, Mom — What's a New Democrat," *Washington Post*, June 6, 1993.

4. William Galston and Elaine Ciulla Kamarck, *The Politics of Evasion: Democrats and the Presidency* (Washington, D.C.: The Progressive Policy Institute, September 1989, pp. 3–4.

5. Ibid., p. 5.

6. Donald Lambro, "Insurgent DLC Sees Victory Within Grasp," *Washington Times*, May 4, 1992.

7. Ibid.

8. W. John Moore, "On the March Again?," *National Journal*, December 12, 1992, p. 2824.

9. Howard Kurtz, "In Instant Replay, Clinton's Unvarnished Emotion," *Washington Post*, February 29, 1992.

10. Ibid.

11. "Golf Club Where Clinton Played Retains Ways of Old South," *New York Times*, March 23, 1992.

12. "Clinton to Boycott All–White Club," *Washington Post*, March 20, 1992.

13. Ingrid Sturgis, "Blacks More Involved in National Conventions," *Black Enterprise*, July 1992, p. 16.

14. "Blacks Help Democrats Prepare for Largest Convention Ever, *National Chronicle*, July 1–18, 1992, p. 4.

15. Ibid., Bositis, *Blacks and the 1992 Democratic National Convention*, p. 1.

16. Ibid., p. i.

17. Ibid., p. 45.

18. Jackson used the term "new covenant" during his 1984 race to describe what he perceived to be the new and more reciprocal relationship between blacks and the Democratic Party. He also used the term during his Operation PUSH days in labelling the relationships he brokered between white corporations and black businesses. See Katherine Tate, *From Protest to Politics: The New Black Voters in American Elections* (Cambridge: Harvard University Press, 1993), p. 61.

19. See "The Platform: Party's Statement of Policies of Mirrors Clinton's Goals," *Congressional Quarterly*, July 4, 1992, pp. 59–67.

20. "Both Sides with Jesse Jackson," television program, July 11, 1992.

21. Jesse Jackson speech to DNC in *Washington Post*, July 17, 1992.

22. See William Schneider, "The Suburban Century Begins," *The Atlantic Monthly* July 1992, pp. 33–44.

23. Author's interview with Cecil McDonald; and "General Election Summary: African American Component," final report, November 1992.

24. See Jeffery M. Elliot, "Half Truths and Whole Lies: A Conversation with Willie Horton,"*Emerge*, November 1993, pp. 30–34; Jeffrey M. Elliot, "The 'Willie Horton Nobody Knows,"*The Nation*, August 23/30, 1993, pp. 201–205.

25. Ibid., p. 19.

26. Adrienne T. Washington, "Black Republican Not Necessary Oxymoron," *Washington Times*, August 21, 1992.

27. Ibid., p. 16.

28. Ronald Walters, "The Truth About Truman," *Black Political Agenda '92*, September 1992, p. 1.

29. Jack M. Bloom, *Class, Race & the Civil Rights Movement* (Bloomington and Indianapolis: Indiana University Press, 1987), p. 76.

30. Manning Marable, *Race, Reform and Rebellion: The Second Reconstruction in Black America, 1945–1982* (Jackson, MS: University of Mississippi Press, 1984), pp. 24–27.

31. Ibid., Bloom, p. 82.

32. See Editorial, *Amsterdam News*, October 9, 1948, p. 10 cited in Charles Hamilton, ed., *The Black Experience in American Politics* (New York: Capicorn Books, 1973), p. 301.

33. Ibid., Bloom, p. 81.

34. Benjamin J. Wallace, "The Negro People's Liberation Movement," *Political Affairs*, September 1948, pp. 880–98.

35. Rick Hampson, "Private Letters Reveal Truman's Racist Attitudes," *Washington Times*, October 25, 1991.

36. Ibid.

37. See transcript of interview in "King and Perot," *Campaign*, June 1992, pp. 31–35.

38. Ronnie Dugger, "Electoric Caesar?," *The Nation*, June 15, 1992, p. 813.

39. Ibid., p. 814.

40. Ibid., p. 1.

41. "Perotism," *Left Business Observer*, No. 53, June 9, 1992, p. 1.

42. Ibid., Dugger, p. 813.

43. Adam Nagourney, "Big Daddy Image, Wealth are Concerns," *USA Today*, June 8, 1992.

44. Steven A. Holmes, "Perot Makes Plea for Racial Harmony," *New York Times*, June 19, 1992.

45. Ibid., p. 9.

46. Michael Isikoff, "Perot's Rhetorical Drug War Raises Questions," *Washington Post*, June 10, 1992.

47. Ronald Walters, "A Breakthrough Among Blacks?," *USA Today*, June 9, 1992.

48. Ibid., Nagourney.

49. Richard L. Berke, "Some Gaps Emerge in Perot's Appeal," *New York Times*, June 10, 1992.

50. Ibid., Walters.

51. Michael Isikoff, "Perot Offends Many NAACP Delegates," *Washington Post*, July 12, 1992

52. Ibid.

53. Debbie Howlett and John Hanchette, "Perot Trips on Tactics, Remarks," *USA Today*, July 13, 1992.

# Notes to Chapter 12

1. Michael McQueen, "While Blacks Loom Large in Democratic Race, They Have No Natural Home Among the Rivals," *Wall Street Journal*, February 21, 1992.

2. Mack Jones, "The Black Underclass as Systemic Phenomenon," in James Jennings, ed., *Race, Politics, and Economic Development: Community Perspectives* (New York: Verso, 1992), p. 63.

3. See Manning Marable, *Black American Politics* (New York: Verso, 1985) pp. 125–190.

4. Adolph L. Reed, Jr., *The Jesse Jackson Phenomenon: The Crisis of Purpose in Afro-American Politics* (New Haven, CT: Yale University Press, 1986), p. 134.

5. "Clinton Support Among Blacks Lags Behind Jackson's in 1988," *Washington Times*, April 3, 1992.

6. Ibid.

7. Jesse Jackson, "Message from the President," *Campaign '92 Update*, April 3, 1992, p. 1.

8. Jesse Jackson, "Delighted to be United," speech to the Democratic Leadership Council, March 24, 1990, pp. 1–2, 4.

9. Ibid.

10. Ibid.

11. "National Politics," *The American Political Report*, July 19, 1991, p. 4.

12. John E.Smith and Donald Lambro, "Jackson Makes Decision at Last; Will Run for 'Shadow Senator,' Won't Rule Out White House," *Washington Times*, July 6, 1990.

13. Nathan McCall, "Jackson Hails Election as a Boost for Statehood," *Washington Post*, November 7, 1990.

14. "Democratic Presidential Preference Polls," *The American Political Report*, October 25, 1991, p. 7.

15. Ibid.

16. "National Politics," *The American Political Report*, October 25, 1991, p. 5.

17. Ibid., p. 6.

18. Ibid.

19. Chinta Strausberg, "Jackson Considers Third Try at the Presidency," *The Capital Spotlight*, June 13, 1991, p. 5.

20. See Steve Cobble, "Phoenix," unpublished paper, 1991.

21. "Jackson Ordered to Repay '88 Funds," *Washington Post*, April 16, 1993.

22. Jesse Jackson, "We Are Campaigning to Build a New Democratic Majority and Rebuild America," speech, November 2, 1991, p. 9.

23. Ibid., p. 6.

24. Ibid., p. 8.

25. Ibid., p. 5.

26. Bill Carpenter, "Jackson Beats It," *The Washington New Observer*, November 9, 1991, p. 1.

27. See Bill Whalen, "92 Race Gets Wilder," *Insight*, October 14, 1991.

28. Nat Hentoff, "Hard Line on the Death Penalty," *Washington Post*, March 21, 1992.

29. Jesse Jackson letter to Bill Clinton, January 24, 1992.

30. "Reverend Jesse Jackson and Rainbow Coalition Ask Clinton to Spare Rector," National Rainbow Coalition, press release, January 24, 1993.

31. *It's Easy to Believe in the Death Penalty—If You Ignore the Facts*, National Coalition to Abolish the Death Penalty brochure, 1990.

32. Ibid.

33. Ibid.

34. Ibid., Hentoff.

35. David Margolick, "In Land of Death Penalty, Accusations of Racial Bias," *New York Times*, July 19, 1991.

36. "Politicians Distort Death Penalty Issue," Death Penalty Information Center, press release, October 1990.

37. Douglas Wilder, announcement speech, September 13, 1991 in *Democratic Caucus Bulletin*, U.S. House of Representatives, October 7, 1991.

38. Ibid.

39. Ibid.

40. Ibid.

41. Dwayne Yancey, *When Hell Froze Over: The Untold Story of Doug Wilder, A Black Politician's Rise to Power in the South* (Dallas: Taylor Publishing, 1988), p. 34.

42. Ibid.

43. Ibid., p. 369.

44. Charles E. Jones and Michael L. Clemons, "A Model of Racial Crossover Voting: An Assessment of the Wilder Victory," in Georgia Persons, *Dilemmas of Black Politics: Issues of Leadership and Strategy* (New York: Harper Collins, 1993), p. 135.

45. Ibid., p. 140.

46. Ibid.

47. L. Douglas Wilder, "A Plunge into the New Mainstream," *The Mainstream Democrat*, December 1989, p. 16.

48. Ibid., p. 17.

49. Steve Cobble, "A Short Walk on the Wilder Side," *Extra*, April/May 1992, p. 24.

50. Ibid.

51. Robert Jordan, "Is the Jackson Political Era Ending?"*Boston Globe*, December 3, 1989.

52. Juan Williams, "One–Man Show, "*Washington Post*, June 9, 1991.

53. Bill Whalen, "'92 Race Gets Wilder," *Insight*, October 14, 1991, p. 24.

54. Ibid.

55. John F. Harris and Donald p. Baker, "Wilder Accuses Jesse Jackson of Working Against Campaign," *Washington Post*, December 23, 1991.

56. Paul Taylor, "Decades of Damning Torpedoes Finally Takes Its Too on Wilder," *Washington Post*, January 12, 1992.

57. Ibid., Harris and Baker.

58. DeWayne Wickham, "Jackson and Wilder: Strategies for Defeat," *USA Today*, January 6, 1992.

59. Donald Baker, "Wilder Woos Supporters in Clinton's Back Yard; Black Arkansas Lawmakers Endorse Virginian," *Washington Post*, December 9, 1991.

60. Ibid.

61. Ibid.

62. Donald Baker, "Wilder Says Campaign Was a Mistake," *Washington Post*, January 10, 1992.

63. Ibid.

64. Ibid.

65. "Presidential Campaign Funds," *PACs & Lobbies*, March 4, 1992, p. 6.

66. Donald p. Baker, "Wilder Ends Campaign," *Washington Post*, January 9, 1992.

67. Ibid., Harris and Baker.

68. Ibid., Baker, "Wilder Says Campaign Was a Mistake."

69. "The Wooing of Minority Voters," *USA Today*, January 13, 1992.

70. Thomas Byrne Edsall, *Chain Reaction: The Impact of Race, Rights, and Taxes on American Politics* (New York: Norton, 1992), p. 290.

71. Ibid., p. 290.

# Notes to Chapter 13

1. W. John Moore, "On the March Again?," *National Journal*, December 12, 1992, p. 2825.

2. Art Pine, "92 National Elections; President Vetoes Urban Aid Measure; Inner City: He Carries Through On Promise To Reject Legislation, Which Would Have Created New Enterprise Zones In L.A. And Other Big Cities, Saying It Constituted A Tax Hike," *Los Angeles Times*, November 5, 1992.

3. David Bositis, *Blacks and the 1992 Democratic National Convention* (Washington, D.C.: Joint Center for Political and Economic Studies, 1992), p. 29.

4. "Presidential Vote Totals," Associated Press, November 5, 1992.

5. All data comparing voter behavior is taken from the Voter Research and Survey exit polls published in the *New York Times*, November 5, 1992.

6. James Barnes, "Tainted Triumph?," *National Journal*, November 7, 1992, p. 2541.

7. "1992 Presidential Results in Southern States," *Southern Political Report*, November 1992, p. 4.; Jack W. Germond and Jules Witcover, "Due Bills," *National Journal*, November 7, 1992, p. 2550.

8. Manning Marable, "Race and Class in the U.S. Presidential Election," *Race and Class*, January–March 1993, No. 3, p. 78.

9. Ibid., Barnes, p. 2539.

10. Milton D. Morris and Eddie N. Williams, "African Americans and the Making of the Clinton Victory,"Joint Center for Political and Economic Studies, December 9, 1992, p. 3; Ron Walters, "Clinton and the African American Vote," *Government & Politics*, March 1993, p. 3.

11. *National Rainbow Coalition/Democratic National Committee Voter Project*, Report, Washington, D.C., November 1992, p. vi.

12. Ibid.

13. Ibid., Morris and Williams, p. 3.

14. Ibid.

15. Lorenzo Morris, "The Racial Factor in the 1992 Elections," Government & Politics, March 1993, pp. 4–5.

16. Ibid., Walters, p. 3.

17. Mike Davis, "Who Killed L.A.?: The War Against the Cities," *Crossroads*, June 1993, p. 7.

18. Ibid.

19. *It's Time to Reinvest in America* (Washington, D.C.: The Campaign for New Priorities, 1992), p. 4.

20. "Recipe for An Upset," *Campaign*, October 1992, p. 22.

21. Paul M. Green, "The Brains of Braun," *Campaign*, October 1992, p. 23.

22. Ibid., p. 22.

23. pp. 5–6

24. See *New Democratic Members*, Democratic Study Group, U.S. House of Representatives, November 1992.

25. "Final California Election Returns," *Los Angeles Times*, November 5, 1992.

26. William Schneider, "A Loud Vote for Change," *National Journal*, November 7, 1992, p. 2542.

27. William Schnieder, "Who Voted for Clinton, Bush and Perot," *National Journal*, November 7, 1992, p. 2543.

28. Matthew Morrissey, "Taking the Initiative," *National Journal*, November 7, 1992, p. 2585.

29. Ibid.

30. Richard Cohen, "What Coattails?," *National Journal*, May 29, 1993.

31. Ibid.

32. Margaret L. Usdansky, "Minority Majorities in One in Six Cities," *USA Today*, June 9, 1993.

33. Ibid.

34. James Barnes, "Tainted Triumph," *National Journal*, November 7, 1992, p. 2541.

35. Jesse Jackson, "Analyzing and Interpreting the Clinton & Gore Win: Moving Toward Transition, Cabinet and the First 100 Days," in *National Rainbow Coalition/Democratic National Committee Voter Project*, Report, November 1992.

36. Ibid.

## Notes to Chapter 14

1. Black Leadership Family, *The Black Family Leadership Plan for Unity, Survival, and Progress of Black People* (Washington, D.C.: National Black Leadership Roundtable, February 1982).

2. Hanes Walton, Jr., *Black Political Parties: An Historical and Political Analysis* (New York: The Free Press, 1972), p. 40.

3. Ibid., p. 43.

4. See August Meier, Elliott Rudwick, and Francis L. Broderick, *Black Protest Thought in the Twentieth Century* (New York: MacMillan, 1971); Harold Cruse, *The Crisis of the Negro Intellectual* (New York: Quill, 1984); C. Eric Lincoln, *The Black Muslims in America* (Boston: Beacon Press, 1961).

5. See Ruth–Marion Baruch and Pirkle Jones, *The Vanguard: A Photographic Essay on the Black Panthers* (Boston: Beacon Press, 1970), pp. 42–47, and James Boggs, *Manifesto for a Black Revolutionary Party* (Detroit: Advocators, 1976). For a controversial communist critique of these and other nationalist–oriented proposals, see Henry Winston, *Strategy for a Black Agenda: A Critique of New Theories of Liberation in the United States and Africa* (New York: New World Paperbacks, 1973).

6. "Manifesto of the National Black Economic Development Conference," in Meier, Rudwick, and Broderick, op. cit., pp. 536–549.

7. Robert C. Smith, "'Politics' is not Enough: The Institutionalization of the African American Freedom Movement," in Ralph C. Gomes and Linda Faye Williams, *From Exclusion to Inclusion: The Long Struggle for African American Political Power* (New York: Greenwood Press, 1992), p. 111.

8. Ibid., Black Leadership Family.

9. Ben Chavis, "Leadership at the Community Level," *The Urban League Review*, Vol. 9, No. 1, Summer 1985, p. 89.

10. Ibid., pp. 88–89.

11. Ibid., Black Leadership Family, p. 3.

12. Jeffrey M. Elliot and Mervyn M. Dymally, *Fidel Castro: Nothing Can Stop the Course of History* (New York: Pathfinder, 1985), pp. 31, 35.

13. Congressional Task Force on the Future of African Americans, *The Future of African Americans to the Year 2000 Summary Report* (Washington, D.C.: 1988), p. 26.

14. James M. Washington, ed., *A Testament of Hope: The Essential Writings and Speeches of Martin Luther King, Jr.* (New York: Harper Collins, 1986), p. 308.

15. William Tabb, *The Political Economy of the Black Ghetto* (New York: W. W. Norton, 1970), p. 135.

16. Billy J. Tidwell, *Playing to Win: A Marshall Plan for America* (Washington, D.C.: National Urban League, 1991), p. 32.

17. Ibid.; Tidwell, p. 4.

18. Robert Reich, "Two Facts, One Article of Faith," *Roll Call*, June 28, 1993, pp. 19, 34.

19. See "Report on the Proceedings of the Rebuild America—1992 and Beyond National Leadership Summit, June 11–13, 1992," National Rainbow Coalition, July 1992.

20. See "Congressional Black Caucus 1992 Urban Package," U.S. House of Representatives, 1992.

21. See *Investing in Children and Youth, Reconstructing Our Cities: Doing What Works to Reverse the Betrayal of American Democracy* (Washington, D.C.: The Milton S. Eisenhower Foundation, 1993) and Barbara Vobejda, "Little Progress is Seen on Urban Ills Since 1968," *Washington Post*, February 28, 1993.

22. "Report Faults U.S. in Handling Riots," *New York Times*, March 1, 1993.

23. Ibid., *Investing in Children and Youth*, p. xx.

24. David S. Broder, "Still Two Societies," *Washington Post*, March 3, 1993.

25. "National Campaign to Win Payment for Slavery Takes Quantum Leap," *News Dimensions*, June 25, 1993, p. 16.

26. Aurevouche (ps Dorothy Benton–Lewis), *Black Reparations Now!: Solutions to the Crisis in Democracy & Black Survival in the USA* (Rockville, MD: Black Reparations Press, 1990), p. 12.

27. H.R. 40, U.S. House of Representatives.

28. David H. Swinton, "Statement of David H. Swinton," in *The Economic Status of African–Americans*, Hearing Before the Subcommittee on Investment, Jobs, and Prices of the Joint Economic Committee, U.S. Congress, May 24, 1990, p. 53. For a fuller review of black economic history, see Thomas D. Boston, "NEA Presidential Address, 1991: Sixteenth–Century European Expansion and the Economic Decline of Africa (In Honor of Walter Rodney)," *The Review of Black Political Economy*, Spring 1992, pp. 5–38.

29. Ibid., Swinton, p. 52.

30. Ibid.

31. For a discussion of some of the recent changes in racial politics in the South see John Slaughter, *New Battles Over Dixie: The Campaign for a New South* (Dix Hills, NY: General Hall, Inc., 1992).

32. The 1990 figures are adjusted undercount numbers cited in Andrew Hacker, *Two Nations: Black and White, Separate, Hostile, Unequal* (New York: Charles Scribner's Sons, 1992), p. 15. The projected figures are cited in Margaret Usdansky, "Minorities are Headed Toward the Majority," *USA Today*, December 4, 1992.

33. Amos N. Wilson, *Black-on-Black Violence: The Psychodynamics of Black Self-Annihilation in Service of White Domination* (New York: Afrikan World Infosystems, 1990), p. xvii.

34. See Frantz Fanon, *Wretched of the Earth* (New York: Penguin, 1967); Frantz Fanon *Black Skin, White Masks* (London: MacGibbon and Kee, 1968); and William Grier and Price Cobbs, *Black Rage* (New York:Basic Books, 1968).

35. Ibid., Wilson, pp. 202–203.

36. Cornel West, *Race Matters* (Boston: Beacon Press, 1993), p. 15.

37. Ibid., p. 19.

38. Deborah Prothrow–Stith, *Deadly Consequences: How Violence is Destroying Our Teenage Population and a Plan to Begin Solving the Problem* (New York: Harper Collins, 1991), p. 185.

39. "Inside I.B.W.," *Black World View*, Vol. 1, No. 7., p. 21.

40. Darlene Clark Hine, "A History of the Joint Center 1970–1990," Annual Report 1989, Joint Center for Political and Economic Studies, Washington, D.C., pp. 6–15.

41. James Jennings, "Race and the Future of American Politics," Presentation to the Seminar on Future Directions for American Politics and Public Policy, Harvard University, Kennedy School of Government, May 6, 1993, p. 2.

42. Manning Marable, letter to author, May 10, 1993.

43. Steven White, Lisa Sullivan, and Matthew Countryman, "Redefining the Movement: Building a Cross–Class, Multi–Generational Movement for Black Children," *WeSpeak!*, Winter 1992–93, p. 1.

44. "Clinton's Pledges," *Washington Post*, January 20, 1993.

45. Lani Guinier, "What I Would Have Told the Senate," *Washington Post*, June 13, 1993.

46. Joel Bleifuss, "A Good Fight," *In These Times*, June 14, 1993, p. 12.

47. "Text of President Clinton's Comments on Withdrawal of Guinier Nomination," *Washington Post*, June 4, 1993.

48. Ibid.

49. Editorial, "The Lani Guinier Affair," *Washington Post*, June 6, 1993.

50. "Moseley–Braun Feels Guinier Backlash," *Congressional Insight*, June 11, 1993, p. 1.

51. "The Rap on Janet Reno," *Washington Post*, February 12, 1993.

52. Robin D.G. Kelley, "We Are Not What We Seem: Rethinking Black Working-Class Opposition in the Jim Crow South," *The Journal of American History*, June 1993, p. 112.

# Selected Bibliography

Alkalimat, Abdul and Doug Gills, *Harold Washington and the Crisis of Black Power in Chicago: Mass Protest* (Chicago: Twenty-First Century Books and Publications, 1989).

Anderson, J. Lee, *Inside the League* (New York: Dodd, Meade, 1986).

Aurevouche (ps Dorothy Benton-Lewis), *Black Reparations Now!: Solutions to the Crisis in Democracy & Black Survival in the USA* (Rockville, MD: Black Reparations Press, 1990).

Barker, Lucius and Ronald Walters, *Jesse Jackson's 1984 Presidential Campaign: Challenge and Change in American Politics* (Urbana, IL: University of Illinois Press, 1989).

Barlett, Donald L. and James B. Steele, *America: What Went Wrong?* (Kansas City, MO: Andrews and McMeel, 1992).

Baron, Harold, *The Demand for Black Labor: Historic Notes on the Political Economy of Racism* (Somerville, MA: New England Free Press, 1971).

Baruch, Ruth-Marion and Pirkle Jones, *The Vanguard: A Photographic Essay on the Black Panthers* (Boston: Beacon, 1970).

Bennett, Claudett E., *The Black Population in the United States: March 1991*, U.S. Department of Commerce, Bureau of the Census, Current Population Reports.

Bennett, Lerone, *The Negro Mood and Other Essays* (New York: Ballentine, 1965).

Black Leadership Family, *The Black Family Leadership Plan for Unity, Survival, and Progress of Black People* (Washington, D.C.: National Black Leadership Roundtable, February 1982).

Bloom, Jack M., *Class, Race & the Civil Rights Movement* (Bloomington, IN: Indiana University Press, 1987).

Boggs, James, *Manifesto for a Black Revolutionary Party* (Detroit: Advocators, 1976).

Bositis, David, *Blacks and the 1992 Democratic National Convention* (Washington, D.C.: Joint Center for Political and Economic Studies, 1992).

-----, *Blacks and the 1992 Republican National Convention* (Washington, D.C.: Joint Center for Political and Economic Studies, 1992).

Boston, Thomas D., *Race, Class & Conservatism* (Boston: Unwin Hyman, 1988).

Branch, Taylor, *Parting the Waters: America in the King Years, 1954-63* (New York: Simon and Schuster, 1988).

Bunche, Ralph, in Dewey Grantham, *The Political Status of the Negro in the Age of FDR* (Chicago: University of Chicago Press, 1973).

Burgess, Margaret Elaine, *Negro Leadership in a Southern City* (Chapel Hill, N.C.: University of North Carolina Press, 1962).

Cabral, Amilcar, *Return to the Source* (New York: Africa Information Service, 1973).

Clay, William L., *Just Permanent Interests: Black Americans in Congress 1870-1991* (New York: Amistad, 1992).

Collins, Sheila, *The Rainbow Challenge: The Jackson Campaign and the Future of U.S. Politics* (New York: Monthly Review Press, 1986).

Congressional Task Force on the Future of African-Americans, *The Future of African Americans to the Year 2000 Summary Report* (Washington, D.C.: 1988).

Cruise, Harold, *The Crisis of the Negro Intellectual: From Its Origins to the Present* (New York: Quill, 1967).

Daniels, Ronald, "Some Reflections on the Ohio Black Political Assembly on the Occasion of Its First Reunion," *Vantage Point: Articles and Essays by Ron Daniels*, September, 1988.

Davidson, Chandler, ed., *Minority Vote Dilution* (Washington, D.C.: Howard University Press, 1989).

Davis, Mike, *City of Quartz* (New York: Vintage Books, 1992).

-----, *L. A. Was Just the Beginning* (Westfield, N.J.: Open Magazine, 1992).

Denby, Dallas L., Jr., *Statistics of the Presidential and Congressional Election* (Washington, D.C.: U.S. Government Printing Office, 1989).

Edsel, Thomas Byrne, *Chain Reaction: The Impact of Race, Rights, and Taxes* (New York: Norton, 1992).

Elliot, Jeffrey M. and Mervyn M. Dymally, *Fidel Castro: Nothing Can Stop the Course of History* (New York: Pathfinder, 1985).

Fanon, Frantz, *Black Skin, White Masks* (London: MacGibbon and Kee, 1968).

-----, *Wretched of the Earth* (New York: Penguin, 1967).

Galston, William and Elaine Ciulla Kamarck, *The Politics of Evasion: Democrats and the Presidency* (Washington, D.C.: The Progressive Policy Institute, September 1989).

Gomes, Ralph C. and Linda Faye Williams, eds., *From Exclusion to Inclusion: The Long Struggle for African American Political Power* (New York: Greenwood Press, 1992).

Gooding-Williams, Robert, ed., *Reading Rodney King/Reading Urban Uprising* (New York: Routledge, 1993).

Hacker, Andrew, *Two Nations: Black and White, Separate, Hostile, Unequal* (New York: Scribners, 1992).

Hamilton, Charles, *The Black Experience in American Politics* (New York: Capicorn Books, 1973).

Hamilton, Cynthia, Apartheid in an American City (Los Angeles: Labor/Community Strategy Center, 1991).

Henry, Charles, *Jesse Jackson: The Search for Common Ground* (Oakland: The Black Scholar Press, 1991).

Hughes, Langston, *The Panther and the Lash: Poems of Our Times* (New York: Alfred A. Knopf, 1967).

Huston, Aletha, et al., *Big World, Small Screen: The Role of Television in American Society* (Lincoln: University of Nebraska Press, 1992).

*Inside the L.A. Riots* (New York: Institute for Alternative Journalism, 1992).

*Investing in Children and Youth, Reconstructing Our Cities: Doing What Works to Reverse the Betrayal of American Democracy* (Washington, D.C.: The Milton S. Eisenhower Foundation, 1993).

Jaynes, Gerald David and Robin M. Williams, Jr., eds., *A Common Destiny: Blacks and American Society* (Washington, DC: National Academy Press, 1989).

Jennings, James, ed., *Race, Politics, and Economic Development: Community Perspectives* (New York: Verso, 1992).

Jennings, James, *The Politics of Black Empowerment: The Transformation of Black Activism in Urban America* (Detroit: Wayne State University Press, 1992).

Kennedy, Paul, *The Rise and Fall of the Great Powers: Economic Change and Military Conflict from 1500 to 2000* (New York: Vintage Books, 1987).

King, Martin Luther, Jr., *Stride Toward Freedom* (San Francisco: Harper & Row, 1958).

Lewis, David, *The Civil Rights Movement in America* (Jackson, MS: University Press of Mississippi, 1986).

Lincoln, C. Eric, *The Black Muslims in America* (Boston: Beacon Press, 1961).

Maloney, Gary, ed., *The Almanac of 1988 Presidential Politics* (Falls Church, VA: The American Political Network, 1989).

Marable, Manning, *Black American Politics: From the Washington Marches to Jesse Jackson* (London: Verso, 1985).

-----, *Race, Reform and Rebellion: The Second Reconstruction in Black America, 1945-1982* (Jackson, MS: University Press of Mississippi, 1984).

Matthews, Donald R. and James Warren Protho, *Negroes and the New Southern Politics* (New York: Harcourt, Brace and World, 1968).

McAdam, Doug, *Political Process and the Development of Black Insurgency, 1930-1970* (Chicago: University of Chicago Press, 1982).

Marshall, Will and Martin Schram, eds., *Mandate for Change* (New York: Berkley Books, 1993).

Meier, August, Elliott Rudwick, and Francis L. Broderick, *Black Protest Thought in the Twentieth Century* (New York: MacMillan, 1971).

Morris, Aldon D., *The Origins of the Civil Rights Movement: Black Communities Organizing for Change* (New York: The Free Press, 1984).

Morris, Lorenzo, ed., *The Social and Political Implications of the 1984 Jesse Jackson Presidential Campaign* (New York: Praeger, 1990).

Myrdal, Gunnar, *An American Dilemma* (New York: Pantheon Books, 1944).

National Rainbow Coalition, *National Rainbow Coalition/Democratic National Committee Voter Project, Report*, November 1992.

National Urban League, *State of Black America 1986* (New York: National Urban League, 1986).

-----, *State of Black America 1993* (New York: National Urban League, 1993).

Omi, Michael and Howard Winant, *Racial Formation in the United States: From the 1960s to the 1980s* (New York: Routledge, 1986).

Perot, Ross, *Not for Sale at Any Price: How We Can Save America for Our Children* (New York: Hyperion, 1993).

-----, *United We Stand: How We Can Take Back Our Country* (New York: Hyperion, 1992).

Persons, Georgia A., ed., *Dilemmas of Black Politics: Issues of Leadership and Strategy* (New York: HarperCollins, 1993).

Pettigrew, Thomas and Denise Alston, *Tom Bradley's Campaigns for Governor* (Washington, D.C.: The Joint Center for Political Studies, 1988).

Phelps, Timothy, M. and Helen Winternitz, *Capitol Games: The Inside Story of Clarence Thomas, Anita Hill, and a Supreme Court Nomination* (New York: HarperPerennial, 1992).

Piven, Frances Fox and Richard Cloward, *Poor Peoples Movements: Why They Succeed, How They Fail* (New York: Vintage-Random House, 1977).

Pohlmann, Marcus D., *Black Politics in Conservative America* (New York: Longman, 1990).

*Police Brutality in Los Angeles, California* (London: Amnesty International, 1992).

Preston, Michael B., Lenneal J. Henderson, and Paul L. Puryear, eds., *The New Black Politics* (New York: Longman, 1987).

Prothrow-Stith, Deborah, *Deadly Consequences: How Violence is Destroying Our Teenage Population and a Plan to Begin to Solving the Problem* (New York: HarperCollins, 1991).

Reed, Adolph L., Jr., *The Jesse Jackson Phenomenon: The Crisis of Purpose in Afro-American Politics* (New Haven, CT: Yale University Press, 1986).

Ridgeway, James, *Blood in the Face* (New York: Thunder's Mouth Press, 1990).

Rose, Arnold M., ed., *Human Behavior and Social Process* (Boston: Houghton Mifflin, 1962).

Slaughter, John, *New Battles Over Dixie: The Campaign for a New South* (Dix Hills, NY: General Hall, Inc., 1992).

Smith, Robert C., *Black Leadership: A Survey of Theory and Research* (Washington, D.C.: Mental Research and Development Center, Institute for Urban Affairs and Research, Howard University).

Sonenshein, Raphael, J., *Politics in Black and White: Race and Power in Los Angeles* (Princeton, NJ: Princeton University Press, 1993).

Stern, Philip, *The Best Congress Money Can Buy* (New York: Pantheon, 1988).

Tabb, William, *The Political Economy of the Black Ghetto* (New York: W.W. Norton, 1970).

Tate, Katherine, *From Protest to Politics: The New Black Voters in American Elections* (Cambridge: Harvard University Press, 1993).

Thompson, Donald, *The Negro Leadership Class* (Englewood Cliffs, NJ: Prentice-Hall, 1963).

Tidwell, Billy J., *Playing to Win: A Marshall Plan for America* (Washington, D.C.: National Urban League, 1991).

*The Voting Rights Act: Ten Years After* (Washington, DC: The United States Commission on Civil Rights, January 1975).

Walters, Ronald, *Black Presidential Politics: A Strategic Approach* (Albany: State University of New York Press, 1988 ).

Walton, Hanes, Jr., *Black Political Parties: An Historical and Political Analysis* (New York: The Free Press, 1972).

-----, *Invisible Politics: Black Political Behavior* (Albany: State University of New York, 1985).

Washington, James M., ed., *A Testament of Hope: The Essential Writings and Speeches of Martin Luther King, Jr.* (New York: HarperCollins, 1986).

West, Cornel, *Race Matters* (Boston: Beacon Press, 1993).

Wilson, Amos N., *Black-on-Black Violence: The Psychodynamics of Black Self-Annihilation in Service of White Domination* (New York: Afrikan World Infosystems, 1990).

Wilson, James Q., *Negro Politics: The Search for Leadership* (New York: The Free Press, 1960).

Wilson, William Julius, *The Truly Disadvantaged: The Inner City, the Underclass, and Public Policy* (Chicago: University of Chicago Press, 1987).

Winston, Henry, *Strategy for a Black Agenda: A Critique of New Theories of Liberation in the United States and Africa* (New York: New World Paperbacks, 1973).

Yancey, Dwayne, *When Hell Froze Over: The Untold Story of Doug Wilder, A Black Politician's Rise to Power in the South* (Dallas: Taylor Publishing, 1988).

# Index

Jackson, 153-54, 155; and Joint Center for Political and Economic Studies, 200; monitoring of, 205; and new radicals, 39; and 1992 elections, 153-54, 155, 158, 163; and Republican Party, 134; and Sister Souljah incident, 121; and Wilder, 163. *See also* Black leadership; Electoral politics; Voting; *specific people*

Black independent politics: and accommodationism, 38; Bevel's activities, 59-61; Chavis on, 29; Committees of Correspondence, 55-56; Daniels campaign, 48-49, 53; "Democracy and its Discontents" conference, 52; Horne campaign, 50, 51; importance of, 195; as independent leverage, 68-69; National Emergency Conference on Black Independent Politics, 51-52; NBIPP, 47; and NBPA, 45-47; New Alliance Party, 56-59; and new radicals, 39; Patton campaign, 50-51; People's Progressive Convention, 52-55; and Perot movement, 182

Black leadership: agenda-setting role, 190-97; and Civil Rights movement, 17-18, 19-20; collective, 199; and criminal justice system, 11; crisis of, 183-84, 199; criticism of, 3-4, 24-26, 34, 183; definitions of, 18-19; and Democratic Party, 142-43; and end of Cold War, 5-6; future of, 34-36, 189; and gang-truce movement, 15-16; harassment of, 12; and Los Angeles rebellion, 105, 107-9; media images of, 34-35; and 1992 elections, 142; structure of, 17-22, 29-34; and Thomas nomination, 85-86; and Voting Rights Act, 20-22; women's role, 44, 213. *See also* Black agenda; Black elected officials; Civil rights establishment; *specific organizations and people*

Black Leadership Family Plan (BLFP), 187-88

Black Leadership Forum (BLF), 29-30, 187

Black Leadership Round Table, 187

Black Manifesto (1969), 186-87

Black mayors, 23-24, 31, 43, 113. *See also specific people*

Black nationalism, 32, 34, 40, 47, 117. *See also specific people and groups*

Black Panther Party, 21-22, 186

*Black Power: The Politics of Liberation in America* (Hamilton & Carmichael), 70

*Black Presidential Politics* (Walters), 68-69

*The Black Scholar*, 205

Black Student Leadership Network, 203

Black-Jewish relations, 32-33

Black-on-Black Violence (Wilson), 198

Blackwell, Lucien, 178

BLF. *See* Black Leadership Forum

BLFP. *See* Black Leadership Family Plan

Bloice, Carl, 55

Bloods/Crips Proposal, 108-9

Boggs, James, 186, 200, 201

Bond, Julian, 12, 26, 45

Booker, Chris, 10

Bork, Robert, 79

Boston, Thomas, 71

Bradley, Bill, 147

Bradley, Tom, 23, 43, 96; and deracialization, 97; and economic crisis, 98-99; and King beating, 103; and LAPD, 94; response to Los Angeles rebellion, 105; withdrawal of, 112

Braun, Carol Moseley, 175, 209

Briseno, Theodore, 102

Brown, Jerry, 56, 141, 157, 159

Brown, Jesse, 212

Brown, Lee, 212

Brown, Ron, 130, 153, 212

Brown, Tony, 109, 142

Buchanan, Patrick, 91, 110, 134, 145

Bunche, Ralph, 35

Burnham, Linda, 202

Bush, George, 109-10, 147; racism of, 133, 167. *See also* Bush campaign (1992); Reagan-Bush administrations

Bush campaign (1992), 147, 149, 170; defeat of, 167, 169, 173, 174, 176-77, 179, 180; and Duke candidacy, 89; and 1948 elections, 134-35

Butts, Calvin, 49, 138

# C

Cabral, Amilcar, 115

Camp, Billy Joe, 50

Campaign for a New Tomorrow, 48, 52, 70. *See also* Daniels, Ron

Campbell, Luther, 123

Campbell, Ralph, 176

Capitalism, 194

Carmichael, Stokely, 70

National Association for the Advancement of White People, 87-88
National Baptist Convention, U.S.A., 31
National Black Caucus of Local Elected Officials, 31
National Black Caucus of State Legislatures, 31
National Black Convention (1972), 187
National Black Economic Development Conference, 186-87
National Black Independent Political Party (NBIPP), 47
National Black Political Assembly (NBPA), 45-47
National Black Republican Council, 134
National Coalition of Blacks for Reparation in America (NCOBRA), 193
National Committee for Independent Political Action (NCIPA), 49, 52
National Conference of Black Lawyers (NCBL), 80, 82-83
National Conference of Black Mayors, 31
National Council of Negro Women, 117
National Council of the Churches of Christ in the USA, 15
National Emergency Conference on Black Independent Politics, 51-52
National mobilizations, 30
National Negro Congress, 186
National Negro Convention Movement (NNCM), 185-86
National Organization for Women (NOW), 69-70
National People's Progressive Network (NPPN), 53, 54-55
National Rainbow Coalition (NRC), 47; disempowerment of, 148; influence of, 29, 55; and New Alliance Party, 57; and 1992 elections, 27, 154, 156-58, 160-61, 181; and People's Progressive Convention, 55; vs. Perot movement, 136; "Rebuild America" conference, 118-19; "Ten Commitments," 154. See also Jackson, Jesse; Jackson presidential campaigns
National Research Council, 8
National Urban League (NUL), 9, 25, 191
National Urban Peace and Justice Summit (1993), 15
Nationalism. See Black nationalism
NBIPP. See National Black Independent Political Party

NBPA. See National Black Political Assembly
NCBL. See National Conference of Black Lawyers
NCIPA. See National Committee for Independent Political Action
NCOBRA. See National Coalition of Blacks for Reparation in America
Neoconservatism, 37, 38, 66, 71, 81-82, 198
New Alliance Party (NAP), 56-59, 197
New Deal, 67
New Party, 52, 69
New radicals, 39-41, 180-81
Newman, Fred, 56
Newport, Eugene "Gus," 9, 55
Niagara Movement, 186
Nichols, Ben, 156
Niggahs With Attitude (NWA), 116, 117, 123
"Nightline," 90
1948 elections, 67, 134-35
1984 elections. See Jackson presidential campaigns
1988 elections, 56, 57, 133. See also Jackson presidential campaigns
1992 elections: and accommodationism, 37; and Black agenda, 142, 181; and Black elected officials, 153-54, 155, 158, 163; Black progressive challengers in, 50-51; Black vote in, 64-66, 143, 172-74, 175-76; Black voter turnout in, 143-45, 172; Bush defeat, 167, 173, 177, 179, 180; Clinton success, 145, 179-80; and Committees of Correspondence, 55; Daniels campaign, 48-49; Democratic National Convention, 130-31; and economic crisis, 176-77, 179; gay rights in, 177; Jackson role in, 146, 147, 148-55; and Los Angeles rebellion, 109-10, 182; and National Rainbow Coalition, 27, 154, 156-58, 160-61, 181; and New Alliance Party, 56, 57, 58-59; and new radicals, 180-81; and People's Progressive Convention, 53-54, 55; Republican racism during, 132-35; results of, 169-72; significance of, 141-42, 180-84; White voter turnout in, 145; and women, 44, 170-71, 173. See also Bush campaign (1992); Clinton campaign; Perot, H. Ross
Nixon, Richard, 136

and 1992 elections, 44, 170-71, 173; and
Thomas nomination, 85, 175, 179-80.
*See also specific people*
Women in the NAACP (WIN), 26
Woo, Michael, 112
Woodson, Robert, 78
World Anti-Communist League, 83
Wright, Eric. *See* Easy E

# Y

Yeutter, Clayton, 90

Young, Andrew, 60
Young, Andy, 160
Young, Coleman, 23, 43
Young, Whitney, 45
Youth, 108, 112. *See also* Hip Hop culture

# Z

Zepp-Larouche, Helga, 60
Zogby, Jim, 156

# About Clarence Lusane

Clarence Lusane is an author, activist, lecturer, and free-lance journalist. He has worked for nearly twenty years in national black politics, and foreign and domestic policy issues. Lusane, chairman of the board of the National Alliance of Third World Journalists, also edits the newsletter *Black Political Agenda.* Currently, he is pursuing a doctoral degree at Howard University.

Born in Detroit, Michigan in 1953, Lusane now lives in Washington, D.C. As a journalist, he has traveled to Haiti, Panama, South Korea, East Germany, Zimbabwe, Cuba, Mexico, Jamaica, and England. In 1990, his first book, *Pipe Dream Blues,* was described by the director of the Christic Institute as the "single most important book on this crisis in the last few years." The *Black Books Bulletin* noted, "People do not like to read the sort of things that Lusane writes about, but he gives us facts that will not go away."

Lusane has written numerous articles for the *Black Scholar,* and *Crossroads.* He is currently working on the third book in the *Race and Resistance* series by South End Press that deals with the state of African Americans.

# About South End Press

South End Press is a nonprofit, collectively-run book publisher with over 175 titles in print. Since our founding in 1977, we have tried to meet the needs of readers who are exploring, or are already committed to, the politics of radical social change.

Our goal is to publish books that encourage critical thinking and constructive action on the key political, cultural, social, economic, and ecological issues shaping life in the United States and in the world. In this way, we hope to give expression to a wide diversity of democratic social movements and to provide an alternative to the products of corporate publishing.

Through the Institute for Social and Cultural Change, South End Press works with other political media projects—*Z Magazine;* Speak Out!, a speakers bureau; the Publishers Support Project; and the New Liberation News Service—to expand access to information and critical analysis. If you would like a free catalog of South End Press books, please write to us at South End Press, 116 Saint Botolph Street, Boston, MA 02115. Also consider becoming a South End Press member: your $40 annual donation entitles you to two free books and a 40% discount on our entire list.

## Other Titles Of Interest:

*Pipe Dream Blues: Racism and the War on Drugs*
    by Clarence Lusane
*Confronting Environmental Racism: Voices from the Grassroots*
    by Robert Bullard
*The State of Asian America: Activism and Resistance in the 1990s*
    edited by Karin A. San-Juan
*The State of Native America: Genocide, Colonization and Resistance*
    edited by M. Annette Jaimes
*Black Looks: Race and Representation*
    by bell hooks
*Breaking Bread: Insurgent Black Intellectual Life*
    by bell hooks and Cornel West
*How Capitalism Underdeveloped Black America*
    by Manning Marable